OXFORD WORLD'S CLASSICS

CATILINE'S CONSPIRACY, THE JUGURTHINE WAR, HISTORIES

Gaius Sallustius Crispus, known as sallust, is thought to have been born in Amiternum, a town in the Sabine country north-east of Rome, in 86 BC and to have died in 35 BC. We know nothing of his early life. He must have been a quaestor before 52 BC, but when we first hear of him he is one of the unruly tribunes who attacked Cicero in 52. He was expelled from the Senate in 50. He sided with Caesar during the civil war. In the summer of 49 he was sent to aid C. Antonius, who was barricaded on Curicta in the Adriatic; he failed and Antonius was forced to surrender. In 47, as praetor, Sallust was sent to deal with a mutiny in Campania; he barely escaped with his own life. In 46 Caesar made him governor of 'New Africa'. He returned to Rome in 45 with vast wealth which he used to purchase a villa at Tivoli, a mansion in Rome, and the famous 'Gardens of Sallust' that became the property of later Roman emperors. He was tried for extortion, but was acquitted. After Caesar's assassination in 44, Sallust retired from public life and turned to the writing of history. His monographs on Catiline's conspiracy and the Jugurthine War survive complete, and he also began an annalistic history of the late Republic, starting in the year 78, the year Sulla died; he got as far as 67 before he himself died. In antiquity he was considered the greatest of Rome's historians. His style, difficult to read, broken and deceptive, and his perspective, satirical and sarcastic, had a profound influence on Tacitus, and was praised by Nietzsche.

William W. Batstone is Professor of Greek and Latin at The Ohio State University. He has written many articles about the poetry and prose of the Roman Republic, focusing primarily on the relationship between our modern theoretical understanding of ourselves and our historical understanding of the ancient world. He wrote the commentary to *Latin Lyric and Elegiac Poetry*, which he co-edited with Diane Rayor. He co-authored *Caesar's Civil Wars* with Cynthia Damon and co-edited *Genre and Gender in Latin Literature* with Garth Tissol.

T0058827

OXFORD WORLD'S CLASSICS

SALLUST

Catiline's Conspiracy
The Jugurthine War
Histories

Translated with an Introduction and Notes by
WILLIAM W. BATSTONE

OXFORD
UNIVERSITY PRESS

OXFORD
UNIVERSITY PRESS

Great Clarendon Street, Oxford OX2 6DP

Oxford University Press is a department of the University of Oxford.
It furthers the University's objective of excellence in research, scholarship,
and education by publishing worldwide in

Oxford New York

Auckland Cape Town Dar es Salaam Hong Kong Karachi
Kuala Lumpur Madrid Melbourne Mexico City Nairobi
New Delhi Shanghai Taipei Toronto

With offices in

Argentina Austria Brazil Chile Czech Republic France Greece
Guatemala Hungary Italy Japan Poland Portugal Singapore
South Korea Switzerland Thailand Turkey Ukraine Vietnam

Oxford is a registered trade mark of Oxford University Press
in the UK and in certain other countries

Published in the United States
by Oxford University Press Inc., New York

© William W. Batstone 2010

The moral rights of the author have been asserted
Database right Oxford University Press (maker)

First published as an Oxford World's Classics paperback 2010

British Library Cataloging in Publication Data

Data available

Library of Congress Cataloging in Publication Data

Data available

Typeset by Glyph International, Bangalore, India
Printed in Great Britain
on acid-free paper by
Clays Ltd., Elcograf S.p.A

ISBN 978-0-19-282345-8

CONTENTS

ABBREVIATIONS

C   *Catiline's Conspiracy*
J   *The Jugurthine War*
H   *The Histories*

References to other classical works are abbreviated according to *The Oxford Classical Dictionary* 3rd edn. (Oxford, 1996).

INTRODUCTION

Sallust wrote near the end of a century of civil discord and civil war. His first monograph tells the story of Catiline's conspiracy (63 BC), an event that he considered 'especially memorable because of the unprecedented nature of the crime and the danger it caused' (*C* 4.3). In his second monograph, he takes up the history of the Jugurthine War, a period from 118 to 104 BC, 'first because it was great and brutal, with victories on both sides, and second because that was the first time there was any opposition to the aristocracy's abuse of power. This struggle confused all things, human and divine, and proceeded to such a pitch of madness that political partisanship had its end in civil war and the devastation of Italy' (*J* 5.1–2). His final work, the *Histories*, is unfinished and exists for us only in about 500 fragments, four orations, and two letters. In this he undertook to deal with the events between the Jugurthine War and Catiline's conspiracy. He did not, however, write about the Social Wars and Sulla's dictatorship (after the first instances of the 'madness' that resulted in civil war) but began with the year of Sulla's death (78 BC). He got as far as the year 67 before he died.

Historical Background

In all these works, Sallust is concerned explicitly and implicitly with the political and moral decline of the Roman Republic, which he dates to the destruction of Carthage in 146 BC. Others saw different turning points. Livy ascribed the beginnings of luxury to 187, when Manlius Vulso's army returned from Asia. Polybius saw moral standards changing as early as 200, but placed the crisis of the late Republic after the battle of Pydna in 168, when Rome began to achieve world domination. But in Sallust's view the destruction of Carthage began a period of factionalism and luxury. As a result the Roman state 'gradually changed from the most lovely and best and became the worst and most depraved' (*C* 5.9).

Sallust does not ignore the many domestic conflicts that make up the history of the Republic. In fact, he says that civil disputes arose in

Rome from 'a vice of human nature which, restless and indomitable, is always engaging in contests over liberty or glory or domination' (*H* 1.7). But 'the highest moral standards and the greatest harmony were displayed between the second and the last Punic war' (*H* 1.11) because these contests were kept in check by *metus hostilis* ('fear of an external enemy') or more specifically *metus Punicus* ('fear of Carthage'). Then, when the destruction of Carthage made it possible to pursue internal enmities and rivalries, 'the aristocracy twisted their "dignity" and the people twisted their "liberty" towards their desires; every man acted on his own behalf, stealing, robbing, plundering. In this way all political life was torn apart between two parties, and the Republic, which had been our common ground, was mutilated' (*J* 41.5).

Sallust was not original in this view. The importance of *metus hostilis* as the basis of internal cohesion and common interest had often been recognized in Rome. In fact, Scipio Nasica had cited it as a reason to oppose Cato's demand that Carthage be destroyed. But Sallust saw the destruction of Carthage as pivotal because it created the conditions for both factionalism and luxury. 'The young men were so corrupted by luxury and greed that it could be rightly said that men had been born who could neither hold on to their family wealth themselves nor allow others to' (*H* 1.16). 'Men who had easily endured hard work, dangers, uncertainty and adversity found that leisure and wealth, things desirable at other times, were a burden and the cause of misery. And so, at first, greed for money grew, then greed for power. These things were the root, so to speak, of all evils' (*C* 10.2–3). It was the conjunction of wealth and factionalism, greed for money and greed for power, that made 146 BC pivotal. Later ancient writers were to follow Sallust's view.

Modern historians, however, emphasize two institutions that played a central role in the decline of the late Republic: the tribunate and the Roman army. The tribunate was an old republican office going back to 494 BC. It was instituted to protect the rights of the plebeians against abuses of power by the patrician or aristocratic class (which is to say, the Senate). Eventually there were ten tribunes, elected by the plebeian assembly. Their person and body were considered sacrosanct, meaning that they could not be touched or coerced. Their power could be used to halt public business, to veto proposals and actions by other magistrates, to convene the Senate, and to propose legislation directly to the people. By convention, the tribunes deferred to the Senate for legislative review. It was the Gracchi brothers who first used tribunician power (in 133 and again in 123–122) to deprive the Senate of its traditional control of legislative review, of fiscal policy, and even of foreign policy. Later the office was used by commanders to get land for their veterans and to secure commands that they desired or needed. While tribunes most frequently opposed the Senate's authority by appeal to the people, they could easily be bribed and were found promoting the factional interests of both *optimates* and *populares*.

This struggle between the *nobiles* or the *optimates* (members of the ruling aristocracy, senators with family names and histories to honour and live up to) and the *populares* (the 'supporters of the people') should not be thought of as a contest between the Senate and the plebs (Roman citizens without the privileges or power of the aristocracy), that is, between two parties or classes. Since 494 the tribunate had protected the plebs from aristocratic power and by the late Republic not only could plebeians be elected to any office, but it was required that one consul each year be a plebeian. This means that one could and did have plebeian magistrates and senators. The term *nobiles*, then, begins to refer to those who had gained power and wealth and controlled access to power by electoral success and collusion with others. These men were often members of old aristocratic families, but not necessarily. It was not a group with stability and lineage but whoever happened to be the dominant elite at any given time.

The conflict between *optimates* and *populares* was really a conflict among aristocrats themselves, a struggle between senators and magistrates for primacy or even domination. This distinction was not determined by the political agenda of the individuals, but by their base of power. The *optimates* sought support by appealing to the traditional power and privileges of the Senate and 'the powerful few'. The *populares* opposed the privileges or the abuses of power by the 'few' and did so by using the power of the tribunate, which is to say by claiming to protect the freedom of the people and the rights of the citizen voting assemblies. These bases of power entailed certain policies: *populares* tended to be interested in supplying grain to the urban poor and in agrarian laws that would supply land to veteran soldiers, while the *optimates* resisted any new power base, especially that of a successful general like Marius or Caesar. They did what they could to control policy themselves. But it was not about policy; it was about power: 'To put the truth in a few words, after those times whoever stirred up the Republic with honourable claims, some as if they were defending the rights of the people, others to secure the authority of the Senate, pretending to work for the public good while they struggled for their own power. There was no restraint or measure to their efforts. Each side used their victories brutally' (*C* 38.3–4).

In the struggle for power, wealth played an important, if not determinate, role. Those who had money and land used the electoral process to protect it; those who did not have money used political institutions to acquire it. According to Sallust, wealth promoted both luxury and greed, avarice and sloth. It weakened the power, but not the arrogance, of old aristocratic families; it raised to prominence and pre-eminence men who had no investment in the traditional power base of the Senate. Elections could secure lucrative governorships and military commands, and military commands could secure money and political influence. At Rome, everything was for sale; such is the refrain of Sallust's *Jugurthine War*, and that included the especially disruptive powers of the tribunate.

For modern historians, the second important institution that made possible the century of civil wars was the Roman army, or rather the army reforms that were instituted by Marius during the Jugurthine War. Sallust does not show much interest in these reforms per se, but they changed the relationship of commander, Senate, and troops primarily by creating a professional army from the urban poor. This army would be loyal to their commander, not to the foreign policy decisions of the Senate. It was this kind of army that marched on Rome first following Sulla, then Lepidus, and later Caesar.

Sallust's interest, however, was not a modern interest in institutional structures. He was concerned with politics and factionalism, wealth and luxury. For Sallust, the failure of political institutions is to a large extent the moral failure of the men who operated within those institutions. His concern is with the arrogance and violence and the character of men who used and sought power. Similarly, his concern with money is not with the economic base and the creation of wealth, or the financial structure of the Roman electoral process, but with how money is used by individuals and how it affects, on the one hand, the character of the men who have it or seek it and, on the other, the character of the state. For Sallust these elements are interactive. Thus, when he outlines Catiline's character (*de cuius moribus . . . C* 4.5), he finds Catiline's propensities exacerbated 'by the corrupt moral character of the state (*mores civitatis*), which was depraved because of two destructive and internally contradictory evils, extravagance and greed' (*C* 5.8). This leads to a parallel digression on the character of the state (*de moribus civitatis, C* 5.9).

Sallust's Life and Times

Sallust's urgency about the fall of the Republic comes no doubt from the fact that he was born in the middle of the political 'earthquake' (*J* 41.10) that he writes about and he died before Augustus turned the Republic into a 'principate'. But he does not write as an eye-witness to the events of his histories: the Jugurthine War was over before he was born and he seems to have been away from Rome during Catiline's conspiracy. Nevertheless, the events of these years shaped his understanding of politics. St Jerome tells us that Sallust was born in Amiternum, a town in the Sabine country north-east of Rome, in 86 BC; the *Consularia Constantinopolitana* adds the birthday 1 October. This was the year of Marius' last consulship, though Marius had died in January. After the carnage and destruction of 87 which had eventually consolidated Cinna's position in Rome, Cinna now waited and feared the return of Sulla from the east. To understand the world Sallust was born into, we need to look back at the careers of Marius and Sulla.

Marius was the great Roman general who had defeated Jugurtha, defeated the Germans, and held the consulship six times (107, 104–100). Sulla had served with him during the Jugurthine War, and in fact claimed to be the man who actually brought Jugurtha into Roman hands. After considerable success in the Social Wars (91–88), in which Rome's Latin allies fought for citizenship or independence, Sulla was elected consul (88) and was given as his proconsular command the war against Mithridates, an eastern king intent on expanding his empire into Roman territory. Marius, now an old man, was jealous: he convinced a tribune, Sulpicius, to call a referendum on the command. There was fighting in the Forum; Sulla fled to his legions and appealed for their support. A military tribune was sent to claim Sulla's army in Marius' name, but the soldiers stoned him to death. Sulla's officers deserted, but his men remained loyal. Sulla became the first general in the history of Rome to cross into the city with an army. As master of Rome, he now declared Sulpicius' laws invalid; Marius and Sulpicius were declared public enemies. Sulpicius was hunted down and killed. Marius escaped to Africa where many of his veterans were settled, while Sulla went to Asia to fight Mithridates. Already the forces of factionalism, the power of the tribunate, and the loyalties that Marius' military reforms encouraged were shaping events. And, of course, Sulla's command against Mithridates was a bid for power, glory, and wealth.

Before leaving for Asia in 88, however, Sulla allowed the consular elections to proceed. L. Cornelius Cinna, an enemy of Sulla, was elected; his colleague was Cn. Octavius, a loyal optimate. They quarrelled. Octavius drove Cinna from Rome; Cinna sought the aid of Marius and besieged Rome. By the autumn of 87 he had the upper hand: the city was starving, disease was rampant, and the Senate accepted terms of surrender. Marius let his retinue of soldiers and ex-slaves loot and murder. After five days of slaughter, even Cinna was disgusted. Marius and Cinna were declared consuls for 86. Such was the world into which Sallust was born.

Sallust would have been a toddler when Sulla returned to Rome. Sulla had been formally exiled and his laws repealed, but he still commanded a Roman army in the east. He landed at Brundisium in 83 where he was joined by men who would shape the course of the last years of the Republic: M. Licinius Crassus came from Spain; Metellus Pius arrived from Africa; Cn. Pompeius brought three private legions from Picenum. With the help of these armies, Sulla became ruler of Italy by the end of 82. For the first time in 120 years the Senate declared a man dictator, and there was an innovation: this republican office, which was traditionally limited to six months, was granted to Sulla without limit. Furthermore, all his actions were validated beforehand and were not subject to legislative or judicial review.

Sulla needed money for his veterans—at least twenty-three legions—and he wanted to eliminate all political opposition. At first men were murdered indiscriminately. Then proscription lists went up. Those whose names appeared on these lists were condemned without a trial. Anyone could kill them and claim a reward; their property was auctioned off by the state; and their sons and grandsons were barred from seeking political office. We do not know how many were killed; one ancient source gives 9,000 as the figure. At this time, Pompey, Caesar's opponent in Caesar's civil war, was 24 years old. He acted with such cruelty in Sicily that he was called 'the young butcher'. He fancied himself another Alexander, and Sulla called him 'the Great', a name that stuck with him the rest of his life. Many benefited from Sulla's proscriptions, including both Crassus, who gained considerable wealth from them, and L. Sergius Catilina.

As dictator, Sulla's specific charge was 'to pass laws and reconstitute the state'. He began by filling up the ranks of a depleted Senate: of the traditional 300 senators, only about 150 lived. Sulla increased the number to 600, appointing friends and supporters from among the equestrian class. He modified the *cursus honorum*, or sequence of offices that a successful politician could hold. He required men to hold the quaestorship before standing for the praetorship, and to hold the praetorship before running for consul. He added age requirements for these offices: 30 for quaestor, 39 for praetor, and 42 for consul. And, to prevent another man's holding consecutive consulships as Marius had, or consecutive tribuneships as Gaius Gracchus had, he required a ten-year hiatus before repetition of the same office. Then, to break the power of the tribunes, he banned them from holding any other office in the future and limited their ability to initiate or promulgate legislation. The juries were taken from the *equites* (the 'equestrian' or mercantile class) and given to the senators. Grain distributions were abolished. Land was taken from communities that had opposed him and some 80,000 veterans were settled there.

While still holding the office of dictator, he was elected consul for 80—just eight years after his first consulship, making him the first man to violate his own rules. He refused election for 79, and instead resigned the dictatorship and went into retirement as a private citizen. He did not interfere in politics, even when the elections of 79 returned a man he opposed. He died in 78 at the age of 60. The 'Domination of Sulla' was a turning point in the history of Roman violence. Sallust himself would refuse to write of it, saying in *The Jugurthine War*, 'Before his victory in the civil war he was the most fortunate of all men, but his good fortune did not exceed his efforts.

As for what he did afterwards, I do not know whether one should feel more shame or disgust in talking of it' (_J_ 95.4).

During the next eight years, Pompey and Crassus consolidated their power. In 78 Pompey was sent to put down a revolt of farmers in Etruria; they were rebelling against the colonists Sulla had placed on their land. In 77 he was sent to Spain to deal with Sertorius, a supporter of Cinna, whose armies controlled most of Spain. It was not until 73 that Pompey began to gain the upper hand. But it was a war that promoted the military power upon which Pompey built his political power. No sooner was the war with Sertorius concluded than another crisis arose. A group of seventy-four slaves led by Spartacus escaped from a gladiatorial training school in Capua. They were joined by other runaway slaves and agricultural workers and soon numbered 70,000. In 72 the Senate sent the consuls against the slaves; both consuls were defeated. The Senate turned to Crassus, who had served with Sulla in 82. He was given four legions and raised six more. He drove Spartacus south, hoping to corner him in the toe of Italy, but, when Spartacus broke through his lines, the Senate summoned Pompey from Spain. Crassus defeated and killed Spartacus at Lucania; Pompey moving south met and killed about 5,000 fugitives who had fled northward. He then claimed responsibility for ending the war. Crassus was rightly resentful.

Pompey and Crassus had supported Sulla. Both desired to be the first among equals. Both claimed credit for defeating Spartacus. Both wanted the consulship for 70. And both, hoping for triumphs, kept their armies under arms near Rome. The Senate was duly intimidated: Pompey received his triumph and both Crassus and Pompey were elected to the consulship. Crassus was about 45; he had been praetor in 72. Pompey was 36 and had held none of the offices which Sulla's constitution made prerequisite to the consulship. They then proceeded to restore the powers of the tribunate that Sulla had curtailed; they revived the censorship and ended the senatorial monopoly of the law courts. Little was left of Sulla's reforms and reorganization of the state. Sallust would have been about 16 at this time.

Pompey was now identified with the _populares_. The _optimates_ were suspicious of his intentions and powers. In 67, when Sallust would be turning 20, Rome decided to do something about the pirates that infested the Mediterranean, interfering with trade and even attacking cities on the coast of Greece and Asia. An extraordinary command was proposed for Pompey: authority over the entire Mediterranean and the coastline up to fifty miles inland. The *optimates* opposed but the motion was carried. By midsummer the pirates were gone, and Pompey began a reorganization of Asia. Next, the tribune C. Manilius proposed that Pompey take over the Third War against Mithridates. The general in charge was Lucullus, a plebeian aristocrat, who was insulted that this 'new man' would replace him. He called Pompey a 'vulture', referring to the fact that he had already fed off Crassus' victory over Spartacus just as he was trying to feed off Lucullus' successes against Mithridates. Lucullus was essentially right. But he had trouble motivating his army; the war had stalled. It was Pompey's job to bring the war to its conclusion. He pursued Mithridates toward the Black Sea, and then headed toward Jerusalem. In 63 during the Judaean War he heard of the death of Mithridates. Meanwhile, Crassus had been at Rome taking care of his wealth, working with the tax-collectors, and supporting the career of Julius Caesar.

During this period Catiline stood for the consulship (64 BC); it was the same year that Cicero was also a candidate. Cicero and Antonius were elected. Then Catiline stood for the consulship again (63). In his bitterness at a second defeat, he turned to violence. It was said that Crassus helped Catiline; if he did, or when he stopped, we do not know. It is said that Crassus was behind anyone who could oppose Pompey's pre-eminence. And many men were afraid of what might happen when Pompey returned from the east with his armies. Sallust himself leaves the matter of Crassus' involvement undecided. Crassus' money, no doubt, affected many things behind the scenes. Sallust would have been 22, but it is noteworthy that his history of Catiline's conspiracy never relies on personal experience. Presumably he was not in Rome at the time, but we do not know what he was doing.

By the time Sallust was in his mid-twenties, Rome had survived the Catilinarian conspiracy but was facing another internal danger: the first triumvirate. Pompey had returned to Italy in 61. He was hoping for a triumph and a second consulship. In the campaigns from 65 to 62 he had annexed much of Asia, brought back to Rome incalculable tribute, imposed settlements that endured for centuries. Cato, a young conservative, persuaded the Senate to make Pompey choose between a triumph and the consulship. He chose a triumph. But then the Senate dragged its feet. The *optimates* were reluctant to confirm his settlements in Asia. He wanted land for his veterans, but the Senate refused to act. Crassus, who had been cultivating his wealth and promoting the career of Julius Caesar, asked the Senate to adjust the terms for tax-collection in Asia. This would support the *equites*, whom Crassus himself supported. The Senate rejected his request. Finally, Caesar returned from Spain where as propraetor he had been governor. He too wanted a triumph for his military successes and he wanted to stand for the consulship. He too was forced to choose, but he chose the consulship.

Discontent with the Senate's obstructionism made for strange political bedfellows. Pompey and Crassus, though mistrustful of each other's ambitions, were drawn together by Julius Caesar into a political alliance. These three men, backed by armies that were loyal to them, by money and the interests of the *equites*, and by the support of the urban populace, imposed their will on the state and ignored the desires of the Senate. Caesar was consul in 59 and received the two Gauls as his proconsular province. Cato opposed Caesar during his consulship and after. Enmity grew. Cato opposed Caesar's agrarian laws; Caesar had Cato dragged out of the Forum while making a speech against him. Cato attempted to prevent Caesar's second five-year command in Gaul and was instrumental in creating impasses and in dividing the tenuous loyalties between Pompey and Caesar. For the Roman historian Pollio (a supporter of Caesar), the triumvirate was the beginning of Caesar's civil war.

It was during this period, from the first triumvirate to Caesar's civil war, that Sallust appears for the first time as a political figure. The year was 52; Sallust was 34 years old and tribune of the plebs. Cicero, the hero of the war with Catiline, had been exiled in 58 with the help of the tribune P. Clodius, but had returned to acclaim and relative unimportance. In 54 the triumvirate had been weakened by the death of Pompey's wife, who was Caesar's daughter. Then, in 53 Crassus died. Caesar suggested that Pompey marry his grand-niece. Pompey declined, and married Cornelia Metella, the daughter of one of Caesar's enemies. The triumvirate was over.

Political violence and obstructionism prevented elections in 53. On 6 December Clodius was killed by a gang of men led by Milo, a friend and ally of Cicero. Clodius was variously thought to have been an adherent of Caesar, an ally of Pompey, or an enemy of Pompey—he was, no doubt, an opportunist. When his body was placed in the Senate house, crowds were incited by two tribunes to burn the building. Asconius tells us that Sallust was involved. Later in 52, when Cicero defended Milo, Pompey's armies surrounded the trial and so intimidated Cicero that he could barely speak. Two tribunes disrupted the trial, called Cicero a thief and a murderer. Cicero said that they were 'contemptible failures as men'.[1] One of them was Sallust.[2] After their term in office, the other tribunes involved in these incidents were prosecuted, but Sallust seems to have escaped unscathed. A commentary on Cicero's speeches tells us that Sallust settled his quarrel with Milo and Cicero.[3] In 50, however, we hear that he was removed from the Senate by Appius Claudius.[4] We do not know why.

The next we hear of Sallust is during 49 BC. In January of that year, Caesar had crossed the Rubicon—to defend his dignity and the rights of the tribunes, he said. Sallust commanded a Caesarian legion in Illyricum.[5] Scholars assume that Caesar appointed Sallust to a quaestorship at this time, thereby allowing him to re-enter the Senate, but there is no evidence for this. Caesar's legate, C. Antonius, was trapped by Pompey's generals on the island of Curicta; Sallust was asked to bring help but failed. Later, in 47, Sallust was sent to deal with Caesar's mutinous troops in Campania.[6] He barely escaped with his life. The troops marched on Rome and Caesar himself had to intervene. In Caesar's African campaign in 46, Sallust, now a praetor, was put in charge of supplies for the island of Cercina.[7] This time he had some success. As praetor, he would have regained his seat in the Senate (if not before). We next hear that Caesar appointed him governor of New Africa (Africa Nova). It is odd that Sallust would receive this commission: except for his handling of supplies at Cercina, he had failed at all the other tasks we know about. But a governorship provided opportunities.

Caesar brought his war against Pompey to an end with his victory at the battle of Pharsalus in 48. He pursued Pompey to Egypt, but Pompey was assassinated by old comrades while coming ashore. Caesar turned his attention to the remnants of Pompey's support. In 45 he returned to Rome. That was the year Sallust also returned

---

[1] *Mil.* 47. [2] Asc. Mil., p. 44. [3] Asc. Mil., p. 37C, 23–4.
[4] Dio Cass. 40. 63. 4. [5] Oros. 6.15.8.
[6] App. *B.Civ.* 2.92; Dio Cass. 42.53.1–2. [7] *B. Afr.* 8.3; 34.1; 34.3.

from Africa, where he had acquired great wealth. He was prosecuted for extortion but was acquitted. This is the last we hear of Sallust. In March of 44 Caesar was assassinated. Presumably Sallust retired from political life at about that time, at the age of 42. He went on to write *Catiline's Conspiracy*, *The Jugurthine War*, and the unfinished *Histories*. Out of his wealth, either he himself or his adoptive heir created the famous and luxurious Horti Sallustii, or Gardens of Sallust. Jerome tells us that Sallust died on 13 May 36 BC, in the fourth year before the battle of Actium.[8]

The few pieces of information that we have about Sallust's life have attracted elaboration and invention. This is the product of both the complex and tumultuous times in which he lived and the tone of his writings. The contrast between his conservative and moralistic posture and the apparent facts of his life—his wealth, his expulsion from the Senate, the charges of extortion, and his self-serving partisanship—led even in ancient times to stories and rumours of dubious value. It was said that he was caught in adultery with Milo's wife and, after paying some money, got off with a whipping.[9] He was mocked for his ambition and immorality, for a youth spent in dissipation, for the cultic sacrifice of young boys, for his lies and his failure in politics, and for his extravagance and sloth. He is accused of abusing his body to gain the money needed to satisfy his extravagant desires, and then when older abusing others as he had been abused.[10] There is little or no historical value in these accusations, which often seem modelled on his own description of Catiline, but they point to an interest in the apparent contradiction between his life and the moralistic tone of his writing.

This contradiction is also addressed by Sallust himself. In the preface to *Catiline's Conspiracy* he says,

as a young man I was at first attracted like many others to politics, and in politics I was thwarted by many obstacles. In place of shame, self-restraint, and virtue, arrogance thrived and graft and greed. My mind, unaccustomed to wicked ways, rejected these things. But I was young and did not know how to resist. Caught in the midst of such corruption, I too was

---

[8] This date, however, cannot be correct, since the battle of Actium took place on 2 September 31 BC.

[9] Gell. 17. 18.

[10] [Cicero], *Invective against Sallust*.

seized and corrupted by ambition. I rejected the wicked character of others, but nevertheless was troubled by the same craving for honour, and I fell victim to the same reputation and invidious attacks as the others. (*C* 3.3–5)

While noting the 'wickedness' that surrounded any young man in politics, he excuses both his actions and his reputation. Whatever one might think of the excuse, a lifetime lived between Sulla's rule and Caesar's assassination gave him his particular insights into factionalism and wealth, corruption and power.

Catiline's Conspiracy

Catiline was born in 108 BC to one of the oldest patrician families in Rome, the Sergii. The family had not produced a consul, however, since 380 BC. Catiline had hopes of restoring his family dignity and began a relatively successful military career. He served during the Social Wars with the father of Pompey the Great. During Sulla's civil war he attained notoriety as a supporter of Sulla. Early in the 70s he was a legate. In 73 he was accused of committing adultery with the Vestal Virgin Fabia: he was acquitted with the help of the ex-consul Q. Lutatius Catulus (consul in 102). He seems to have held the praetorship in 68, after which he was governor of Africa.

When he returned to Rome in 66 he asked to stand for the consulship. He was blocked by L. Volcacius Tullus (consul in 66). We do not know why, but it may have been because charges of extortion were pending for his conduct as governor. When the consuls designate, P. Autronius and P. Sulla, were convicted of bribery, Sallust reports that a conspiracy was formed by Catiline and Autronius to kill the new consuls on 1 January 65 and take over the government. The plot was discovered and postponed to 5 February, but Catiline gave the signal too quickly and nothing happened. Modern scholars are sceptical about the existence of this earlier conspiracy.

For two years Catiline was quiet. He could not run for the consulship in 65 because he was under prosecution for extortion. But he was supported by many of the most important men in Rome and was acquitted through massive bribery (according to Cicero's brother). In 64 he stood for election with five others, including M. Tullius Cicero and C. Antonius Hybrida. Just before the elections, Cicero

accused Catiline of plotting to murder several leading senators.
Cicero and Antonius were elected.

In the summer of 63 Catiline stood for the consulship again.
He ran on a platform of debt relief. Again, there were rumours of
violence. Cicero showed up at the elections with a bodyguard and
wearing a breastplate. Again Catiline was defeated. Most historians
today believe that this was when Catiline decided on violence. He
sent Manlius to Etruria to set up an armed camp. When rumours
of rebellion and letters warning of a massacre arrived in Rome, the
Senate passed its 'final decree'. Armed forces were sent out and
attempts to capture Capua and Praeneste were foiled.

Catiline sent volunteers to kill Cicero in the early morning of
7 November. Cicero was warned and turned the assassins away. The
next day he delivered his *First Catilinarian Speech*, a brilliant attack
on and mockery of Catiline's aspirations and plans. This speech pre-
cipitated Catiline's departure from Rome to join Manlius in Etruria.
Both Catiline and Manlius were declared public enemies. A week or
so later word arrived that Catiline had joined Manlius. But it was not
until early December that Cicero took decisive action.

Ambassadors from Gaul were in Rome seeking redress of
grievances. They were convinced to join the conspiracy, but then
betrayed it. An ambush at the Mulvian Bridge on the night of
2 December led to the capture of five leading conspirators. They
were placed under house arrest and Cicero was honoured with an
official vote of thanks. After some debate, the Senate voted to have
the conspirators executed. Catiline's army met the Roman army
under Antonius early in January 62 and was destroyed. Later in 62 the
praetor, Cicero's brother Quintus, and his colleague M. Calpurnius
Bibulus put down disturbances in southern Italy. In 61 C. Octavius
was sent to crush refugees from the armies of Catiline and Spartacus
around Thurii.

For his role in putting down Catiline's rebellion, Cicero was hailed
as 'father of the fatherland'. His days of glory, however, were not to
last long. In 60 his refusal to join the first triumvirate left him out
in the cold. Soon after, in 58, the tribune P. Clodius passed a law
threatening exile for anyone who killed a Roman citizen without trial.
Cicero argued that the Catilinarians were no longer citizens but had
become enemies once they took up arms against the state; he claimed
that the Senate's 'final decree' absolved him of guilt. He hoped for

help from Pompey at least, but help was not forthcoming and he went into exile.

Why did Sallust choose to write about this event? It was already well documented in the published speeches of Cicero. As a result, it is inadequate and probably incorrect to think that Sallust wanted to portray Catiline as the epitome of evil. In fact, Sallust presents him as a mirror of his age. And he exercises restraint: stories of perversity that Cicero recounts on several occasions[11] Sallust says cannot be confirmed. He distrusts rumours of drinking human blood (*C* 22.3). Other stories, that Catiline murdered his first wife and married his own daughter,[12] he ignores. Sallust's Catiline is perverse (he murdered his own son, *C* 15), but if Sallust was out to demonize, he missed many good opportunities. In fact, he notes that Catiline 'was a man of great strength, both mental and physical', that 'his body could endure hunger, cold, sleep-deprivation beyond what one would believe' (*C* 5.1, 3). And he adds that Catiline was 'encouraged by the corrupt moral character of the state' (*C* 5.8). This combination of mental strength and twisted character, encouraged by a corrupt body politic, is Sallust's focus; not the demonization of a figure already vilified in the powerful and gaudy rhetoric of Cicero.

Sallust himself explains his choice in terms of the conspiracy: it was 'especially memorable because of the unprecedented nature of the crime and the danger it caused' (*C* 4.4). But what was unprecedented about Catiline's conspiracy? Sulla had marched on Rome with an army, twice, and ruled Rome with a murderous hand. His proscriptions had made many rich, including perhaps Catiline. Thousands had died, including half the Senate. Cinna and Marius had starved the city and slaughtered Sulla's supporters. Lepidus, too, had led an army against Rome. Sallust's claim might seem excessive. And yet there appear to have been unprecedented dangers.

First, there are the men involved. Sallust begins his narrative with a catalogue of conspirators (*C* 17): it includes senators and *equites*, a praetor, an ex-quaestor, one of the consular candidates in 64, and a tribune elect. Elsewhere we hear of Crassus' support and the belief that Caesar was involved. The plebs at first favoured war (*C* 48.1); and from the provinces the Allobroges were at first persuaded to join

---

[11] Cic. *Cat.* 2.8, 2.23; *Red. Sen.* 10; *Dom.* 62.
[12] Cic. *Cat.* 1.14; *Tog. Cand.* ap. ASC. 91C.24–6.

Catiline. 'Catiline gathered around him, like a bodyguard, crowds of vices and crimes' (*C* 14.1). But there was also uncertainty: no one knew all who were involved. At the beginning of November, the Senate offered rewards for information (*C* 30.6); in mid-November they offered immunity (*C* 36.2). No one came forward. Even Cicero was troubled by this uncertainty: he said he would not take action until he could eradicate the entire danger. But men of power and wealth easily hide their activities and purposes. Sallust illustrates the problem when he describes the Senate's response to the charge by a certain Tarquinius that Crassus was involved (*C* 48). Some did not believe it; others thought he was involved but were afraid of his power; many owed him money. Disbelief, fear and financial self-interest are added up: the Senate voted that he was not involved.

Second, there is the obscurity of Catiline's purpose. He says he wanted to restore his family dignity, to bring aid to those who, like him, had suffered at the hands of 'the powerful few'. Some think he wanted to solve his own financial problems, to fulfil a desire for power and domination, to satisfy his hatred for those who succeeded where he had failed. In June 64 (*C* 20) he speaks of wealth and glory; he recalls the spoils of war; then, he promises to act as consul. Manlius, his ally, says that they do not seek power or wealth; they want freedom from the cruelty of the praetor; they do not want to fight (*C* 33). Catiline writing to Catulus (*C* 35) speaks of injustice, loss of dignity and office, false suspicions and the cause of the poor. In his final speech to his troops (*C* 58), he says, 'We are fighting for our homeland, for freedom, for our lives.' One may say that this is just rhetoric, but the grievances that his programme of debt relief addressed were real and had popular support, and the abusive power of the few concerned others, including Caesar. And Catiline's diagnosis of power and corruption at Rome is oddly similar to Sallust's own view. We cannot tell where a real political programme ends and mere rhetoric begins.

Finally there is Cicero's view of the conspiracy's unique danger. Others had sought power in the state, had even displayed cruelty, but they had done so as magistrates, as tribunes and generals. Only Catiline had wanted to be consul without being elected, general without earning or even being given a command. Only Catiline wanted domination for the sake of destroying the state, not for the purpose of being powerful within the state. And this was a conspiracy that had seeped over the Alps to Gaul and Spain and Mauretania.

The danger of the conspiracy arose from its ambition to gain civil authority from the violence of civil war and from the impossibility of containing it or defining its goals beyond power and greed.

We can see what interested Sallust in these events by comparing his version of the narrative with what Cicero himself wanted. In 56, seven years after the conspiracy, Cicero asked L. Lucceius, a Roman historian, to compose a monograph that covered the period from the beginning of the conspiracy to his return from exile: 'a single theme and a single persona'.[13] He recommends not only elaboration but exaggeration; he notes the treachery and grief, the opportunities for praise and blame: 'the risky and varied circumstances of real men, often superior men, contain wonder, suspense, joy, trouble, hope, fear; but if they arrive at a noteworthy end, the reader's soul is filled with a most delightful pleasure'.[14]

So far as we know, Cicero never got his monograph from Lucceius, and critics and scholars have found it easy to laugh at his uneasy combination of self-importance and embarrassed neediness. However, his request puts Sallust's monograph in perspective. They share a sense that this conspiracy was in some sense equal to, if not more important than, the external wars with foreign enemies that occurred at the same time. They disagree about the focus on a single man. But this is not a matter of contempt: Sallust refers to the political reaction against Cicero as *invidia* (hateful envy) and to his election as a victory over that *invidia* (*C* 22.3; 23.5–24.1). He calls the *First Catilinarian Speech* 'brilliant' (*C* 31.6) and describes Cicero as 'our very fine consul' (*C* 43.1). This hardly adds up to contempt or disdain, but it is not the kind of praise Cicero wanted. The reason is that Sallust is not focused on a single person; he is exploring a traumatic event, one that entailed the actions, virtuous and vicious and obscure, of several men, and one that did not arrive at 'a noteworthy end'.

For Cicero, the story of heroism and closure ended with his own triumphant return from exile. Sallust, however, brings his narrative to a stop on the battlefield where Catiline is defeated and his army crushed. But the strong closure of victory and death is undermined by the continuing animosities of Roman politics. After the final battle, when Romans come onto the battlefield, they do so in order to plunder other Romans. They are glad to see the corpse of a political

---

[13] Cic. *Fam.* 5.12.2.   [14] Ibid. 5.12.5.

enemy, sad to see the corpse of a friend. The war is over but the body politic is still at war and the Republic is still divided by murderous enmities. The desire for power and money, the forces of factionalism and greed, are thriving in this scene, and they are the same forces that continued to thrive long after the 'noteworthy end' that Cicero imagined.

In fact, in Sallust's writing these forces are inherent in history itself. He says that men should not pass through life in silence, that glory and fame, the goal of human life, require all the resources of body and soul, and that mind should rule body. He says that the history of warfare proves this. When 'craving for domination' was considered a justification for war and 'the greatest glory was held to consist in the greatest military command (*imperium*)' (2.2), Cyrus in Persia and the Greek city-states, Athens and Sparta, showed the superiority of the mind. They won glory; they became the subjects of history: Herodotus wrote of Cyrus; Thucydides of Athens and Sparta. But the craving for domination and military command is the prerequisite.

Sallust goes on to say that political life would be more stable if kings and generals acted in peacetime as they did in war. The obvious problem with this paradigm is that men, especially Roman men, do act in peacetime just as they act in war: 'craving for domination' justified conflict in both the Forum and in Gaul; for both Pompey and Sulla the greatest military command (*imperium*) was the greatest glory. But the problem is deeper. If men should not pass through life in silence, if the goal of human life is to win fame, then Catiline is an example. His speeches and his actions inspire his men to impressive acts of military prowess. He won from history what all men should want, the memory of things done. And he was able to do this at least in part because he had remarkable physical and mental strength, his mind ruled his body with incredible rigour. It is, of course, an irony that Sallust's history is what rewards his crime. But, the process of history rewards 'manliness' (*virtus*), not virtue (another meaning of *virtus*).

Sallust, then, is telling a story about Roman virtue. The result is civil war, an image of Rome destroying herself, of Roman standards hostile to each other, of two armies, veterans remembering their former acts of bravery (*virtus*), the enemy showing incredible daring and mental toughness. This, then, is a story of virtue that does not

cohere, that is already at war with itself. The great image of this inco-
herence is Sallust's comparison of Caesar and Cato (*C* 54), two men
of extraordinary virtue, enemies who will soon try to destroy each
other. These men do not together have the whole of Roman virtue,
because together these two men represent civil war. The problem is
that there is no harmony, no larger virtue that pre-empts and directs
the 'craving for domination' that created, governed and destroyed
the Republic. This lack of *concordia* (harmony) clearly contradicts
Cicero's claim to have created a 'harmony of all', but it nevertheless
points to a basic agreement between Cicero and Sallust about what
was needed.

In the end, Sallust's Roman reader might ask how he is to use
history, especially this history, to prevent further decline, another
act of civil war, Romans plundering Romans, or even the destruction
of the Republic. The conservative platitudes of the preface do not
help. By the time Sallust was writing *Catiline's Conspiracy*, he had
himself lived through Caesar's civil war, Pompey's assassination and
Caesar's, Cato's suicide and the slaughter of Cicero. There was no
way that Sallust's preface could add up to an explanation of history,
glory, and virtue. History was, like Rome herself, filled with 'craving
for domination' and Catiline's conspiracy was a particularly twisted
example, 'especially memorable because of the unprecedented nature
of the crime and the danger it caused'.

The Jugurthine War

During the Second Punic War (218–201 BC), the Numidian king
Masinissa (Jugurtha's grandfather) allied himself with Rome, while
Syphax, another Numidian king, was a Carthaginian ally. After the
Roman victory Masinissa was given as his reward the entire territory
of Numidia, a territory which now acted as a buffer to Carthaginian
expansion on the east, west, and south. Masinissa died in 148, just
after the beginning of the Third Punic War, and his son, Micipsa,
succeeded him as ruler of Numidia. Upon Micipsa's death in 118, the
territory was divided between his two sons, Adherbal and Hiempsal,
and his adopted son, Jugurtha. Jugurtha, however, was ambitious
and ruthless. First, he killed Hiempsal and forced Adherbal to flee.
When Adherbal appealed to Rome, Rome responded without much
urgency by sending Opimius (consul in 121) with a commission

of ten legates. The embassy divided Hiempsal's kingdom into two parts: the western part went to Jugurtha, the eastern to Hiempsal. The embassy effectively restored the Numidian territory to the division that had preceded the Second Punic War. Bribery was suspected, but foreign kings were expected to bring gifts to Rome, and Rome was reluctant to become involved in dynastic disputes. That changed when Jugurtha killed Roman and Italian traders at Cirta in 112.

After the conclusion of the Jugurthine War, Bocchus, the king of Mauretania, was given western Numidia, while Gauda, Jugurtha's half-brother, received the eastern half. The former had been persuaded by Sulla to betray Jugurtha; the latter had been persuaded by Marius to undermine Metellus' command. This arrangement again looked very much like the situation at the beginning of the war, when Opimius divided Numidia, giving the western kingdom to Jugurtha and the eastern kingdom to Adherbal. Clearly, Jugurtha's tactics were arrogant and irritating, but there was not much at stake. In other words, the outcome only stabilized Numidia, an old ally of Rome, in the same way it had been stabilized before. To be sure, a stable boundary between Numidia and Egypt was important, and the outcome restored Roman honour, but it did not increase Roman holdings or Roman wealth in any significant degree.

So why does Sallust write a history of this war? He himself gives two reasons: 'first because it was great and brutal, with victories on both sides, and second because that was the first time there was any opposition to the aristocracy's abuse of power' (*J* 5.1). The first reason seems to be a bit of self-advertising, especially when one thinks of other threats: the Cimbri and Teutones, Mithridates in the east, Sertorius in Spain, Spartacus in Italy, or even the Social Wars. But the war did drag on from, say, the massacre at Cirta (112 BC) until Jugurtha's capture (105). More important, however, is Sallust's political reason. In fact, he goes on to say, 'This struggle confused all things, human and divine, and proceeded to such a pitch of madness that political partisanship had its end in war and the devastation of Italy' (*J* 5.2).

But what does Sallust mean by saying that it was 'the first time there was any opposition to the aristocracy's abuse of power'? Sallust himself notes (*C* 33, *J* 31.6) that the plebs had seceded from the government: in 494 when they gained the tribunate, in 449 to protest abuses of power, and in 287 when they gained the right to pass legislation at the plebeian assemblies. More recent were the struggles of the *optimates* against the Gracchi brothers, young aristocrats who found in the tribunate a way to circumvent senatorial power. In 133 Tiberius Gracchus had used the tribunate to begin a programme of land reform and to fund it with money bequeathed to the Roman people. His actions ignored the traditional senatorial control of fiscal and foreign affairs. When he sought a second term as tribune, the *optimates*, led by Scipio Nasicaa, killed him and about a hundred of his followers. They feared the power base he had developed and his actions both in opposing the Senate and in removing by plebiscite another tribune whom they had put up to oppose him.

In 122 the Senate, led by the consul Opimius, again used violence to meet the challenge of Gaius Gracchus, another tribune and Tiberius' brother. Sallust characterizes their struggle in terms of class interests: 'after they began to assert the freedom of the plebs and expose the crimes of the oligarchy, the aristocracy, which was guilty and therefore frightened, opposed their actions' (*J* 42.1). But it is clear that Sallust considers the Gracchi to be aristocrats: 'For as soon as men were found among the aristocracy who put true glory above unjust power, the state began to tremble and civil strife began to rise up like an earthquake' (*J* 41.1). Perhaps Sallust means that Marius was the first man without aristocratic credentials, the first 'new man', to succeed in opposing the Senate and then to ensure his prestige and power through six consulships.

Sallust's two reasons for writing about the Jugurthine War present two sides to the conflict: one, a contest that takes place in the strange country of Africa with its shifting sands, ambiguous boundaries, treacherous landscape, and Jugurtha; and another contest that takes place in Rome with its duplicities, power struggles, and treacherous allegiances. Rome and Roman politics can, of course, be read as a place with shifting sands, ambiguous boundaries, treacherous land-scapes . . . and a considerable amount of guerrilla warfare. It is at least worth noting that, while the war did little to change the African political landscape, it did set in motion, at least according to Sallust, the internal power struggles that would change for ever the Roman political landscape.

The Jugurthine War is a story of corrupted virtue, an education in treachery on both sides. 'When Jugurtha first reached manhood, he was strong in body, handsome to look at, but above all powerful in his intellectual talents. He did not allow himself to be corrupted by extravagance or idleness' (*J* 6.1). But he was corrupted, first by his own desire for honour and power. When insulted by Hiempsal, he began to plot murder. Then he was infected by the corruption of Rome, where partisan interests pre-empted the common good and everything was for sale (*J* 9, 20, 28, 31.25, 35). He learned to play the Roman game of bribery.

On the other side, the Roman contest is carried on by three major players. The first is Metellus, a representative of the old aristocracy at Rome, 'a great and wise man', according to Sallust. In the past fifteen years, seven members of his family had been consul. After the fall of Cirta (112), when he inherits the Senate's failed and lackadaisical war effort, he restores traditional discipline in the Roman army, even at the cost of delaying the war (*J* 44); he undoes the apathy and laziness he finds among Albinus' men (*J* 45). He learns to use Jugurtha's methods against him: promising peace but preparing war (*J* 48), using the treachery of friends and promises of wealth (*J* 61). And finally he marches to Thala (*J* 75–6) for a surprising and stunning victory. Metellus brings to the war both the strengths of ancestral discipline and, like Jugurtha, an ability to learn treachery from the enemy.

But Metellus would not brook the success of a 'new man' like Marius. And Marius is mentioned as soon as Metellus enters the narrative (*J* 46.7). In fact, throughout Metellus' successes Marius is usually there: behind the front line at the river Muthul (*J* 50), leading half the army to Zama (*J* 55.6); routing Jugurtha at Sicca (*J* 56.6). At Zama, Metellus in tears begs him to save the Roman army (*J* 58–60). Like Jugurtha, Marius had been a young man of great promise and ability: 'he was hard-working, honest, had great knowledge of the military; his spirit was prodigious in war but moderate at home; he was not a victim of lust or wealth, all he really longed for was glory' (*J* 63.2). Like Jugurtha, he served with Scipio Numantinus in Spain and won the praise and admiration of Scipio. He wanted to be consul, but, like Jugurtha, he was provoked to treachery by an insult. But he too had learned from the Numidians. He persuaded Gauda (another man insulted by Metellus) with promises of empire and security to begin a letter-writing campaign. Soon, Marius was elected consul and Metellus was replaced.

Metellus' participation in the war ends with a stalemate at Cirta (*J* 83.3), the very place where the war began (*J* 23, 26) and where it will end (*J* 104). In 107 he returns to Rome (*J* 88). Marius takes up the war and sets his sights on taking Capsa, that is, on equalling Metellus' achievement at Thala (*J* 89.6). He succeeds brilliantly and thereafter 'Every poorly planned action was treated as a sign of courage' (*J* 92.2). Soon he undertakes a risky attack on a well-protected mountain fortress. Luck brings success, but this is the very moment that L. Cornelius Sulla arrives as Marius' quaestor (*J* 95), 'Sulla Felix', Sulla the Lucky, the man who will drive Marius from Rome.

Sulla's role in *The Jugurthine War* is not nearly as large or as impressive as that of Marius or Metellus, but one cannot mention his name without recalling his presence in the history of the late Republic. Sallust's history of the beginnings of factionalism already extends beyond the boundaries of *The Jugurthine War*: 'As for what he did afterwards, I do not know whether one should feel more shame or disgust in talking of it' (*J* 95.4).

After the fall of Capsa and the Numidian stronghold, Marius sets off toward his winter quarters (*J* 100). On the way to Cirta, he defeats Jugurtha and Bocchus in two engagements. Bocchus decides to negotiate, and Marius sends Sulla. What follows is a competition in bribery: Jugurtha bribes Bocchus' friends (*J* 102.15); Sulla's generosity persuades Bocchus' legates: 'And so the barbarians came to believe that the Roman reputation for avarice was false and that Sulla was, given his munificence, a friend. Clearly, at that time many men did not understand the purpose of largesse' (*J* 103.5). The war ends with a charade of diplomacy: Aspar spying on Dabar for Jugurtha; Sulla pretending to talk openly with Dabar about Bocchus; Sulla having a secret meeting with Dabar; and Bocchus pretending to negotiate while making up his mind whom to betray. As luck would have it, Bocchus decides to betray Jugurtha, not Sulla. Marius returns to Rome for his second consulship. 'On 1 January the consul had a glorious triumph. At that time the hopes and resources of the state were in his hands' (*J* 114.3–4).

Sallust uses his preface, as he did in *Catiline's Conspiracy*, to give this story a moral context. He isolates general points about human nature and action which not only have a particular relevance to the story that he is going to tell, but which seem to be contradicted by that very story. This contradiction is a problem in Sallust studies: it has led to a general refusal to take Sallust's prefaces seriously. Quintilian in the second century AD had already concluded that Sallust's prefaces have nothing to do with what follows. Modern scholars follow suit, and treat the moral philosophy on its own terms without relating Sallust's argument to his narratives. A few, however, see the relationship as pointed, polemical, and ultimately satirical.

In the preface to *The Jugurthine War* Sallust claims that the soul is the leader and ruler of life, that the soul has all the resources it needs for fame and success, and that it does not need the help of chance (*J* 1.1–5). Men make a mistake, Sallust says, when they blame misfortune for their own failings. But this austere faith in self-determination is defeated by the narrative. First, the conflict between Marius and Metellus came to a head when 'Marius was by chance offering sacrificial animals to gods at Utica. The soothsayer told him that . . . he should test his fortune as often as possible; all would turn out well' (*J* 63.1). Now, whether we focus on the encouragement which happened 'by chance' or the efforts Marius should make to 'test his fortune', it is hard to get chance and fortune out of the equation. Second, after taking Capsa, when Marius' risky attempt to capture a mountain stronghold near the river Muluccha only ends well because a Ligurian hunting for snails found a way up the mountain, Sallust says, 'In this way Marius' recklessness was amended by chance, and in place of blame he found glory' (*J* 94.7). Third, at the end of the monograph, while Sulla is waiting for Jugurtha, he does not know that Bocchus is trying to decide whether to betray Jugurtha to Sulla or Sulla to Jugurtha. When Bocchus finally decides to betray Jugurtha, it is not clear how this depends upon Sulla's 'virtuous ways' or how 'Sulla the Lucky' controls what happens rather than is controlled by it. 'Before his victory in the civil war he was the most fortunate of all men' (*J* 95.4). And finally, if we ask what gave Metellus the upper hand against Jugurtha, or Marius against Metellus, or Sulla against Jugurtha, we find in place of manly virtue treachery and largesse.

One may believe in the urgency of Sallust's moral agenda without believing that Sallust thinks the world actually works that way. The conflict between a conservative notion of virtue, action, and 'the memory of things done' (history) and the reality of fame and power (history) is a stubborn conflict within Sallust's work, as important as the explicit conflict between *optimates* and *populares*.

Sallustian History

Sallust says that it was not his intention, upon leaving public life, to indulge in hunting and agriculture, servile pastimes. His disdain is surprising: hunting had the recommendation of no less a man than Scipio Aemilianus, the general who brought the Third Punic War to an end by sacking and destroying Carthage, and agriculture was praised by both Cato the Censor and Cicero. But perhaps that was the point: Sallust was an outsider, a 'new man' from Amiternum, not a member of the Roman aristocracy. He did not want an easy aristocratic retirement. And, if we are to trust his words, he wanted to do something both glorious and useful. One can serve the Republic in action and in words, he said; one could win glory by writing about what others had accomplished (*C* 3.1–2).

Subject and Purpose

Sallust's personal reasons for turning to history may be easy enough to understand: he had failed in politics, which had become dangerous, and history, by virtue of its inherent difficulties, was another path to fame and glory (*C* 3.1–2). But we should not assume that history for him was an academic discipline that privileged disinterested objectivity. He is on occasion concerned about evidence, but, when he speaks of the difficulties of his profession, he says that deeds must be equalled by words, and praise and blame must be persuasive (*C* 3.2). This means that it is a mistake to consider Sallust's history as 'analytical' in any modern sense. For Roman writers and readers, history was a branch, not of knowledge, but of rhetoric. It was the memory of things done. And its purpose was ultimately praise and blame.

But the rhetorical nature of this enterprise should not lead one to think that it must be small-minded and political in the pejorative sense. Partisan and mean-spirited attacks are just what Sallust opposes. Our modern world does not endorse a form of history that is self-consciously rhetorical, and the rhetorical tracts that we are familiar with fall mainly into the category of political pamphlets. But Sallust's world was different, and his putative partisanship, whether it is construed as loyalty or enmity with individuals or with political alliances, cannot be proved. He praises an aristocrat like Metellus (*J* 45) and is explicit about the shame and disgust he feels for Sulla (*J* 95). He recounts the partisan roles of tribunes: Memmius against Jugurtha and against the Senate's handling of the war (*J* 31) and Baebius, who protected Jugurtha and the Senate (*J* 34). He condemns the ruling oligarchy (*C* 39, 41; *J* 80), and has the aristocratic villain Catiline repeat the very terms of his own condemnation (*C* 20, 58) and both are recalled by the irresponsible and inflammatory rhetoric of tribunes (*J* 30.3, 31.19–20, 37.1).

If we try to account for both sides of this picture, there is no better place to begin than with Sallust's own words when he steps back to look at both sides: 'At that time were many in our army, both "new men" and old aristocracy, who thought wealth preferable to virtue and honour; they were politically factious at home, powerful among the allies, more famous than honourable' (*J* 8.1). 'To put the truth in a few words, political agitators used honourable explanations: "defending the people's rights" or "securing the authority of the Senate", and they pretended to work for the public good while they struggled for their own power. There was no restraint or measure to their efforts. Each side used their victories brutally' (*C* 38.3–4).

It is in this context that one can and should appreciate Sallust's concern with the rhetorical problems of history. The first problem is to make the words equal to the events. This is not a technical matter of representation or of naming. Sallust does not mean that it is hard to find the right word for, say, manly virtue. He is concerned with the problem that words change things and deeds: they magnify or diminish; they give the confusing and the obscure an apparent stability, while the actions themselves are rich with contradictions and subterranean forces. When Sallust has the villain Catiline say that he knows the virtue of his men, is that just cynical rhetoric? It turns out to be true: his men do display both fidelity to the cause and military prowess. But how can a wicked cause display virtue? And if it does, should we call it virtue? And when Catiline's men die displaying the manly virtue that made Rome great, the problem is not just words. Sallust struggles to achieve some equivalence to and with the confusions, contradictions and intractable impasses of what he saw happening.

Then there was the problem of persuasion: 'many will think that what you castigate as offences are mentioned because of hatred and envy; but, when you speak of the great virtue and glory of good men, what each one thinks is easy for himself to do, he accepts with equanimity; what goes beyond that—he construes like fictions made up for lies' (*C* 3.2). Sallust is concerned that his history could be dismissed for three reasons: as partisanship, as uncompelling, or as lies. This means that he wants his readers to feel the pressure of his praise and blame. He does not write history to explain away the events of the past, to put them in some apparently objective, unemotional, even-handed prose. He expects and provokes his readers to care about the processes by which the Roman state 'gradually changed from the most lovely and best and became the worst and most depraved' (*C* 5.9).

Sallust's Style

Sallust's monographs have been called epoch-making, not for their historical accuracy or detail, but for their achievement as literature, creating a new style and manner, and putting Latin historiography in competition with Greek historiography. Sallust's style opposed both the balanced parallelisms and ornamented periods of Cicero and the clear, elegant prose of Caesar. Quintilian, who considered Sallust the greatest Roman historian, found his style to be brief, abrupt (or broken), and deceptive. He said that it was not well understood when read aloud; 'perhaps he deceives less the leisurely reader, but he flies past the listener, and does not wait for repetition'. Seneca comments on his truncated clauses, distorted word order and obscure brevity. In all of this, Sallust emulates the great Greek historian Thucydides: dense, brief, pressing. In fact, the elder Seneca says that brevity was Thucydides' special virtue, but that Sallust was superior in this and defeated the great historian in his own camp.[15]

Sallust's brevity depends upon inconcinnity (lack of parallelism), broken phrases, ellipses, and parataxis (unconnected lists without subordination). To describe the end of a battle he uses a paratactic sequence of infinitives (here translated as participles):

> Finally, the enemy was now routed everywhere. Then a horrible
> sight on the open plains: pursuing, fleeing, falling, being captured;
> horses and men afflicted, and many, wounded but not able to flee
> or to stay still, now struggling up and immediately collapsing back;
> finally, everything, wherever you looked, strewn with weapons,

---

[15] Quint. *Inst.* 10.1.101, 4.2.45; Sen. *Ep.* 114.17; Quint. *Inst.* 10.1.73; Sen. *Controv.*

armour, corpses, and between them the ground drenched with blood.
(*J* 101.12)

To describe Catiline's character a list of traits is given:

> L. Catiline, born in a noble family, was of great strength of mind and
> body but of character wicked and perverse. . . . His body tolerant
> of hunger, cold, wakefulness beyond what anyone would believe.
> His mind daring, crafty, versatile, simulator and dissembler of
> whatever he wanted, greedy for others', lavish of his own, burning
> in his passions; sufficient eloquence, wisdom little. His vast mind
> was always desiring the immoderate, the incredible, the too lofty.
> (*C* 5.1–5)

(My translations here attempt to emphasize Sallust's verbal techniques and the strangeness of some of his effects; they are not the
same as the translations offered in the text, which attempt to be more
accessible.)

Sallust also aims at effects in diction that imitate Thucydides'
austerity and majesty. Thucydides had adopted and manipulated
the resources of a well-developed poetic idiom. To produce a similar
result in Latin prose, Sallust turned to archaism. And his contem-
poraries noticed: Asinius Pollio (a military man and also a historian)
described his style as 'mired with an excessive affection for archaic
words'. Quintilian records an epigram that calls Sallust 'a great thief
of the words of ancient Cato'. It is said that he had an assistant, Ateius
Praetextatus Philologus, who collected archaic words and figures of
speech for him.[16] In fact, he adopted the language as well as the tone
of Cato the Censor, the great-grandfather of the younger Cato, the
austere 'new man' who demanded that 'Carthage must be destroyed'.
Ironic, of course, since for Sallust the destruction of Carthage was
the beginning of Roman decline (*C* 10).

Archaism appears in Sallust's vocabulary and pronunciation,
syntax, and sentence structure. He often prefers antique and majestic
words (e.g. *mortales*, 'mortals', for *homines*, 'humans'; *opulentia*,
'opulence', for *opes*, 'wealth'). Some common words are used with a
sense different from their usual meaning (*tempestas*, which can mean
'storm', is used for the more common *tempus*, meaning 'time'). He
tends to use archaic endings for abstract nouns (something like

---

[16] Suet. *Gram.* 10, Quint. *Inst.* 8.3.29.

'beatitude' instead of 'blessedness'), and he expands the use of the substantive adjective in place of abstract nouns (as in 'the good' or 'the lofty'). He shows a preference for simple verbs like 'do', 'make', and 'have' in new phrases and he enjoys archaic-sounding alliterative phrases ('the glory of wealth and beauty is *fluid and fragile*', *fluxa atque fragilis*, *C* 1.4). In Latin, nouns are declined in cases with differing endings, some of which had changed their pronunciation over the years. Thus, at a time when most Romans would have said '*omnes*', Sallust begins *Catiline's Conspiracy* with '*omneis*' and when the term for 'greatest' was generally pronounced '*maximus*', Sallust wrote '*maxumus*'.

The effect of these archaisms is to produce a prose that is austere and unfamiliar. This effect is complemented by Sallust's invention of new terms (noted by Valerius Probus[17]) and his use of bold metaphors and similes (noted by Ateius Philologus)[18]: 'Such was the force of the disease [i.e., treasonous self-interest and fear] that like a plague had invaded the minds of many citizens' (*C* 36.5); 'the state began to tremble and civil strife began to rise up like an earthquake' (*J* 41.10). He also enjoyed changing the order of idiomatic phrases: 'land and sea' becomes 'seas and lands', 'consul designate' becomes 'the designated consuls'.

The moralistic and conservative austerity of Sallust's archaisms and the edginess of his broken phrases and ellipses, his innovations and metaphors are often intensified by a penchant for antithesis, or rather what sounds antithetical. He opposes body and soul in the preface to *Catiline's Conspiracy* as he tries to secure both a practical and a moral orientation toward action. The clarity of the antithesis is belied by the facts of history and even by the virtues of Catiline. He opposes the oligarchy (the aristocracy, the nobles, the few) to the plebs (the crowd), the *optimates* to the *populares*, as their impassioned oppositions dissolve the structure of republican governance. He opposes the strengths and virtues of two extraordinary men, Cato and Caesar, as they debate the future of the Catilinarians. He opposes the doing of deeds to the speaker and writer of deeds in terms of fame and service to the state.

Finally, we come to Sallust's sentence structure. For the most part he avoids the balanced and ornamented periods of Cicero. But even

---

[17] Gell. I.15.18.   [18] Suet. *Gram.* 10.

in antiquity his style was noted both for its structure and for the effort he put into it. He could produce the typical historical period, one that gathers the context of an event into subordinate clauses: 'Volturcius at first encouraged the others and with his sword defended himself from the crowd; then, when he was deserted by his legates, having first made many demands to Pomptinus concerning his own safety, because Pomptinus knew him, finally, timid and uncertain of his life, just like an enemy, he handed himself over to the praetors' (*C* 45.4; the translation here reflects Sallust's periodicity but differs from the text). But Sallust could also, and more typically, write an awkward but powerful sentence: 'And in fact, to set out the truth in a few words, after that time whoever agitated the Republic with honourable slogans, one part as if they were defending the rights of the people, some in order that the Senate's authority be greatest, pretending the public good they struggled every man for his own power' (*C* 38.3; the translation in the text has been altered to reflect Sallust's style). Here, agitation and 'honourable slogans', pretence ('as if') and real purpose ('in order that'), inconcinnity ('one part . . . some . . .'), and ellipsis ('pretending the public good' for 'pretending to defend the public good') gather together in the simple but cynical conclusion, 'every man for his own power'.

Sallust's Achievement

Sallust's life was troubled personally and politically. He did not succeed at politics or at warfare; he faced criminal charges, was removed from the Senate, and finally retired. He saw the madness of the late Republic, when civil strife rose like an earthquake, and his state, the loveliest and best, became the worst and most vicious. But out of those experiences he forged a broken, abrupt and deceptive style that was the perfect vehicle for his moral urgency, his bitter condemnation, and his satirical cynicism. Nietzsche praises, as many have, his 'compact' and 'severe' style, 'with as much substance as possible'. But there was more than style at work—or, rather, style is more than just style. The monumental history that Sallust alludes to when he refers to the waxen images of aristocratic ancestors is not the history Sallust writes. The totalizing certainty of the conservative morality he gives voice to in his prefaces is not supported by the history he writes. His history is nowhere a story of greatness; it is nowhere inspiring or comforting. This might align Sallust with Foucault's satirical historian, the one who knows that all heroes have feet of clay, except that in Sallust it is not the hero who is exposed; it is the criminal who dies ferocious, mindful of his dignity, displaying all the Roman manliness of Rome's glorious past. Virtue, a word that is so impossible to translate, is the issue that will not go away. Nietzsche again: he shows 'a cold malice for all "beautiful words" and "beautiful sentiments".'

The anger and grief of Sallust's narrative, the cynicism and despair of his conceptual framework, and the power of his style had an immediate effect. One hears Sallust's voice in Horace's *Epodes*: 'Rome herself is collapsing under [with, from] her own strength.'[19] In this epode Syme finds allusions to Sallust's Sertorius (*H* 1.100 ff.) and the Allobroges (*C* 40). On the shield in Virgil's *Aeneid* one finds Catiline suffering and Cato giving laws. Sallust and Livy were proclaimed 'equals rather than similar'. But it was Sallust who influenced L. Arruntius (consul in 22) when he wrote his history of the First Punic War. Martial considered Sallust 'number one in Roman history', and Quintilian said he was the greater historian, although he should be kept from young boys because understanding him required maturity.[20] He remained influential throughout antiquity: admired by Augustine and Macrobius, quoted by grammarians and commentators. Later, in 'What I Learned from the Ancients' Nietzsche would say that Sallust awakened in him his own sense of style. But, perhaps most important was his influence on Rome's third great historian, Tacitus. He adopted (and some think improved) Sallust's manner and perspective. Thereafter, Sallust was imitated and studied throughout late antiquity and the Renaissance. His own writings, his 'memory of things done', finally became the written image that enkindled the flame of emulation in orators, philosophers, and politicians.

[19] Hor. *Epod.* 16.2, 39.   [20] Mart. 14.199.2; Quint. *Inst.* 2.5.19.

NOTE ON THE TRANSLATION

There are probably about as many views of translation as there are translators, and for good reason. Not only does each language divide the world in different ways, but each author and translator uses the resources of his or her language, its sounds and rhythms as well as its vocabulary and syntax, in ways that cannot be duplicated in different sounds, vocabulary, rhythm, and syntax. Translation is one of the arts of compromise, and as such may seem to be now a form of betrayal, now an act of love.

Many of the features of Sallust's style outlined in the Introduction do not survive well in translation. This is partly because of our expectation that translations should be accessible and clear, and partly because similar techniques have different effects in different languages. If we find an English translation that is filled with awkward word order, the syntax is disturbed, but word order in Latin does not typically determine syntax. Sallust's awkward word order achieves different effects: the unexpected, the edgy.

Similarly, if Sallust creates a resonance between all his repetitions of *virtus* (meaning 'manliness', 'courage', 'virtue', 'determination', and 'ability') we simply cannot create the same effect in English by finding some single word that will always translate *virtus*. There are two reasons for this: first, no English word has this range of meanings, and to make some word do that work distorts English where the Latin is not distorted; second, we have and use different terms for these instances of Roman *virtus* and we cannot pretend that we do not. English simply divides up the world differently, and it has a vocabulary many times that of Latin. So to translate any Latin word with the same English word regardless of context is to emphasize Sallust's resonance, his repetitions, the way he struggles with a concept. But such a translation also sacrifices the very concept that Sallust struggles with. Of course one can say that translation at this level always sacrifices something. It is an art of compromise.

Here, the primary goal set for the translation has been to make Sallust's intensity, energy, and 'cold malice' accessible. When Sallust is jagged, I have tried to find or create a jaggedness in the English—not the same jaggedness, because that seems to me futile, if not misleading, but something that feels out of joint. When Sallust is archaic, I have rarely been able to duplicate the effect. What would it mean for my version of Sallust's Cato to sound at times like the King James Bible, at times like the United States Constitution? Something would be gained, but something would be lost or distorted as well. When his word order is misleading, broken, and deceptive, I have generally hoped that the narrative and his moral logic (which can also be broken and deceptive) will be enough to alert the reader to the fact that something is wrong. It has always been a judgement call and I have especially tried not to allow any mannerism or norm of translation to pre-empt the overall effect of a passage. A couple of areas in which those judgement calls are particularly important are discussed below.

Vocabulary. Latin vocabulary is limited: smaller than Greek, much smaller than English. This means that Latin words not only divide the world differently from English words, but they often have more 'meanings' than their English counterparts and overlap with other terms in different ways. A common example would be the word mentioned above, *virtus*, which is the origin of the English word 'virtue' and derived from the Latin term *vir*, 'man' (as in 'virility'). The term refers to those qualities which are 'manly': courage and bravery, strength and persistence, excellence or ability in general; by extension, the term also refers to moral virtue, even the kind of virtue a Roman would find in a wife or a woman. We find it in Sallust's preface to *Catiline's Conspiracy*, where he speaks of 'the mind's *virtus*' as superior to 'the body's strength', and again in Catiline's speeches where he says that he knows his men's *virtus* and that they should rather die through *virtus* than live in disgrace. In the first instance, 'mental excellence' seems adequate, although it obscures the need for moral excellence. But that is precisely the problem, for it is just this moral component that is lacking throughout *Catiline's Conspiracy*, perhaps most poignantly at the end, when Catiline's army dies fighting with 'mental toughness' and the veterans fight 'remembering their long-established virtue'. On the other hand, 'mental virtue' sounds rather medieval and is not particularly clear. Similarly, when Catiline says that his men's *virtus* encourages him (*C* 58.21), he means primarily 'courage' and tenacity. Better to die through courage than live in disgrace. But this precision obscures the further point that Catiline is using the language of moral virtue in a vicious cause. Throughout Catiline's speech I have translated *virtus* as 'manly virtues' because I thought the reference to 'virtue' was important, but neither this translation nor a more precise translation, like 'courage', allows Catiline's words to echo with Sallust's moral concerns in the preface. As should be clear, I do not think that there is a wholly adequate solution to these problems. In the main, I have tried to reflect the meaning in context without losing the larger meaning that comes from Sallust's repetitive style.

Another example would be *ambitio*, the word from which we derive 'ambition'. The word literally means 'going about', for example, going about the Forum canvassing for votes, and so it has a common and specific meaning: to solicit or canvass for votes. Since one needs to be pleasing and flattering when soliciting votes, the term comes to mean 'flattery', 'ingratiation'. Sallust uses the term or its cognates seventeen times, and, given the explicitly political concerns of his histories, these echoes should be important. But these repetitions cannot be rendered by the same word into English: Sallust says that his youth was corrupted by *ambitio* (*C* 3.4); that *ambitio* compels men to be liars (*C* 10.5); when things began to go downhill, it was *ambitio* rather than 'avarice' that worked men's souls, and *ambitio* was a vice closer to a *virtus* (*C* 11.1); that Metellus held a moderate course between *ambitio* and savagery (*J* 45.1); and that, when Marius appealed to his soldiers' sense of shame rather than punish them, many said this was done through *ambitio* (*J* 100.5). I have not been able to find any term in English that captures the self-serving, determined, fawning, and potentially duplicitous nature of Latin *ambitio* and at the same time can simply mean 'to canvass for votes'.

In fact, many of the terms that Sallust uses to refer to the powerful forces at work in the Roman Republic are words that have wide application. The Latin term *ingenium* may refer to 'innate qualities', 'character', 'intelligence', 'mind', 'talent', or 'genius'. *Anima* may be 'life principle' or 'soul' and *animus* may be 'soul', or 'self', or 'mind'. A crime is a *facinus*, but the word can also mean simply a 'deed', and, when Sallust has Catiline encourage his men to a 'very great and most beautiful *facinus*' (*C* 20.3), the irony is obvious but untranslatable. The interplay of these words and concepts is rich and is further enhanced by the fact that political rhetoric, especially when scrutinized later as 'a period of crisis and decline', perverts or co-opts the usual meaning of terms (see *C* 52.11 and note). Thus, the vicious Catiline speaks of *virtus* and 'good faith', of liberty and fatherland; and Cato turns 'compassion' into a crime, 'liberality' into murder, and 'generosity' into bribery. Much of this eludes any translator.

Sentence structure. Sallust's brevity and speed were mentioned earlier. This is often achieved by paratactic lists, a series of infinitives, a set of parallel phrases or clauses. Whenever possible, I have tried to keep the paratactic nature of these lists, modifying them as necessary; for instance, English prefers participles for listing actions, while Latin uses the infinitive. But Latin has other resources for moving ideas along with great speed and point, resources that are possible but often awkward in English.

These resources include participles which can stand for clauses, appositions which can make identifying statements within a sentence, word order which can bring one part of a modification or even a single word into the kind of prominence that would require an entire sentence in English. Since Latin word order does not mark syntactic relationships, it is free to mark many other aspects of communication: predication, emphasis, ironic juxtaposition, surprise. The result of these resources is that the complex and periodic sentence structure that all Romans used cannot be reproduced in English without writing some sort of 'translationese'. And to produce translationese would be a misrepresentation of Sallust's powerful native idiom.

Ultimately, a translation cannot substitute for the original. The difficulties and pleasures of Sallust's style can only be fully enjoyed (if that is the right word) by a direct confrontation (if that is the right word) with the Latin text. There, readers will find much more repetition than here, especially of terms that emphasize moral qualities, terms that are frequently glossed as 'virtue', 'ambition', 'crime', 'greed', 'pride', 'talent', 'intellect', 'character'. They will also find an idiom that is restless, broken, filled with ellipsis and innovation at the same time as it indulges in archaism and subordination. If something of Sallust's urgency and austerity, his moral intensity, and his satiric malice comes through the English of this translation, and if that encourages a few to grapple with the original, then my own labour will have been rewarded.

The Text

The Latin text is that established by L. D. Reynolds, Oxford Classical
Texts (Oxford, 1991). The few readings that deviate from Reynolds
are listed below. The paragraph numbers in the margins are also
those of the OCT.

	This translation	*Reynolds*
Catiline's Conspiracy:		
19.2	putabant: etiam tum	putabant et iam tum
22.2	idque eo fecisse quo	[atque eo dictitare fecisse] quo
25.2	Graecis et Latinis	Graecis [et] Latinis
43.1	agrum Aefulanum	agrum #faesulanum#
53.5	magnitudine sua	magnitudine sui
	effeta parente	#effeta parentum#
59.3	quemque [armatum]	quemque armatum
The Jugurthine War:		
15.5	polluta licentia	#polluta# licentia
113.3	voltu colore motu corporis	voltu [corporis] <et oculis>
The Histories:		
1.11	[. . .].	<causaque . . . non amor iustitiae, sed stante Carthagine metus pacis infidae fuit>
1.77.17	intellegat	intelleget
2.47	plebes abalienata fuerat	#plevis avalia funera#
3.48.20	iniuria	iniuriae
4.69.17	pesti	peste

Acknowledgements

I would like to thank all those who have supported this surprisingly
long project. Special thanks to Cynthia Damon, whose perspective
on all sorts of things is always valuable, to graduate students who read
the translation at various stages, especially Mark Wright and Joey
Lipp, and to the Department of Greek and Latin for twenty hours
of proofing, and to Leah Batstone for providing the perspective of a
thoughtful undergraduate. Mary, this is for you.

SELECT BIBLIOGRAPHY

General

Badian, E., *Publicans and Sinners: Private Enterprise in the Service of the Republic* (Oxford, 1972).

Brunt, P. A., *The Fall of the Roman Republic and Related Essays* (Oxford, 1988).

Crook, J. A., Lintott, A., and Rawson, E. (eds.), *The Last Age of the Roman Republic, 146–43 B.C.*, vol. ix of *The Cambridge Ancient History*[2] (Cambridge, 1994).

Feldherr, Andrew, *The Cambridge Companion to Roman Historiography* (Cambridge, 2009).

Gruen, Eric, *The Last Generation of the Roman Republic* (Berkeley and Los Angeles, 1974).

Lintott, A. W., *Violence in Republican Rome*[2] (Oxford, 1999).

Rosenstein, Nathan, and Morstein-Marx, Robert, *A Companion to the Roman Republic* (Oxford, 2006).

Seager, R. (ed.), *The Crisis of the Roman Republic* (Cambridge, 1969).

Syme, Ronald, *The Roman Revolution* (Oxford, 1939).

Taylor, L. R., *Party Politics in the Age of Caesar* (Berkeley and Los Angeles, 1949).

Wirszubski, C., *Libertas as a Political Idea at Rome during the Late Republic and Early Principate* (Cambridge, 1950).

Wiseman, T. P. (ed.), *Roman Political Life: 90 B.C.–A.D. 69* (Exeter and Chicago, 1985).

Sallust

Allen, W., 'Sallust's Political Career', *Studies in Philology*, 51 (1954), 1–14.

—— 'The Unity of the Sallustian Corpus', *Classical Journal*, 61 (1966), 268–9.

Earl, D. C., *The Political Thought of Sallust* (Cambridge, 1961).

Scanlon, T. F., *The Influence of Thucydides on Sallust* (Heidelberg, 1980).

—— *Spes Frustrata: A Reading of Sallust* (Heidelberg, 1987).

Syme, Ronald, *Sallust* (Berkeley, 1966).

Catiline's Conspiracy

Allen, W., 'In Defense of Catiline', *Classical Journal*, 34 (1938), 70–85.

Batstone, W. W., '*Incerta pro certis*: An Interpretation of Sallust's *Bellum Catilinae* 48.4–49.4', *Ramus*, 15 (1986), 105–21.

—— 'The Antithesis of Virtue: Sallust's Synkrisis and the Crisis of the Late Republic', *Classical Antiquity*, 7 (1988), 1–29.

—— 'Intellectual Conflict and Mimesis in Sallust's *Bellum Catilinae*', in J. W. Allison (ed.), *Conflict, Antithesis and the Ancient Historian* (Columbus, Ohio, 1990), 112–32, with notes 189–94.

Brunt, P. A., 'The Conspiracy of Catilina', *History Today*, 13 (1963), 14–21.

Drummond, A., *Law, Politics and Power: Sallust and the Execution of the Catilinarian Conspirators* (*Historia Einzelschriften*, 93; Stuttgart, 1995).

Gunderson, E., 'The History of Mind and the Philosophy of History in Sallust's *Bellum Catilinae*', *Ramus*, 29 (2000), 85–126.

Levine, D. S., 'Sallust's "Catiline" and Cato the Censor', *Classical Quarterly* (2000), 170–91.

MacKay, L. A., 'Sallust's "Catiline": Date and Purpose', *Phoenix*, 3 (1962), 181–94.

Phillips, E. J., 'Catiline's Conspiracy', *Historia*, 25 (1976), 441–8.

Seager, R., '*Iusta Catilinae*', *Historia*, 22 (1973), 240–8.

—— 'The First Catilinarian Conspiracy', *Historia*, 13 (1964), 338–47.

Sklenár, R., 'La République des signes: Caesar, Cato, and the Language of Sallustian Morality', *TAPA* 128 (1998), 205–20.

Yavetz, Z., 'The Failure of Catiline's Conspiracy', *Historia*, 12 (1963), 485–99.

Wilkins, A. T., *Villain or Hero: Sallust's Portrayal of Catiline* (New York, 1996).

The Jugurthine War

Claasen, Jo-Marie, 'Sallust's Jugurtha: Rebel or Freedom Fighter? On Crossing Crocodile Infested Waters', *Classical World*, 86 (1993), 273–97.

Due, Casey, 'Tragic History and Barbarian Speech in Sallust's Jugurtha', *Harvard Studies in Classical Philology*, 100 (2000), 311–25.

Keitel, Elizabeth, 'The Influence of Thucydides 7.61–71 on Sallust Cat. 20–21', *Classical Journal*, 82 (1987), 293–300.

Levene, D. S., 'Sallust's Jugurtha: An "historical fragment" ', *Journal of Roman Studies*, 82 (1992), 53–70.

Morstein-Marx, R., 'The Alleged Massacre at Cirta and its Consequences (Sallust Bellum Jugurthinum 26–27', *Classical Philology*, 95 (2000), 468–76.

—— 'The Myth of Numidian Origins in Sallust's African Excursus (Jugurtha 17.7–18.12)', *American Journal of Philology*, 122 (2001), 179–200.

Parker, Victoria, 'Romae omnia venalia esse: Sallust's Development of a Thesis and the Prehistory of the Jugurthine War', *Historia*, 53 (2004), 408–23.

Scanlon, T. F., 'Textual Geography in Sallust's The War with Jugurtha', *Ramus*, 17 (1988), 138–75.

von Fritz, Kurt, 'Sallust and the Attitude of the Roman Nobility at the Time of the Wars against Jugurtha (112–105)', *TAPA* 74 (1943), 134–68.

Wiedemann, Thomas, 'Sallust's "Jugurtha": Concord, Discord, and the Digressions', *Greece and Rome*, 2nd ser., 40/1 (April, 1993), 48–57.

Sallust's Histories

Alheid, F., 'Oratorical Strategy in Sallust's Letter of Mithridates Reconsidered', *Mnemosyne*, 41 (1988), 67–92.

Badian, E., 'Waiting for Sulla', *Journal of Roman Studies*, 52 (1962), 47–61.

Badian, E., 'Lucius Sulla, the Deadly Reformer', in A. J. Dunston (ed.), *Essays on Roman Culture: The Todd Memorial Lectures* (Toronto, 1976), 35–74.

Rawson, E., 'Sallust on the Eighties?', *Classical Quarterly*, 37 (1987), 163–80.

Further Reading in Oxford World's Classics

Caesar, Julius, *The Civil War*, trans. John Carter.
—— *The Gallic War*, trans. Carolyn Hammond.
Cicero, *Defence Speeches*, trans. D. H. Berry.
—— *Political Speeches*, trans. D. H. Berry.
—— *Selected Letters*, trans. P. G. Walsh.
Livy, *Rome's Mediterranean Empire* (Books 41–45 and the Periochae), trans. Jane D. Chaplin.
Plutarch, *Roman Lives*, trans. Robin Waterfield, ed. Philip A. Stadter.

A CHRONOLOGY OF THE LATE REPUBLIC

All dates are BC.

157 Birth of C. Marius.

146 End of Third Punic War; destruction of Carthage.

138 Birth of L. Cornelius Sulla.

133 T. Gracchus tribune of the plebs; death of T. Gracchus; destruction of Numantia by Scipio; Jugurtha and Marius with Scipio in Spain.

123 C. Gracchus tribune of the plebs (to 122).

122 Senate's 'final decree'; death of C. Gracchus.

120 Birth of M. Aemilius Lepidus.

115 Birth of M. Licinius Crassus.

112 Jugurtha takes Cirta.

111 L. Calpurnius Bestia consul. Jugurthine War begins.

109 Q. Caecilius Metellus consul.

108 Birth of L. Sergius Catilina (Catiline).

107 Marius consul for the first time; Sulla quaestor.

106 Birth of Cn. Pompeius (Pompey); birth of M. Tullius Cicero.

105 P. Rutilius Rufus consul; Jugurthine War ends; battle of Arausio (against the Cimbri).

104 Marius consul for the second time; his triumph brings Jugurtha to Rome; death of Jugurtha.

103 Marius consul for the third time; L. Saturninus tribune of the plebs.

102 Marius consul for the fourth time.

101 Marius consul for the fifth time; defeat of the Cimbri.

100 Marius consul for the sixth time; birth of C. Julius Caesar; L. Saturninus tribune of the plebs; Senate's 'final decree'; death of Saturninus.

97   Sulla praetor.

95   Birth of M. Porcius Cato.

93   Birth of P. Clodius Pulcher.

91   Social Wars (to 87).

88   Sulla consul for the first time.

88   First Mithridatic War (to 86).

87 Cinna consul for the first time.

86 Marius consul for the seventh time; death of Marius; L. Cornelius Cinna consul for the second time; birth of C. Sallustius Crispus (Sallust).

85 Cinna consul for the third time.

84 Cinna consul for the fourth time; death of Cinna.

83 Second Mithridatic War (to 81).

82 Sulla dictator (to 81).

81 War with Sertorius (to 72).

80 Sulla consul for the second time.

78 M. Aemilius Lepidus and Q. Lutatius Catulus consuls; death of Sulla.

77 Lepidus revolt; Senate's 'final decree'; death of Lepidus.

77 Pompey in Spain (to 71).

74 Third Mithridatic War (to 65).

70 Pompey consul for the first time; Crassus consul for the first time.

67 Pompey's extraordinary command against pirates.

66 'First Catilinarian conspiracy'.

66 Pompey in east (to 62).

63 Cicero consul; birth of C. Julius Caesar Octavianus (the future emperor Augustus); Catiline's conspiracy; Senate's 'final decree'.

62 Death of Catiline.

60 First triumvirate.

59 Caesar consul for the first time.

58 Clodius tribune of the plebs; Cicero in exile (to 57).

56 Triumvirate renewed at Luca; Caesar's proconsular command extended.

55 Pompey consul for the second time; Crassus consul for the second time.

53 Death of Crassus.

52 Pompey consul for the third time; trial of Milo; death of Clodius; Sallust tribune of the plebs.

50 Sallust expelled from the Senate.

49 Caesar crosses the Rubicon: civil war begins; Senate's 'final decree'.

48 Caesar consul for the second time; battle of Pharsalus; death of Pompey; Caesar dictator.

46 Caesar consul for the third time; death of Cato; Sallust praetor, then governor of Africa.

45 Caesar consul for the fourth time; Sallust charged with extortion.

44 Caesar consul for the fifth time, dictator *perpetuus*; death of Caesar.

43 Second triumvirate (Antony, Lepidus, Octavian); death of Cicero.

42 Battle of Philippi; Sallust probably begins his career as a historian.

36 Death of Sallust.

MAPS

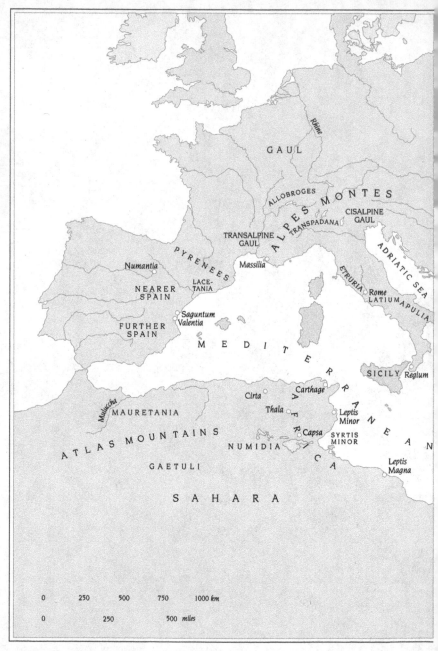

MAP 1. The Mediterranean world in the first century.

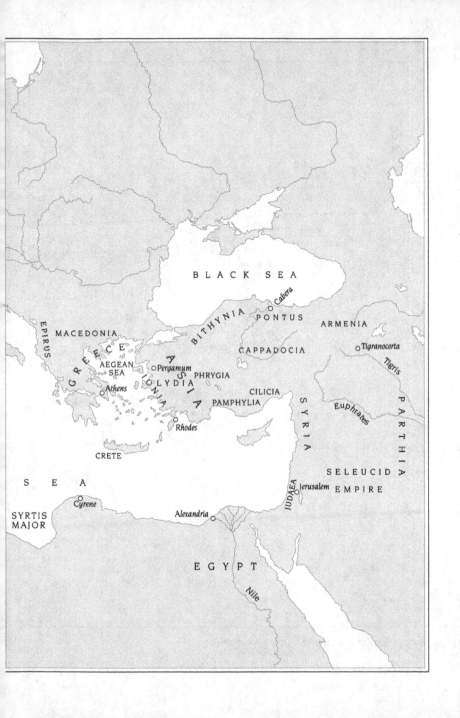

MAP 2. Italy at the time of Catiline's conspiracy.

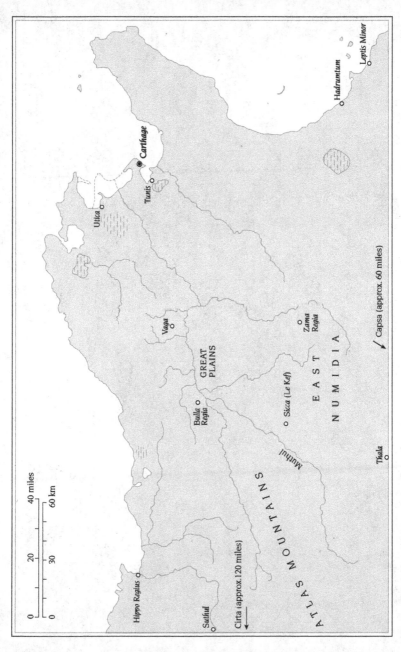

MAP 3. Africa at the time of the Jugurthine War.

CATILINE'S CONSPIRACY,
THE JUGURTHINE WAR,
HISTORIES

CATILINE'S CONSPIRACY

INTRODUCTION

Summary and Outline

The structure of *Catiline's Conspiracy* is anything but clear. Scholars even disagree about where the preface ends. Sallust begins with a philosophical brief on the purpose of human life (to win fame and glory) as the natural functioning of history, virtue and success (1–2). He then adds history itself as a field in which one may win glory (3), an unusual choice for a Roman. This leads to a defence of his own life and present choice of career (3–4). The preface might end here and the body begin with his portrait of Catiline ('I will, therefore, give an account of Catiline's conspiracy . . .', 4.3–5.8), except that the circumstances of Catiline's success requires a digression on Rome's growth and subsequent moral decline (5.8–13.5). Some scholars take this to be the end of the preface, but Sallust complicates neat divisions by returning to a general portrait of Catiline and his associates (14–16). At ch. 17 we seem to begin the narrative proper: 'Therefore, about 1 June . . .', but this is interrupted for another background narrative, the so-called 'first Catilinarian conspiracy' (18–19). Sallust then returns to the June meeting and Catiline's speech to his followers (20). By the time this speech is over we are well into Sallust's narrative, but one cannot say exactly where that narrative began. In fact, the concerns of Catiline's speech continue after he concludes with his further promises of consular power, booty, and armies (21). This scene ends with rumours that the followers drank blood together (22). The story of Curius' over-confidence and Fulvia's revelations (23) follow, all of which leads to the election of Cicero and Antonius: 'Therefore, when the elections were held, M. Tullius and C. Antonius were declared consuls' (24.1).

The meeting in June 64 and Catiline's speech create some dissonances that are worth noting. First, the men Catiline gathers together are not insignificant malcontents. They represent all orders of Roman society. This catalogue of villains at the beginning of Sallust's narrative is itself an emblem of the depth and breadth of the problems in Rome that Catiline both represents and preys upon. Second, Catiline's language recycles Sallust's concerns in the preface with virtue, body and soul, talent, money, power, and other moral–political qualities. The speech seems to challenge the reader to separate the true critique of Roman factionalism from the slogans of demagoguery. But the separation will not be simple: sometimes villains really have suffered wrongs and sometimes real wrongs lead to demagoguery. Finally, Catiline's strategy is simultaneously a military strategy and a political strategy. This may either reflect Sallust's own recognition of the contradictory nature of Catiline's project at this point, or it is an element of Catiline's unprecedented danger and crime: he was not using military power to claim the consulship as the reward of his success or aiming at the consulship for the opportunities of a proconsular command. He was seeking the consulship precisely for the purpose of having an army to enforce his political agenda.

The election of Cicero and Antonius causes Catiline to renew his efforts, both as a revolutionary and as a candidate (24). Sallust begins anew describing Catiline's followers; he adds a portrait of Sempronia (25) and describes the traps Catiline tried to lay for Cicero during Cicero's consulship in 63 (26). Cicero, informed of Catiline's plans, again by Fulvia, asked that the election be postponed in order to investigate rumours of violence. The Senate was convened. Catiline refused to cooperate and uttered some veiled threats. The elections were held, probably within a few days. Cicero appeared in the Campus Martius with a bodyguard and wearing a breastplate. He claimed later that Catiline and his followers were planning to assassinate him. If so, his measures prevented them from acting. In any event, his display seems to have ensured Catiline's defeat.

The conspiracy finally turns to outright violence after the elections of 63. Catiline sends Manlius to Etruria to enlist an army (27.1). Sallust relates (out of order; see below) a secret meeting at the house of Laeca, after which two *equites* go to Cicero's house and attempt to kill him (28). News that Manlius was gathering an army in Etruria (ch. 29), which caused the Senate to issue its 'final decree' on 21 October), was followed by news of an uprising in Etruria on 27 October (30), which caused omens and panic at Rome. Catiline was then accused of violence (31, probably on 1 or 2 November), after which, according to Sallust, Catiline appeared in the Senate on 8 November, where he was attacked by Cicero in the *First Catilinarian*. According to Sallust, Catiline left the Senate threatening a general demolition (31.9). (According to Cicero, however, this particular remark was made, not to Cicero, but to Cato, in July 63 when Cato threatened him with prosecution.) The narrative moves from a secret meeting to rumours to uprisings to fear and panic ending with Catiline storming out of the Senate house on his way to Manlius' camp.

Sallust then reports two letters, both of which complicate any clear notion of the conspiracy. First, C. Manlius writes to Marcius Rex (consul in 68): we are not seeking power or money, he says; we want freedom from debt and from the abuses of the praetor (33). The grievances of this letter are in many ways justified, and are even mentioned elsewhere by Cicero himself. Its inclusion serves to blur the boundaries between a merely vicious and self-serving desire for power and money, and the legitimate grievances that allowed such revolutionary actions to thrive. Next, Catiline writes to Catulus (consul in 78), the ex-consul who had helped in his defence against adultery charges (35). Here, Catiline complains about injuries and insults, the state of his 'dignity' (*dignitas*), his customary avowal of the cause of the wretched, and his own financial solvency. Without what we know of the conspiracy, he seems a sympathetic figure.

After another digression, on the state of Roman society (36–9), Sallust focuses on the negotiations with the Allobroges (39–49). They were a Celtic tribe that had come to Rome to seek debt relief from the Senate. Their appearance not only brings about the exposure of many conspirators at Rome, but it also demonstrates the extent to which real problems of power and money lay behind Catiline's conspiracy. In the first place, this mismanagement of external affairs made possible further allies for Catiline's revolutionary project. Not only that, but when the Allobroges decided to expose the conspirators to the Senate, they still did not get any relief for their grievances. They revolted in 62. Second, when the Senate met in the Temple of Harmony (*Concordia*) to examine the captured conspirators, a certain Tarquinius reported that Crassus was involved. Sallust does not say whether the accusation was true or not. Fear and money are more important than the truth, and the Senate decides instead to investigate why Tarquinius 'lied'. The narrative devolves into rumours and suspicions, first about the role of Crassus, then about Cicero's purpose, and finally about the patriotism of Caesar. This passage ends with some Roman *equites* drawing their swords on Caesar as he leaves the Temple of Harmony.

In the next section, the Senate debates the fate of the conspirators. Here, in place of the harmony (*concordia*) that made Rome great, we find two irreconcilable responses to the problem. Caesar presents a moderate view: passion can mislead, he says, and history is filled with examples that warn us of the dangers of setting bad precedents. He echoes and recalls the speeches of Cato's great-grandfather. Then Cato speaks: we cannot wait for these criminals to act; that will be the death of us. Besides, Rome was made great by examples of severe discipline; fathers even killed their own sons for disobedience. Among other things, these two men are arguing about how one uses history: do we learn from disasters like Sulla or from the discipline of Torquatus? About how we take care of the future: do we avoid bad precedents or do we protect our present condition? About what is ultimately at stake: the virtue of our own actions or the danger-ous intentions of others' actions? This section ends with the famous comparison of Caesar and Cato. Both exhibit *virtus* but in different ways. It is important to note that these men do not have two halves of a complete virtue, as if we would arrive at harmony by putting together their moral characteristics. Their characteristics, like the men themselves, are already at war. What is lacking is some greater principle (harmony, Republic, common good) that would direct and orient their strengths. And this is not just an ideological war. Being out to destroy each other these two men eventually did destroy the Republic.

The final section (55–61), after a brief account of the execution of the conspirators in Rome (55), turns to the military conflict with Catiline's army. As far from the end of the monograph as Catiline's first speech is from the beginning, we hear Catiline speak for the last time. From this moment to the end Sallust not only seems to emphasize the extraordinary virtues that Catiline placed at the service of his criminal scheme, the Roman toughness and daring of his army, and Catiline's memory of his own dignity, but he draws a less than flattering picture of the Roman general who was sent to meet Catiline. Antonius (consul in 63) had a sore foot, it turns out.

Perhaps it was gout: we know he was a heavy drinker. So he passes command to his legate, Petreius. Petreius, of course, wins, but the model commander's speech is given to Catiline as is the final description of Roman valour.

Historical Veracity

Sallust reports that before the conspiracy of 63 there was 'an earlier conspiracy' in 66–65 (18–19). Cicero refers to this conspiracy in his speech as a candidate in 64 and his First Speech against Catiline. But the facts do not add up and modern historians remain sceptical. For instance, if Catiline conspired to kill the incoming consuls in 65, why would Torquatus (an alleged victim) defend Catiline at his extortion trial? Why would Cicero consider defending Catiline, and then in 64 consider an alliance with Catiline against another candidate, Antonius? And what new information made clear the extent of Catiline's guilt just before the elections in 64? Furthermore, Catiline wanted to stand for the consulship in 66; he did stand for the consulship in 64 and in 63. It seems unreasonable and incoherent to believe that he was seeking to overthrow the government at the same time he was seeking electoral office, and that he continued to do this for two or three years.

If we conclude, as most historians do, that Catiline decided to take violent action after his defeat at the elections during the summer of 63, then the meeting in June 64 (17–22) is also either a fiction or an event displaced from 63.

There is one other distortion in Sallust's chronology: Sallust reports the meeting of the conspirators on 6/7 November at the house of M. Laeca (27.2) and the failed assassination attempt against Cicero on 7 November (28.1–3). He follows this with Manlius' activity in Etruria, which refers to the period from mid-July to mid-October (28.4). These actions resulted in the Senate's 'final decree' on 21 October (29.2). Manlius' revolt (30.1) began on 27 October; it was reported in Rome on 1 November (30). In Sallust, the terror and confusion in Rome caused by Manlius' revolt leads to Cicero's *First Catilinarian* (31.6), when in fact it was the assassination attempt that preceded the speech. There seems to be no agenda in this chronological displacement.

CHRONOLOGY OF THE CONSPIRACY

Italics mark events reported by Sallust but generally disputed by modern scholarship.

68 L. Sergius Catilina praetor.

67 Catiline governor of Africa.

66 C. Manlius tribune of the plebs; M. Tullius Cicero praetor. Catiline returns from Africa; not allowed to stand for consulship. L. Vargunteius convicted of electoral fraud.

66 Summer: election of Sulla and Autronius as consuls. Autumn: conviction of Sulla and Autronius for bribery; Autronius attempts to disrupt the court; election of Cotta and Torquatus. 29 December: trial of Manlius before the praetor Cicero; mob demonstrations, postponement.

65 1 January: *'first conspiracy': plot to kill the consuls: Catiline, Sulla, Autronius, Piso, Vargunteius.* Manlius' trial continued; gangs disrupt trial; Catiline and Piso implicated. Piso sent to Spain. Catiline tried for extortion; the consul Torquatus speaks in his defence.

64 Piso killed by Spaniards.

64 June: *Catiline's meeting with conspirators, and speech.* Electoral candidates (according to Asconius): Catiline, Antonius, Cicero, Longinus, Sulpicius, Cornificius, and Licinius; Antonius and Cicero win. Catiline tried for violence during the 'Domination of Sulla'.

63 Cicero and Antonius consuls. Summer: Catiline's threats; election postponed. July: elections held; Catiline defeated. Manlius gathers forces in Etruria. 20 October: Crassus and others pass letters to Cicero warning of attacks. 21 October: Senate's 'final decree'. 27 October: Manlius begins revolt in Etruria. 28 October: planned massacre in Rome. P. Sestius, quaestor, sent to secure Capua. 1 November: attempt to seize Praeneste foiled; military commanders dispatched. Catiline indicted for violence. 6/7 November: meeting at house of Laeca. 8 November: Cicero's *First Catilinarian Speech.* 8/9 November: Catiline leaves Rome. 9 November: Cicero's *Second Catilinarian Speech.* Mid-November: Catiline and Manlius declared public enemies. Lentulus recruits the Allobroges; disturbances put down in Gaul, Picenum, and Apulia. Late November: Catiline leaves camp in Faesuli. 2/3 December: ambush at Mulvian Bridge: arrest of the Allobroges and Volturcius. 3 December: Senate meeting in the Temple of Concord; Cicero's *Third Catilinarian Speech.* 4 December: debate about conspirators; Cicero's *Fourth Catilinarian Speech*; five

conspirators executed. 10 December: Bestia's planned attack on Cicero as signal for attacks in Rome. 15 December: news reaches Catiline; desertions. 25 December: Catiline prevented from leaving Etruria. 29 December: tribunes Bestia and Nepos prevent Cicero from addressing the Roman people.

62 3 January: Nepos attempts to recall Pompey to put down Catiline; Senate's 'final decree'. Early January: Catiline and his army destroyed near Pistoria. Mid-January: Catiline's head brought to Rome. Spring: Q. Cicero and M. Bibulus, praetors, put down last uprisings in central and southern Italy.

CATILINE'S CONSPIRACY

1 **1.** All human beings who want to be superior to the other animals ought to struggle with every resource not to be like cattle passing silently through life. It is natural for the cattle to hang their heads
2 and obey their stomachs, but all our strength is situated in our mind as well as our body: we use the mind more for control, the body for servitude; the one we have in common with the gods, the other with
3 the beasts. And so I think it more upright to seek glory with our inner resources than with our physical strength and, since life is itself brief,
4 to make the memory of our lives as long as possible. I say this because the glory of wealth and physical beauty is fluid and fragile; but virtue is held brilliant and eternal.*

5 For a long time, however, there was a dispute among mortals as to whether physical force or mental excellence was most responsible for
6 success in military affairs. The reason: you require both a plan before
7 you begin and timely action when you have made a plan. Thus, each element, insufficient in itself, needs the help of the other. [**2.**] And so
1 it was that at the beginning kings—this being the first name for political command on earth—pursued their goals in different ways, some using their intellect, others using physical resources. Besides, at that time humans passed their lives without being covetous; each person was
2 happy enough with what he had. But afterwards, when Cyrus* in Asia, and the Lacedaemonians and Athenians* in Greece began to subjugate cities and nations, when craving for domination began to be considered a justification for war, and the greatest glory was held to consist in the greatest military command, then, finally, it was discovered through danger and trouble that in war the intellect had the most potent power.

3 But if the mental excellence of kings and commanders were valued as much in peacetime as it is in war, there would be more justice and stability in human affairs; you would not see everything either
4 moving helter-skelter nor changing and confused. For, political command is easily retained by the same means that created it in the first
5 place. But when sloth supplants hard work, and in place of restraint and equity lust and pride march in, then fortune changes along with
6 character. Consequently, command is always being transferred to the best individuals from the less good.

All that men accomplish in farming, sailing, and building is 7
obedient to the law of virtue.* But many mortals are devoted to their 8
bellies and to sleep; without learning and without culture they pass
through life like tourists. Their bodies are for pleasure, their soul*
a burden, and I say that is contrary to nature. I consider their life
and their death equally meaningless, since no one has anything to say
about either. But what is more, that man alone seems to me to live 9
and enjoy the breath of life* who is focused on some undertaking and
seeks fame for an illustrious deed or for good character.

Still, there is a great diversity in the world, and nature shows
different people different paths. [3.] It is a beautiful thing to serve 1
the Republic with good deeds; but to speak well* is also not without
importance. One can achieve brilliance either in peacetime or in war.
And many win the praise of others, both those who act and those who
write up their actions. As for me, although the glory that comes to 2
the writer is not equal to the glory that comes to the author of deeds,
still it seems especially difficult to write history: First of all, deeds
must find an equivalence in words.* Then, there are readers: many
will think that what you castigate as offences are mentioned because
of hatred and envy; but, when you speak of the great virtue and
glory of good men, what each one thinks is easy for himself to do,
he accepts with equanimity; what goes beyond that he construes like
fictions made up for lies.

But in my own case, as a young man I was at first attracted like many 3
others to politics, and in politics I was thwarted by many obstacles.
In place of shame, self-restraint, and virtue, arrogance thrived and
graft and greed. My mind, unaccustomed to wicked ways, rejected 4
these things. But I was young and did not know how to resist. Caught 5
in the midst of such corruption, I too was seized and corrupted by
ambition. I rejected the wicked character of others, but nevertheless
was troubled by the same craving for honour, and I fell victim to the
same reputation and invidious attacks as the others.

4. Consequently, when my mind found peace after a multitude of 1
miseries and dangers,* I decided to pass what remained of my life far
from the public world. But, it was not my plan to waste the benefits 2
of leisure in idleness and indolence, nor to pass my time engaged in
the slavish occupations* of farming or hunting. Rather, I decided to
return to the very study from which my failed ambition had diverted
me at the beginning: to write out the history of the Roman people,

selecting the parts that seemed worthy of memory. I was encouraged all the more to do this because my mind was free from political hopes,
3 fears, and partisanship. I will, therefore, give an account of Catiline's
4 conspiracy in a few words and as accurately as I can. I consider this event especially memorable because of the unprecedented nature
5 of the crime and the danger it caused. But, first, before I begin my narrative, a few things must be said about that man's character.

1   **5.** L. Catiline was born in an aristocratic family.* He was a man of great strength, both mental and physical, but his nature was wicked
2 and perverse. From early adulthood on, he took pleasure in civil wars, murders, plunder, and political discord, and this was where
3 he exercised his youth. His body could endure hunger, cold, sleep-
4 deprivation beyond what one would believe; his mind was arrogant, clever, unstable. He could pretend or dissemble whatever he liked. He coveted others' property but was profligate with his own; he burned with passionate desires. He had some eloquence, but little
5 wisdom. His mind was vast, always longing for the extravagant, the
6 unbelievable, the things beyond his reach. After the 'Domination of Sulla'* he was overcome by an extraordinarily powerful desire to seize control of the state. He did not care at all about how he attained
7 his goal as long as he got a 'realm'* for himself. Daily he grew more agitated. His family's poverty and his own guilty conscience made his spirit violent, and both of these problems were exacerbated by
8 the practices I have mentioned above. He was further encouraged by the corrupt moral character of the state, which was depraved because of two destructive and internally contradictory evils, extravagance and greed.

9   Since there has been an occasion to call to mind the moral character of the state, my subject seems of itself to suggest that I should go further back in time and briefly discuss the institutions of our ancestors, both at home and in the military, and to set forth how they governed the Republic, how great a state they left us, and how it gradually changed from the most lovely and best and became the worst and most depraved.

1   **6.** The city of Rome, as I understand it,* was founded and controlled at first by Trojans. They had no fixed home and were wandering about with Aeneas as their leader. They founded the city together with the Aborigines,* a wild race of men, without law, without polit-
2 ical institutions, free and unrestrained. These peoples, though they

were of different races, dissimilar languages, living each in a different way, after they came together within a single city's walls, it is
incredible to relate how easily they coalesced: in so short a time did a
disparate and wandering crowd because of internal harmony become
a state.* But after their community increased in citizens, morality, 3
and territory and began to seem quite wealthy and quite powerful,
envy was born from their prosperity, as is usually the case among
mortals. Therefore, neighbouring kings and peoples* began to test 4
them in war. Of their friends, only a few came to their aid, the rest
were shaken by fear and avoided danger. But the Romans kept their 5
focus at home and in the field: they hurried about, made preparations,
urged each other on, went to meet the enemy, and with their weapons
protected their freedom, their fatherland, and their parents. Afterwards, when courageous virtue had driven off danger, they brought
aid to their allies and friends; they established alliances more by
conferring kindnesses than by receiving them. Their political power 6
was based on law; its name was monarchy. Men were chosen to give
advice to the state, men whose bodies were weak with age, but whose
minds were strong in wisdom. These men were called 'Fathers',*
either because of their age or from the similarity of their care. At 7
first this regal power served to preserve freedom and to increase the
commonwealth; but, after it turned into arrogance* and domination,*
the Romans changed their custom and created for themselves annual
offices* and two executive officers:* they thought that restricting
political licence in this way would prevent men's minds from becom-
ing arrogant.

7. But that was the time when individuals began to elevate them- 1
selves and to display their native ability more readily. The reason 2
is that kings are always more suspicious of good men than wicked
men and they fear the virtue they do not have. But once liberty was 3
attained, it is incredible to recount how great the state became in a
short time. So strong was the desire for glory that came over them.
Now for the first time the young men, as soon as they could endure 4
battle, entered camps and began to learn the hard work of a military
life; they had passionate desires, but those desires were for splendid
armour and warhorses, not for prostitutes and parties. And so for 5
men like this no hard labour was unfamiliar, no place was harsh or
difficult, no armed enemy brought fear: their manly virtue had dominated everything. But competitions for glory were among them the 6

toughest competitions. Each man was in a hurry to strike the enemy, to climb a wall, to be noticed doing such deeds. They thought that this was true wealth; this meant a good reputation and great nobility. They were greedy for praise, but with money they were generous:

7 they wanted glory that was huge, wealth that was honourable. I could mention the places where the Roman people with a small band routed the enemy's greatest armies, the cities fortified by nature that they seized, were this not to take us too far from our project.

1 8. Still, it is my experience that Fortune governs everything; she exalts and obscures according to her pleasure, not according to the

2 truth. Athenian history, in my estimation, was quite grand and mag-

3 nificent, but still it was a little less grand than people say. It is because writers of great talent flourished there* that the deeds of the Athenians

4 are celebrated as if they were the greatest. And so, the virtue of those who acted is held to be as great as has been the ability of brilliant

5 talents to glorify it in words. The Roman people, on the other hand, never had those resources, because their most thoughtful men were most engaged in public business. No one used their intellectual talents independent of their body, and the best men preferred action to words. They preferred that their activities be praised by others rather than that they themselves tell another's story.

1 9. And so at home and in the military good moral character was cultivated; maximum harmony, avarice was minimal. Justice and goodness was strong among those men not because of the law more

2 than because of their nature. They engaged in quarrels, disputes, competition with the enemy, but among citizens the contest was over manly virtue. In their offerings to the gods, they were lavish; at home

3 they were sparing; with friends they were trustworthy. They cared for the constitution and themselves in two ways: they were fearless

4 in war, and, when peace arrived, they were fair. I take the following as the greatest proof of what I say: first, in war disciplinary action* was more often taken against those who attacked the enemy without orders and against those who withdrew too slowly when recalled from the battle than against those who abandoned the standards or dared to

5 give ground when beaten back; second, in peacetime they exercised political power more often with kindness than with fear and, when they received an injury, they preferred forgiveness to prosecution.

1 10. But, when hard work and just action had increased the Republic, when great kings were defeated in war, uncivilized nations and vast

peoples subdued by force, when Carthage,* the rival to Roman power, had been eradicated, when all the sea and all the lands were accessible, Fortune began to grow cruel and confuse everything. Men who had 2 easily endured hard work, dangers, uncertainty and adversity found that leisure and wealth, things desirable at other times, were a burden and the cause of misery. And so, at first, greed for money grew, then 3 greed for power. These things were the root, so to speak, of all evils. For avarice undermined trust, goodness, and other noble qualities, 4 and in their place taught pride and cruelty, taught men to neglect the gods and to put a price on everything. Ambition forced many men 5 to become liars, to hide one thing in their heart and have something else ready on their tongue, to value friendship and enmity according to convenience, not substance, and to put up a good face rather than have a good heart. At first, these things grew gradually, they were 6 punished occasionally; afterwards, when this contagion invaded like a plague, the state changed, and political power which had been most just and best became cruel and intolerable.

11. At first, however, more than avarice it was ambition that worked 1 the souls of men, which, although a vice is nearer a virtue. For both 2 the good man and the worthless man desire for themselves glory, honour, power. But the former labours on the true path, while the latter, having no honourable abilities, competes using treachery and deception. Avarice entails a zeal for money, which no wise man covets; 3 it is dripping, so to speak, with dangerous poisons and makes the manly body and soul effeminate; it is boundless and insatiable, and is not diminished by wealth or poverty. But after L. Sulla took con- 4 trol of the Republic* and from good beginnings created a disastrous outcome, everyone began to steal and rob. One man wanted a house, another fields; they did disgusting and cruel things to their fellow citizens. In addition to this, L. Sulla had let his army, the one he had 5 led in Asia, live contrary to the custom of our ancestors in luxury and excessive licence.* He did this to make them faithful to his cause. The charming and voluptuous locales easily softened the ferocious spirits of the soldiers when there was no work to do. There for the 6 first time the army of the Roman people grew accustomed to making love, drinking, admiring statues, painted tables, and embossed vases, stealing public and private possessions, plundering temples, pollut- ing all things sacred and profane. And so those soldiers, after they 7 attained victory, left nothing for the defeated. Success, to be sure, can 8

try the souls of wise men; those of corrupt character were much less able to temper their victory.

12. After wealth began to be considered an honour, and after glory, political authority, and power followed in its wake, manly virtue began to lose its lustre, poverty was considered a disgrace, innocence was taken for malevolence.* And so, as a result of our wealth, extravagance and greed with arrogance assaulted our youth: they raped and devoured; they considered their own possessions worthless and desired the possessions of others; decency and chastity, things human and divine alike, they held nothing of value or moderation. When you consider our homes and villas built to the size of cities, it is worthwhile to visit the temples of the gods which our ancestors made. They were very devout men. But they adorned shrines to the gods with their piety, their own homes with glory, and they did not steal from the vanquished anything beyond their freedom to do harm. But today's men, the most worthless of human beings, do the opposite; in the most criminal way they take from our allies everything which the bravest men had left when they were victorious: it is as if the ability to do injustice is what magisterial power really means.

13. Why should I bother to mention things which no one can believe except those who have seen them: mountains dug up by private men, seas paved over?* To these men wealth seems to be a toy: what they could have used honourably, they were quick to abuse shamefully. But that is not all: other excesses advanced as well, a passion for promiscuous sex, for gluttony. Men accepted the woman's role, women put their chastity up for sale, all the land and sea was scoured for the sake of feeding; they slept before the body wanted sleep; without waiting for hunger or thirst, for cold or weariness, they self-indulgently anticipated all these things. These desires incited the young men to criminal actions when the family wealth was gone. A soul imbued with wicked tendencies does not easily do without what it craves. And so they became in every way all the more inordinately addicted to acquisition and expenditure.

14. In such a great and corrupt city, Catiline gathered around him, like a bodyguard, crowds of vices and crimes; it was most easy to do. His companions and friends were those who had wrecked their patrimony with their hand, stomach, penis; any who had enkindled an enormous personal debt in order to purchase immunity from his perversions and crimes; in addition, all murderers and infidels

anywhere, convicted in court or fearing prosecution for their deeds; furthermore, those who lived by hand and tongue off perjury and the blood of citizens; and, finally, all who were stirred by perversity, poverty, and guilty conscience. If anyone still innocent of guilt 4 fell into friendship with him, daily experience and temptations easily rendered that man equal and similar to the rest. But Catiline especially 5 sought out intimacy with young men: their minds were still malleable and pliable and easily snared by his treachery. As each man's passion 6 burned in accordance with his age, so Catiline responded: to some he offered whores, for others he purchased dogs and horses; in short, he spared neither expense nor his own modesty, provided he could make them dependent on him and faithful to him. I know that there 7 were some people who concluded that the young men who frequented Catiline's home did not handle their chastity very honourably, but people said this more for other reasons* than because there was any evidence of it.

15. Already as a young man Catiline had engaged in much unspeak- 1 able debauchery with a virgin from a good family,* with a Vestal priestess,* and other things of this type which are contrary to divine and natural law. Finally, he fell in love with Aurelia Orestilla.* No 2 good man praised anything about her except her figure. She hesitated to marry Catiline, fearing a full-grown stepson. Because of this it is believed to be certain that Catiline made his home ready for his criminal nuptials* by killing his son. In fact, this event seems to me 3 to have been the primary reason that hastened his conspiracy. For 4 his soul, stained with guilt and hated by gods and men, could not find peace either in waking or in sleeping. Thus, his conscience irritated 5 and devastated his mind. And so his face was pallid, his eyes bloody, his gait now quick, now slow; in short, there was madness in his face and features.

16. The young men whom—as we said above—he had lured, 1 learned from him many wicked types of criminal behaviour. From 2 them he supplied false witnesses and signatories; their credit, wealth, trials were considered insignificant. After he had destroyed their reputation and their moral sense, he made other greater demands. If 3 the present circumstances did not provide any reason for crime, he nevertheless asked them to trap and slaughter the innocent as well as the guilty.* One assumes he preferred to be gratuitously wicked and cruel lest their hands or hearts grow listless through inactivity.

4   These were the friends and allies Catiline trusted. Furthermore, debt was rampant throughout the whole world, and most of Sulla's soldiers, having squandered their own property, were thinking about plunder and their former victories and hoping for civil war. And so
5 Catiline formed a plan for overthrowing the government. In Italy there was no army; Cn. Pompey* was waging war at the ends of the earth. Catiline himself was seeking the consulship* and had great hopes. The Senate, clearly, had no pressing business: everything was safe and peaceful. But this was exactly what suited Catiline.

1   17. Therefore, about 1 June,* when L. Caesar and C. Figulus were consuls,* he first summoned certain individuals; he encouraged some, others he sounded out, he pointed to his own resources, the state's lack
2 of preparation, and the great rewards of a conspiracy. When he had gathered the information that he wanted, he called together everyone who suffered from extraordinary need or possessed unusual daring.
3 The senators* he convened were: P. Lentulus Sura,* P. Autronius,* L. Cassius Longinus,* C. Cethegus,* P. and Ser. Sulla, sons of Servius,*L. Vargunteius,*Q. Annius,* M. Porcius Laeca,*L. Bestia,*
4 and Q. Curius*; and from the equestrian order:* M. Fulvius Nobilior, L. Statilius, P. Gabinius Capito, and C. Cornelius; in addition there were many from the colonies and townships who were aristocrats
5 at home.* There were also many aristocrats who participated more secretly in his plan; they were encouraged more by hope of power
6 than by poverty or any necessity. But in general it was the young men who favoured Catiline's goals, especially the aristocratic youth: they had the resources to live at ease either lavishly or elegantly,
7 but they preferred uncertainty to certainty, war over peace. At the time, there were also those who believed that M. Licinius Crassus* was not unaware of Catiline's plans: that, because his enemy Pompey was in charge of a great army,* he was willing to let anyone's resources increase in opposition to Pompey's power; and that he firmly believed he would easily become the leader among the conspirators if the conspiracy succeeded.

1   18. Earlier, however, a few men likewise conspired* against the
2 state and Catiline was among them. I will speak as accurately as I can* about this. When L. Tullus* and M'. Lepidus* were consuls, P. Autronius and P. Sulla,* the consuls elect, were arraigned under
3 bribery laws and fined.* A little later, Catiline was prevented from seeking the consulship because he was a defendant on charges of

extortion and was not able to submit his petition before the legal deadline.* At the same time, there was a young aristocrat, Cn. Piso,* 4 full of daring, lacking resources, interested in violence, who was moved by poverty and wicked character to attack the government. Piso 5 shared his plan with Catiline and Autronius, who joined him around 5 December.* They were prepared to kill the consuls,* L. Cotta and L. Torquatus, on the Capitoline Hill on 1 January,* to seize the fasces, and to send Piso with an army to take possession of the two Spanish provinces.* The plot was discovered and they postponed their mur- 6 derous plan to 5 February.* This time they were plotting the death 7 not only of the consuls but of many senators. And on that day, if 8 Catiline standing in front of the Senate house had not given his allies the signal too soon,* the most wicked act since the founding of Rome would have been accomplished. Because armed men had not yet fully assembled, the plan fell apart.

19. Afterwards, Piso was sent to Nearer Spain as a quaestor with 1 praetorian powers.* Crassus helped in this because he knew that Piso 2 was a bitter enemy of Pompey.* Nor was the Senate unwilling to give him the province: this was because they wanted this repugnant man as far from the state as possible, and at the same time because many good men were thinking he could provide some protection: even then Pompey's power was a source of fear. But this Piso, as he was march- 3 ing through the province, was killed by the Spanish cavalry under his command. There are some who claim that the barbarians were 4 unable to endure his unjust, haughty, and cruel exercise of power; others, however, say that those horsemen, old and faithful clients of 5 Pompey,* attacked Piso on Pompey's orders; further, they point out that the Spaniards had never before perpetrated any such crime,* but had endured many savage acts of power. We will leave this matter undecided. Enough has been said about the earlier conspiracy.

20. When Catiline saw gathered together the men I have just 1 mentioned,* although he had often discussed many things with them as individuals, still he believed it was important to address them as a group and encourage them. He withdrew to an inner room of the house and there, with all witnesses far removed, he delivered a speech like this:

'If your manly virtue and loyalty were not already known to 2 me, this opportunity would have arrived in vain; our high hopes and political dominance would be frustrated while within our reach.

Nor would I rely upon men of weak and fickle character and grasp
3 at uncertainties instead of what is certain. But because I have found
you to be brave and faithful to me in many difficult circumstances,
therefore my heart dares to attempt a very great and beautiful action,
also because I understand that you and I agree about what is good
4 and bad. Indeed, this is unshakable friendship: to want and to reject
the same things.

5   'You have all already heard individually what I have been consid-
6 ering. But, daily my heart grows more passionate as I think about the
7 terms of our future life, if we do not lay claim to freedom. For after
the Republic handed over justice and authority to a powerful few, it
is to these men that kings and rulers always bring tribute, to them
peoples and nations pay taxes. All the rest of us, hard-working good
men, aristocrats and plebeians, we are a common crowd, without
favour and without prestige. We are dependent upon those who would
8 be afraid of us if the Republic meant anything. And so all influence,
power, honour, and wealth lie in their hands or where they want it;
we are left with dangers, electoral defeats, litigation, and poverty.
9 How much longer are we still going to put up with this,* I ask you,
O bravest men? Isn't it better to die with manly courage than to live
wretched and dishonoured, the playthings of other men's arrogance,
and, then, with disgrace to lose our lives?

10   'But in fact, and I swear by the faith of gods and men, victory
really is in our hands. We are young and vigorous, our spirit is valiant;
they, on the other hand, are utterly decrepit, the result of money and
years. All we need do is start, the outcome will take care of itself.
11 Indeed, what mortal with a manly heart can endure it! They squander their superior wealth in building upon the seas and levelling the
mountains,* while we don't even have family possessions sufficient
for the necessities. While they connect one home to another or more,
12 we have no place for our family shrine. They buy paintings, statues,
reliefs; they destroy what they just bought and build something else;
they plunder and waste their money any way they can; still, their
13 extreme desires cannot overcome their wealth. But for us there is
poverty at home, debts everywhere; our circumstances are bad, our
hopes are worse. What do we have left but our miserable breath?

14   'So, why don't you wake up? The things you have often hoped for,
liberty, and then wealth, honour, and glory are right before your eyes.
15 All these Fortune has made the prizes of victory. The circumstances,

the time, the dangers, poverty, the magnificent spoils of war, these
offer more encouragement than my words. Use me as your general or 16
as a foot soldier; I will aid you with mind and body. When I am your 17
consul, this is what I hope to help you accomplish—unless my mind
is deceived and you are more ready to be slaves than to be rulers.'

21. The men who listened to Catiline were rich in troubles but had 1
neither resources nor any good hope. Although they thought that the
disruption of the status quo was a great reward in itself, still, after
they had listened, they demanded that he lay out the terms of the war,
what rewards their weapons would be seeking, what resources or hope
they could have and where. Then Catiline promised clean slates,* 2
proscription of the wealthy,* priesthoods, plunder, everything else
that war and the caprice of victors can offer. Furthermore, he said 3
that Piso* was in Nearer Spain, P. Sittius Nucerinus* was with an army
in Mauretania, and they were aware of his plans; that C. Antonius,*
a family friend broken by poverty, was seeking the consulship and
he expected him to be his colleague; and that he as consul would set
things in motion with Antonius. In addition, he attacked and maligned 4
all good citizens, he named and praised individually his followers,
reminding one of his poverty, another of his desires, most of their
danger and ignominy, and many of Sulla's victory, which had brought
them booty. After he saw that their hearts were eager, he urged them 5
to take care of his election, and he dismissed the gathering.

22. There were at that time some who said that after his speech, 1
when he wanted to bind those privy to his crime with an oath, he passed
around a bowl that had in it human blood mixed with wine, that then, 2
when all had tasted the blood and sworn a solemn oath, just as is the
custom in holy rites, he disclosed his plan, and that he did this to create
a common bond that would make them more faithful to each other,
each one being conscious of the other's guilt. Some were of the opinion 3
that these and many other things were invented by men who thought
that, if they exaggerated the atrocity of the crimes of those whom Cicero
punished, they could mitigate the hatred that later rose up against him.*
Considering its importance, we have too little information.

23. Now one of the members of the conspiracy was Q. Curius. He 1
was not born in obscurity, but he was shrouded in shame and crimes,
a man whom the censors had removed from the Senate* for his disgraceful actions. This man was as fickle as he was reckless; he did not 2
keep silent about what he heard or conceal his own crimes; he did

3 not care a whit about what he said or what he did. Fulvia,* an aristocratic woman, had been his partner in promiscuity for some time,
but he was no longer in her favour, because his limited resources had
made him less generous. Suddenly he began to swagger and promise oceans and mountains, and to threaten her occasionally with his
sword if she did not yield to him. Ultimately, he became much more
4 ferocious than had been his custom. But when Fulvia discovered the
cause of Curius' abusiveness, she did not keep secret such a danger to
the Republic. Hiding the name of her informant, she told many the
5 details she had heard about Catiline's conspiracy. It was this event
that made men particularly eager to entrust the consulship to Cicero.*
6 In fact, before this the aristocracy was in general seething with jealousy; they thought that the consulship was polluted if a 'new man',*
regardless of how outstanding, should attain it. But when danger was
at hand, jealousy and pride took second place.

1   **24.** Consequently, when the elections were held, M. Tullius* and
C. Antonius were declared consuls. At first this event shook the
2 confidence of the members of the conspiracy. And yet Catiline's
madness did not diminish; rather he grew more agitated daily:* arms
were placed throughout Italy in strategic places, money was borrowed
in his own name or that of his friends and was taken to Faesulae
to a certain Manlius,* who afterwards was the first to begin fighting.
3 It is said that he enlisted on his side at that time many men of every
class, and even some women. These were women who covered their
enormous expenses by selling their bodies; afterwards, when age limited their income but not their extravagant desires, they contracted
4 huge debts. Through them Catiline believed that he could bring
the urban slaves* to his side, set fire to the city, and either get their
husbands to join his cause or get them killed.

1   **25.** Now among these women was Sempronia,* a woman who had
2 committed many crimes with the arrogance of a man. She was fortunate enough in her birth and her figure, also in her husband and
children, learned in Greek and Latin literature, lyre-playing and
dancing more pleasingly than a proper woman should. She knew
many other things that were the accoutrements of luxury, but there
3 was nothing she liked less than propriety and restraint. You could
not tell whether she cared less about her money or her reputation.
Her sexual appetite was such that she more often took the initia-
4 tive with men than they with her. Before this conspiracy, she had

often betrayed faith, defaulted on loans, been accessory to murder.
Her expenses and her lack of resources headed her toward disaster.
Nevertheless, her abilities were not despicable: she could write 5
verses, make a joke, converse modestly, or tenderly, or raucously; she
possessed many pleasant characteristics and much charm.

26. Although Catiline had made his preparations, he still sought 1
the consulship for the following year.* He was hoping that, if he
was consul designate, he could use Antonius* as he wished. In the
meantime he was not idle, but laid traps for Cicero in every way possible. But, Cicero had sufficient guile and cunning to avoid them. 2
At the beginning of his consulship, he made many promises through 3
Fulvia to Q. Curius, whom I mentioned above, and got him to betray
Catiline's plans to him. In addition, he reached an agreement about 4
provinces* with his colleague Antonius and so prevailed upon him
not to oppose the Republic. Secretly, he kept around himself a
bodyguard of friends and clients. The election day came.* Catiline 5
succeeded neither in his campaign nor in the plots that he had laid for
the consuls in the Campus Martius. Then, since his covert attempts
had resulted in exasperation and disgrace, he decided to make war
and to let nothing stand in his way.

27. Therefore he sent C. Manlius to Faesulae* and the adjacent 1
parts of Etruria, a certain Septimius of Camerinum* to the Picene
district, C. Julius* to Apulia, and others elsewhere, wherever he
thought they would be useful to him. Meanwhile in Rome he was 2
working on many things at the same time: he set traps for the consuls, planned arson, posted armed men in strategic places; he himself
was armed and ordered others to do likewise, he urged them to be
always alert and ready; he had hurried about day and night, he did
not rest, and did not weary of sleeplessness or toil. Finally, when his 3
many activities produced no result, he called on M. Porcius Laeca* to
convene again the leaders of the conspiracy in the dead of night.* And 4
there, after he had complained at length about their ineffectiveness,
he told them that he had readied a body of men to take up arms and
had already sent Manlius ahead to join them, that he had sent others
to various strategic places to begin the fighting; and that he himself
was eager to get to his army, if he could first do away with Cicero: that
man, he said, was a significant obstacle to his plans.

28. And so, although the others were terrified and hesitant, 1
C. Cornelius, a Roman *eques*, promised his help. L. Vargunteius,*

a senator, agreed to go with him. They would go to Cicero's house a little later that night as if to make a ceremonial visit;* they would take with them armed men and without warning they would stab him
2 unprepared in his own house. When Curius heard the extent of the danger that hung over the consul, he quickly told Cicero through
3 Fulvia of the treachery that was under way. And so those men were turned away from the door and the great crime they had undertaken was frustrated.

4 Meanwhile in Etruria Manlius was stirring up a populace that was eager for revolution because of their poverty and the pain of injustice: during the domination of Sulla they had lost all their fields and property.* Furthermore, Manlius solicited robbers of any kind. There were a great number in that region; some came from Sulla's colonists, men who had nothing left from all their plunder because of their appetite and extravagance.*

1 **29.** When these events were reported to Cicero, he was deeply disturbed by the twofold danger: he was no longer able through private efforts to protect the city from these plots, and he did not have clear information about the size of Manlius' army or his intentions. He brought the matter, already the subject of excited rumours among
2 the people, before the Senate.* And so the Senate passed a decree, the one which is customary in times of deadly peril: Let the con-
3 suls prevent any damage to the Republic.* This is the greatest power which the Senate by Roman custom grants to a magistrate: power to raise an army, wage war, coerce allies and citizens in any way necessary, to exercise complete authority and jurisdiction at home and in the military. Otherwise, without an order of the people, the consul has no right to any of these actions.*

1 **30.** After a few days, L. Saenius,* a senator, read in the Senate a letter which he said had been brought to him from Faesulae. The letter said that C. Manlius had taken up arms with a large number
2 of men on 27 October. At the same time, some men announced portents and prodigies—a common occurrence at such times—others told of meetings, the movement of arms, slave insurrections in Capua
3 and Apulia.* Consequently, Q. Marcius Rex* was sent to Faesulae by senatorial decree, Q. Metellus Creticus* to Apulia and neighbouring
4 places—both of these men were in command of armies outside the city walls where they had been prevented from celebrating triumphs by the malice of a few men who habitually put everything up for sale

whether honourable or dishonourable. The praetors, Q. Pompeius 5
Rufus and Q. Metellus Celer,* were sent to Capua and the Picene
district respectively, and they were given authority to raise an army
according to the circumstances and the danger. In addition to this, a 6
reward was decreed, if anyone had any information about the conspiracy against the state: for a slave, freedom and a hundred *sestertia*; for
a free man, impunity and two hundred *sestertia*.* They also decreed 7
that gladiatorial troops* should be distributed throughout Capua and
other towns in accordance with the resources of each place; at Rome,
watches were to be posted throughout the city and the minor magistrates* were to be in charge of them.

31. These events terrified the citizens and changed the appear- 1
ance of the city. In place of the great joy and abandon which years
of peace had produced, suddenly gloom overcame all. People hur- 2
ried, trembled, trusted little in any place or person; they were neither
waging war nor enjoying peace; each measured the danger in accordance with his own anxiety. In addition, fear of war, unfamiliar to the 3
women because of the greatness of the Republic, overwhelmed them:
they beat their breasts, raised their hands to the heavens in suppli-
cation, wailed over their little children; they questioned everything,
trembled at every rumour, grabbed everything they could, and setting aside pride and pleasure they despaired of themselves and their
country.

Defences were readied against Catiline. He was arraigned by 4
L. Paulus under the *lex Plautia*.* But his cruel spirit was not moved to
change his plans. Finally, he came into the Senate, either to dissemble 5
his intentions or to clear his name as if he had been challenged in some
private quarrel. At that time M. Tullius the consul, either because 6
he was afraid of Catiline's presence or because he was carried away by
anger, delivered a speech that was brilliant and useful to the Republic,
a speech which he later wrote down and published.* But when he sat 7
down, Catiline, who was prepared to dissemble everything, began to
speak with downcast eyes and suppliant voice. He asked the senators
not to form any hasty opinions about him: he was born into a very
great family and had lived since adolescence in such a way that he had
nothing but good prospects. He was a patrician, he said; he himself
and his ancestors had performed a great many services for the Roman
plebs. They should not think that he needed to destroy the Republic,
when M. Tullius, a rental resident citizen of the city of Rome,* said

8 he was going to save it. When he tried to add other insults to this, everyone shouted him down; they called him an enemy and a par-
9 ricide. Then he became enraged and said, 'I'm trapped and I'm being pushed over the edge by my enemies: I'll extinguish my inferno with a general demolition.'*

1   32. He then rushed from the Senate chamber and went home. There he thought over many things: his plots against the consul were not making progress and the city was protected from arson by watchmen. He concluded that the best thing to do was to increase his army and to gather many provisions for war before Roman legions could be enlisted, and so he set off with a few men in the dead of night to
2 Manlius' camp. But first, he gave orders to Cethegus and Lentulus and others whose recklessness he knew was prepared for action. He told them to strengthen the resources of their faction in whatever way they could, to implement the plots against the consul, to arrange for slaughter, arson, and other acts of war; as for himself, he said that he would soon be at the city's gates with a large army.
3   While this was going on in Rome, C. Manlius sent some of his men as legates to Marcius Rex with the following request:

1   33. 'General, we call upon men and gods as our witnesses: we have not taken up arms against our country and we intend no danger to others. Instead, our purpose is to keep our own bodies free from harm. We are humiliated, impoverished by the violence and cruelty of the moneylenders; most of us have lost our fatherland, but all have lost fame and fortune. None of us has been allowed to enjoy legal protections according to ancestral custom,* none has retained his personal freedom once he lost his patrimony: such has been the savage
2 indifference of the moneylenders and the urban praetor.* Often your ancestors pitied the common people of Rome, and by their decrees made resources available to the resourceless.* Most recently, within our own lifetime,* good respectable men were willing to let silver
3 be paid in bronze because of the magnitude of the debt. Often the common people themselves, spurred on by the desire to dominate or by the arrogance of the magistrates, took up arms and seceded from
4 the senatorial fathers.* But it is not political power or wealth that we seek, things which are the cause of all wars and struggles among mortals; rather, it is freedom, which no respectable man gives up except
5 with his life. We beg you and the Senate, think about the suffering of the citizens, restore the protection of law which the inequity of

the praetor has stolen; and do not force us to ask how we can get the greatest vengeance from the loss of our blood.'

34. Q. Marcius responded to this, saying that, if they wanted to 1 make any petition to the Senate, they should put down their arms and set off for Rome as suppliants. The Senate and the Roman people had always shown such compassion and pity that no one had ever sought their help in vain.*

Catiline, on the other hand, while on the road sent letters to 2 several ex-consuls, also to all the most respectable men: he said that he was cornered by false charges; that he was yielding to fortune since he could not counteract his enemies' faction; that he was going into exile at Marseilles,* not because he was guilty of any great crime, but so that the Republic could be at peace and that an insurrection might not arise from his personal struggle. Q. Catulus* read a very different 3 letter in the Senate, one that had been brought to him in Catiline's name. The following is a copy of that letter:

35. L. Catiline to Q. Catulus. Your loyalty is extraordinary, I know this by 1 experience,* and in my many great difficulties I have been grateful for it. It gives me confidence in my commission to you. For this reason, I have 2 decided not to defend my new course of action,* but offer instead an explanation, and not from any sense of guilt, but one that I swear you can recognize as true. I have been provoked by injustice and insult, deprived of 3 the benefits of my labour and efforts; I have not attained the dignified status I deserve,* and so in accordance with my inclination I have publicly taken up the cause of the poor.* It is not because I didn't have enough to pay off my own debts from my own possessions—Orestilla would have generously used hers and her daughter's resources to pay even the debts countersigned by others—but because I kept seeing men of no worth* honoured with honourable offices and was aware that I was myself rejected by false suspicions. On this account, I have pursued hopes of preserving what is 4 left of my dignity. And those hopes are honourable enough given my circumstances. Though I would like to write much more, I have heard that 5 violence against me is under way. Now, I commend Orestilla to you and 6 your loyalty. Defend her from injury, I ask in the name of your children. Take care.

36. Nevertheless, Catiline himself stayed a few days with 1 C. Flaminius* near Arretium* to supply weapons to an area already restless. He then hurried to join Manlius' camp with the fasces and other signs of military authority.* When these events were known at 2

Rome, the Senate decreed that Catiline and Manlius were enemies of the state.* They set a day before which most of the army could lay down their weapons without harm; the exceptions were those who
3 had already been convicted for capital offences. Furthermore, they decided that the consuls should hold a draft, that Antonius should hurry to pursue Catiline with an army, that Cicero should be the city's protection.

4   At that time, it seems to me, the empire of the Roman people was in an especially deplorable state. Everything from the rising sun to the setting sun was dominated by and obedient to Roman arms; and at home there was abundant peace and wealth, things that humans consider most important. But nevertheless there were citizens who with unwavering hearts were intent on destroying themselves and
5 their state. Indeed, in spite of two decrees that were passed by the Senate,* no one from that great multitude of men was induced to expose the conspiracy and no one at all left the camp of Catiline. Such was the force of the disease that like a plague had invaded the minds of many citizens.

1   **37.** This disaffection was not confined to those who were involved in the plot: in general all the plebs were eager for revolution and
2 approved of Catiline's intentions. Indeed, they were seeming to do
3 this in their particular way: for it is always the case in a community that the poor despise respectable men, they exalt the disreputable, they hate tradition and call for innovation; they are eager to change everything because they despise their own circumstances; they feed on turmoil and rebellion, and they do not care, since poverty does not
4 cost much and cannot lose much. But the urban plebs* were reck-
5 less for many reasons. First of all, there were those who excelled in dishonour and derision; likewise others, who had disgracefully lost their family money; finally, all the felons and fugitives who had been exiled from their homes: these flowed into Rome as if into a sewer.
6 Second, there were many who remembered Sulla's victory. They saw that some common soldiers had become senators,* others so wealthy that they passed their time surrounded by kingly feasts and culture. Everyone expected for himself the same kind of outcome from
7 victory, if it should come to war. Next, the young men, who used to alleviate their poverty with the rewards of hard work in the fields, were attracted by private and public doles and preferred urban leisure
8 to thankless labour. Our public disorder nourished these and all

the others. And so it is not surprising that men with no money, bad character, extravagant hopes considered the future of the Republic no more important than their own future. Further, those whose 9 parents had been proscribed during Sulla's victory, who had lost their wealth and found their freedom diminished,* were looking forward to the outcome of war with the same expectations. In addition to this, 10 whoever was not affiliated with the senatorial party preferred public chaos to their own diminished power. This in fact was the evil* that 11 had returned to the state after many years.

38. The reason was that tribunician power had been restored 1 during the consulship of Pompey and Crassus.* Thereafter, certain young men, whose youth and heart were implacable, attained that high position; they began to arouse the common people by attacking the Senate; then, they fanned the flames with public gifts and promises. In this way, they became famous and powerful. Against 2 them most of the aristocracy struggled using every resource: for the Senate's sake, so it seemed, but really for their own aggrandizement. To put the truth in a few words, after those times whoever stirred up 3 the Republic with honourable claims, some as if they were defending the rights of the people, others in order to secure the authority of the Senate, pretending to work for the public good, they struggled for their own power. There was no restraint or measure to their efforts. 4 Each side used their victories brutally.

39. Afterwards, when Cn. Pompey was sent to fight the pirates 1 and Mithridates,* the plebs' resources were diminished, the few increased their power. They held the magistracies, the provinces, 2 and everything else. They were themselves secure, flourishing; they lived without fear; they terrified others with criminal prosecutions so as to have more peaceful dealings with the plebs while holding office. But as soon as political uncertainty created hope for change, the old 3 struggle roused their courage. In fact, if Catiline's first battle had 4 been a victory or a draw, I am sure that great slaughter and disaster would have overwhelmed the state; and those who attained the victory would not have been allowed to use it very long before, exhausted and weary, they would have lost their freedom and authority to someone more powerful.* But, even as it was, there were many outside the 5 conspiracy who went to join Catiline when things began to happen. Among these was Fulvius,* the son of a senator. While on his way to Catiline, he was dragged back to Rome; his father ordered him killed.

6 Meanwhile Lentulus was at Rome carrying out Catiline's orders. By himself or through others, he solicited anyone whose character or fortune he thought made them well disposed to revolution, and not only citizens, but men of any type that would be useful in war.

1   40. Accordingly, he gave a certain P. Umbrenus* the job of seeking out the Allobrogian ambassadors* and urging them, if he could, to a war alliance. He was thinking that they were oppressed by debt both public and private, and, since the Gallic people were warlike by

2 nature, they could be easily enticed to join such a plan. Umbrenus had business dealings in Gaul; he was well known to many of their political leaders and they to him. Thus, without delay, as soon as he saw the ambassadors in the Forum, he asked a few questions about the condition of their country and, as if sympathizing with their misfortune, he began to enquire how they expected their troubles to end.

3 He saw that they complained about the greed of the magistrates, they blamed the Senate because there was no help from that quarter, and they expected that death would be the cure for their miseries. Then he said, 'But I can offer a plan that will let you escape such troubles,

4 if only you are willing to be men.' When he said this, the Allobroges became very hopeful and asked Umbrenus to take pity on them: nothing, they said, was so hard or so difficult that they would not be very eager to do it, provided that they could rid their state of debt.

5 He led them to the house of D. Brutus,* which was near the Forum and, because of Sempronia—for Brutus was away from Rome at the

6 time—not inappropriate to his plan. Furthermore, he summoned Gabinius* in order to lend moral authority to his words. In Gabinius' presence he disclosed the conspiracy, and named their allies, and many other men of each class who were not involved, just to give the ambassadors more courage. Then they promised to help* and he sent them home.

1   41. The Allobroges, however, were for a long time unsure what

2 to do. On the one hand, there was debt, desire for war, and, as they hoped for victory, great rewards; but on the other side, there were the Senate's greater resources, a safe plan, and certain rewards* in the place

3 of uncertain hopes. As they thought about these things, it was finally

4 the good fortune of the Republic that gained the upper hand. And so they revealed everything that they knew to Q. Fabius Sanga,* a man

5 whose patronage had been very useful to their country. When Cicero heard of the plans through Sanga, he ordered the ambassadors to

show an enthusiastic interest in the conspiracy, to approach others, to make fine promises, and to attempt to make the guilty as unmistakable as possible.

42. At about this same time, there were disturbances in Cisalpine 1 and Transalpine Gaul, and also in the Picene and Bruttian territory and in Apulia. The reason for this was that those whom Catiline 2 had sent ahead did not plan well and were like madmen trying to do everything at the same time. Meetings at night, movements of offensive and defensive weapons, haste and agitation; they rendered everything more full of fear than of danger. Q. Metellus Celer, the 3 praetor, brought many to trial in accordance with the Senate's decree and put many of them in chains. C. Murena* did the same thing in Cisalpine Gaul, where he was in charge of the province as legate.

43. At Rome, Lentulus and the other leaders of the conspiracy got 1 together what seemed to them a great force and they decided that when Catiline reached the field of Aefula* L. Bestia, the tribune of the plebs, would hold a public address. He would denounce Cicero's actions and try to make people angry with our very fine consul for a most dreadful war. Taking this as their signal, the rest of the conspirators on the next night would execute their individual tasks.* These tasks, it is said, were distributed in the following way: Statilius 2 and Gabinius with a large company of men would simultaneously set fire to twelve important places in the city. The confusion caused by this would create easier access to the consul and others against whom treachery was afoot. Cethegus would besiege Cicero's door and attack him. Others would attack other victims; the sons of certain families, most of whom were aristocrats, would kill their parents. Then, when everyone was stunned by murder and arson, they would break through to Catiline.

While disclosing these plans and decisions, Cethegus kept com- 3 plaining about the faint-hearted allies: he said that their hesitancy and procrastination had wasted great opportunities; that there was a need for action, not planning; that, though the rest cowered, he would himself attack the Senate house, if only a few would help. He was by nature ferocious, passionate, ready to act; he thought the 4 greatest advantage was in speed.

44. Now the Allobroges following Cicero's orders met the rest 1 of the conspirators through the help of Gabinius. They demanded a signed oath from Lentulus, Cethegus, Statilius, and also from

Cassius, to take to their countrymen. Otherwise, they said, they could not easily induce them to join in such a dangerous business.

2 The others gave the oath without suspecting anything, but Cassius, who promised to meet with them soon, left the city a little before

3 the ambassadors did. Lentulus sent with the ambassadors a certain T. Volturcius* of Croton so that the Allobroges by giving and receiving pledges of loyalty could confirm their allegiance with Catiline before

4 they reached home. He himself gave Volturcius a letter for Catiline, a copy of which* is written below:

5 'You will know who I am from the one I have sent to you. Please understand the danger you are in and remember that you are a man.

6 Consider what your plans require. Seek aid from everyone, even the lowest.' In addition to this, he added a verbal message: Why did he reject slaves when he had been declared an enemy by the Senate? He reported that in the city all orders had been followed. He himself should not hesitate to advance closer.

1   **45.** When these matters were taken care of and the night for their departure was established, Cicero learned of everything through the ambassadors and commanded the praetors, L. Valerius Flaccus and C. Pomptinus,* to ambush the Allobrogian entourage at the Mulvian Bridge* and to arrest them. He disclosed to them the purpose of their mission, but let them decide the details as the situation required.

2 Being military men, they quietly put guards in place, and lay in wait

3 at the bridge as ordered. After the legates arrived with Volturcius and both sides began to shout simultaneously, the Gauls quickly understood the situation and without delay handed themselves over

4 to the praetor. Volturcius at first encouraged the others and defended himself against the band of men with his sword; then, when he was deserted by his legates, first, he earnestly begged Pomptinus, who knew him, to save his life, and, afterwards, frightened and despairing of life, he handed himself over to the praetors as if to the enemy.

1   **46.** When it was over,* everything was quickly reported by messengers to the consul. Great concern and great joy came over him

2 simultaneously. He was happy knowing that the conspiracy had been exposed and the state rescued from danger; on the other hand, he was troubled, unsure what should be done when such important citizens had been caught in the commission of very great crimes. He believed that penalty for them would mean trouble for him; impunity for them

3 would be the destruction of the Republic. Therefore, he stiffened his

resolve* and summoned Lentulus, Cethegus, Statilius, Gabinius, and also Caeparius of Terracina,* who was getting ready to go to Apulia to stir up a slave revolt. The rest came without delay, but Caeparius, 4 who had already left home a little earlier, heard that the conspiracy had been exposed and he fled from the city. The consul himself led 5 Lentulus into the Senate, holding him by the hand because he was a praetor. He ordered the rest to come with their guards to the Temple 6 of Harmony.* There, he summoned the Senate,* and, when a great crowd of senators had gathered, he introduced Volturcius with the ambassadors. He ordered the praetor Flaccus to bring to the same place the box with the letters he had received from the ambassadors.

47. Volturcius was questioned about the journey, the letter, and 1 finally what his plan was and why. At first he made up some things and concealed his knowledge of the conspiracy. Afterwards, when he was granted immunity and told to speak, he disclosed everything as it had happened and declared that he had been enrolled as an ally by Gabinius and Caeparius a few days earlier, but that he knew nothing more than the ambassadors, except that he used to hear from Gabinius that P. Autronius, Ser. Sulla, L. Vargunteius, and many others were in the conspiracy. The Gauls made the same confession 2 and in addition to the letter refuted Lentulus' dissembled ignorance with the things he used to say: that according to the Sibylline books,* three Cornelii* would rule in Rome; that already there had been Cinna and Sulla; that he was fated to be the third master; and, moreover, that this was the twentieth year since the burning of the Capitol,* a year which because of frequent prodigies the soothsayers had said would be bloody with civil war. And so, after the letters were 3 read, when all had acknowledged their own seals, the Senate decreed that Lentulus should resign his position, likewise the others, and that they should be held in 'free custody'.* Accordingly, Lentulus was 4 handed over to P. Lentulus Spinther, aedile at the time, Cethegus to Q. Cornificius,* Statilius to C. Caesar,* Gabinius to M. Crassus, and Caeparius, who had just been arrested during his attempted escape, to Cn. Terentius,* the senator.

48. Meanwhile, when the conspiracy was revealed the plebs who 1 at first had wanted revolution and eagerly favoured war, changed their mind and cursed Catiline's plans. They extolled Cicero to the sky. They were joyful and happy, as if rescued from slavery. They 2 thought that other crimes of war would lead more to booty than to

losses, but that arson was cruel and excessive, a complete disaster for them, because all their resources consisted in what they used for daily needs and their bodily covering.

3   The next day a certain L. Tarquinius* was brought before the Senate. It was said that he was setting out to Catiline when he was
4 arrested and brought back. When he declared that he would give evidence about the conspiracy if he were granted immunity, the consul ordered him to tell what he knew. He gave roughly the same information as Volturcius about the preparations for arson, the slaughter of respectable men, the enemy's movements. In addition, he said he had been sent by M. Crassus to tell Catiline not to be frightened by the capture of Lentulus and Cethegus and the other members of the conspiracy, but to hurry all the more quickly to the city, so that he could more easily snatch them from danger and rebuild the courage
5 of the rest. But, when Tarquinius named Crassus, an aristocrat, a very wealthy man and a man of unsurpassable power, some thought the claim was unbelievable; others, though they thought it true, still saw that under such circumstances such a powerful man was to be placated rather than irritated; the majority were privately in debt to Crassus. Consequently, all shouted that the informer was a liar and
6 they demanded a vote on the matter. Cicero called the question and the Senate as a body decreed that Tarquinius' evidence was deemed false and that he should be held in prison and not allowed any further liberty unless he indicated who had advised him to lie about such
7 an important matter.* There were at that time some who thought that the allegation had been devised by P. Autronius so that, when Crassus was named, by mere association his power would protect
8 the others from danger; others were saying that Tarquinius had been set up by Cicero to prevent Crassus from supporting the wicked and
9 throwing the state into turmoil in his usual fashion. Later, I heard Crassus himself claiming that this extraordinary slander had been imposed on him by Cicero.

1   **49.** At the same time, however, Q. Catulus and C. Piso* were unable to force Cicero either by money or influence to get C. Caesar falsely
2 implicated by the Allobroges or some other witness. Their motivation was the bitter hatred they had for Caesar: Piso because he had been attacked in his extortion trial for the illegal 'punishment' of a certain Transpadane;* Catulus was furious that he, a man of advanced age and great accomplishments, as a candidate for the priesthood, had

been defeated by Caesar who was just a young man.* Moreover, they 3
thought the time was right: Caesar was deeply in debt from his personal generosity, which was extraordinary, and his public largesse
which was exceptional. But when they could not force the consul 4
to such an action, they went about canvassing men individually,
circulating falsehoods, things that they said they had heard from
Volturcius or the Allobroges. This caused such hostility to flare up
against Caesar that some Roman *equites*, who were posted as an armed
guard around the Temple of Harmony, threatened Caesar with their
swords as he left the Senate. They did this to display more clearly 5
their commitment to the Republic, compelled either by the gravity
of the danger or by their own inconstant impulsiveness.

50. While this was going on in the Senate, and they were decid- 1
ing on rewards for the Allobrogian ambassadors and for Volturcius,
since their information had proved true, some of Lentulus' freedmen and a few of his clients were going to different places in the city
urging the craftsmen and slaves to rescue him; others were looking
for gang-leaders, men who were accustomed to torment the state for
a price. Cethegus, however, sent messengers to his slaves and freed- 2
men, men he had selected and trained; he begged them to be bold,
to band together and with their weapons break through to him. The 3
consul, when he heard of these plans, deployed armed guards as time
and occasion required. He convened the Senate,* and formally asked
them what to do about the men held in custody. Just a short time
earlier the entire Senate had judged that these men were traitors.
D. Junius Silanus,* the consul designate, was first asked his opinion* 4
about those held in custody, and also about L. Cassius, P. Furius,*
P. Umbrenus, and Quintus Annius, if they should be captured. He
said that they must pay the penalty.* Later he was moved by C. Caesar's
speech and said he would support the proposal of Ti. Nero* to hold
a referendum after the number of guards had been increased. But
when it came to Caesar's turn, he was asked his opinion by the consul 5
and he spoke as follows:

51. 'All human beings who debate* on matters of uncertainty, con- 1
script fathers,* ought to be free from hatred, enmity, anger, and pity.
The mind cannot easily see the truth when those emotions get in 2
the way, and no one has ever been simultaneously governed by the
demands of his desire and by practical considerations. Wherever you 3
apply your intelligence, it prevails; but, if passion takes over, it becomes

4 master and the mind is powerless. I can recount many examples, conscript fathers, of bad decisions made by kings and peoples under the influence of anger or pity. But I prefer to speak of decisions made correctly and orderly by our ancestors when they resisted their hearts'

5 desires. In the Macedonian War* which we waged with King Perses, the great and opulent state of Rhodes, which had benefited from Roman wealth, treacherously turned against us. But, after the war was over and we took up the matter of the Rhodians' actions, our ancestors let them go unpunished,* lest anyone say that we had started

6 the war more for money than from injury.* Likewise in all the Punic Wars,* though the Carthaginians had often committed many horrible crimes* both in peace and under truces, our ancestors never reciprocated* when they had the opportunity: they preferred to ask what was

7 worthy of them, not what they could justifiably do. You, likewise, must use the same prudential wisdom, conscript fathers. The crime of P. Lentulus and the others should not have more weight with you than your own dignity, and you should not consider your anger more

8 important than your reputation. For, if the penalty can be found that their deeds deserve, I could approve of an unprecedented course.* But, if the enormity of their crime exceeds our ingenuity,* then I say we must use the penalties already established by law.*

9   'Most of those who have given their opinions before me have lamented with great eloquence and grandeur the misfortunes of the Republic. They have listed the savage acts of war, the afflictions of the conquered: the rape of girls and boys; children torn from the arms of their parents; matrons yielding to whatever the conqueror desired; shrines and homes plundered; slaughter, arson; in short, everything

10 filled with weapons, corpses, blood, and grief. But, by the immortal gods, what is the purpose of those speeches? Is it to make you oppose the conspiracy? Do you suppose that a speech will energize someone who is not moved by the enormity and cruelty of the facts?

11 Not true: no mortal thinks his own injuries are small; for many they seem greater than is fair. But not everyone has the same freedom of

12 action, conscript fathers. If the humble who have a life in obscurity become enraged and commit an offence, few know; their fame and their wealth are the same. But the actions of those who are endowed with great power and who live exalted lives are known by all mankind.

13 And so, in the greatest good fortune there is the least licence; neither zealous partiality nor hatred is appropriate, but least of all rage.

What is called anger in others, is named arrogance and cruelty in the 14
powerful. And so this is my assessment, conscript fathers: no tor- 15
ture is equal to the crimes they have committed. But generally men
remember the most recent events, and even in the case of execrable
men, if the punishment is unusually severe, they forget the crimes
and talk about the punishment.

'I am quite certain that D. Silanus, a brave and energetic man, said 16
what he said with the state's interests in mind, and that in a matter
of such importance he shows neither favour nor malice: I know his
character and his composure. But it seems to me his proposal is not 17
so much cruel—what could be cruel against such men?—as it is alien
to our Republic. I am sure that either fear or injustice has forced you, 18
Silanus, a consul designate, to propose an unprecedented punishment. As for fear, there is not much to say, especially since we have 19
so many guards under arms thanks to the diligence of our consul, a
most distinguished man. But concerning the penalty I can speak to 20
the point: in times of grief and affliction death is not a torture but a
release from misery.* It puts an end to all mortal woes; and beyond
that neither anxiety nor joy has any place. But why, in the name of 21
the immortal gods, didn't you add to your proposal that they should
first be whipped? Is it because the *lex Porcia** forbids it? But there 22
are other laws* that similarly forbid taking the life of a condemned
citizen; they allow exile. Or, is it because flogging is worse than death? 23
But what punishment could be too harsh for men convicted of such
a crime? On the other hand, if flogging is less severe than death, why 24
fear the law that forbids the lesser punishment, when you neglect the
law that forbids the harsher punishment?

'But, one might say, who will criticize any decree against the 25
assassins of the Republic? I'll tell you: time, events, fortune, whose
pleasure governs the world. Whatever happens to those men, they 26
have earned it; but you, conscript fathers, think about the example
you are setting for others. Every bad precedent arose from a good 27
case. But when power slips into the hands of those who don't understand it or those less well intentioned, then that new precedent is no
longer appropriately applied to those who deserve it but inappropri-
ately to those who don't. The Lacedaemonians, after they conquered 28
the Athenians,* imposed the rule of thirty men. At first, they began 29
to put to death without trial all the most wicked and those whom
everyone hated. The populace was delighted and they said it was

30 the right thing to do. Afterwards, as their licence to act gradually increased, they began to kill at will good and bad men alike; the rest
31 they frightened and terrified. Thus, the citizen body was reduced to slavery and paid a heavy penalty for their foolish delight.

32   'In our own memory, when Sulla ordered the strangulation of Damasippus* and others like him who flourished to the detriment of the state, who did not praise his actions? People were saying they deserved it, that he killed criminals and insurgents, men who had threatened the
33 government with seditious revolt. But this action was the beginning of a great slaughter. For whenever someone coveted another man's home or villa, or eventually even his dishes or clothes, he would try to get the
34 man proscribed. And soon after those who were delighted at the death of Damasippus were themselves being dragged away and there was no
35 end of carnage until Sulla had glutted all his followers with riches. Now, I don't fear these consequences from M. Tullius nor do I fear them at this time, but in a great city there are many different tempera-
36 ments. It is possible that at some other time, when another man is consul and also has an army at his disposal, a lie will be taken for the truth. When this precedent allows the consul by the decree of the Senate to draw his sword, who will stop or restrain him?

37   'Our ancestors, conscript fathers, were never lacking in intelligence or daring, but neither did their pride prevent them from adopting foreign institutions, provided that they were good institutions.
38 They took our offensive and defensive military weapons from the Samnites;* most of the symbols of civil authority from the Etruscans.* They were very eager, in short, to adopt at home whatever seemed to work among our allies or our enemies: they would rather copy
39 what was good than envy it. But at the same time they imitated the Greek custom* of flogging citizens and executing condemned men.
40 After the Republic reached maturity and, because of its size, factions prevailed, innocent men were convicted, and other similar abuses began to happen. Then, the *lex Porcia* and other laws were passed,
41 laws that allowed exile for the condemned. This, I think, is an especially good reason, conscript fathers, not to adopt a new policy.
42 I am sure that the virtue and wisdom* of those men who created such a great empire from small resources was greater than ours, who have difficulty holding on to what was honourably produced.

43   'And so, is it my opinion that these men should be dismissed and Catiline's army allowed to increase? Not at all. This is my

proposal: their money should be confiscated; they should be held in chains in those towns that have the most resources. Thereafter, there should be no consultation about them before the Senate or referendum presented to the people.* If anyone tries to change this arrangement, it is the Senate's judgement that he will be acting against the interests of the state and against the safety of all.'

52. When Caesar finished speaking, the other senators* expressed 1 aloud their varied approval of one or another proposal. But when M. Porcius Cato* was asked his opinion, he spoke as follows:

'When I consider the facts and the danger we are in, conscript 2 fathers, I'm of a very different mind from when I think of the proposals some have made. They seem to me to be discoursing on the 3 punishment of men who have attempted war against their own fatherland, parents, altars, and hearths; but the facts admonish us to take precautions for the future against these men rather than debate what to do to them. Other crimes can be prosecuted after they are commit- 4 ted; but, if you do not act to prevent this crime, when it does occur, justice will be something you plead for but don't get. When a city is captured nothing is left for the defeated,* by the immortal gods. But I call on you, you who have always valued your homes, villas, 5 statues, and paintings more than the Republic. If you want to keep those possessions, whatever they are that you embrace, if you want to find leisure for your pleasures, then, wake up at last and take control of the state. We are not talking about taxes and the complaints of our 6 allies; your freedom and our life are at risk.

'I have often spoken* at length before this body, conscript fathers, 7 often I have complained about the extravagance and greed* of our citizens, and for this reason I have made many enemies. I am the 8 kind of man who could never indulge in himself even the intention to do wrong, and so it was not easy for me to condone the appetite and the misconduct of others. But you paid little attention to what 9 I said, and still the Republic was strong; our prosperity supported your dereliction. But now we are not asking whether we should live 10 with or without a moral compass, or about the size or magnificence of the empire of the Roman people, but whether this which is ours, however it seems to you, will remain ours or will belong together with our own persons to the enemy.

'At this point does anyone bring up "compassion" and "mercy"? 11 Long ago we lost the true names for things:* squandering the property

of another is called "largesse"; daring to do wicked things is called
12 "courage". And so the Republic is at the edge. By all means let them
be "liberal" with the wealth of our allies, since that's how our morals
are; let them be "compassionate" with thieves who take our treasure;
but do not let them be "generous" with our blood and, while they
spare a few criminals, destroy all the truly good men.

13   'A little while ago before this body Caesar spoke eloquently and well
about life and death, regarding, I believe, the traditional view of the
afterlife as false: that bad people take a path different from that of good
people, and that they inhabit places foul, hideous, revolting, and full of
14 fears. And so he proposed that their money be confiscated, that they
themselves be held under guard in the townships, fearing, I assume,
that, if they were in Rome, members of the conspiracy or some hired
15 mob would use violence to set them free—as if the wicked and the
criminal were only in Rome and not throughout Italy, or as if their
recklessness would be less effective where there were fewer resources
16 to oppose it. And so, if Caesar fears the danger those men present, his
policy is futile. On the other hand, if he alone is not afraid when everyone else is so very afraid, it is all the more incumbent on me to be afraid
17 for you and for me. And so when you decide about P. Lentulus and the
others, know for certain that at the same time you are deciding about
18 Catiline's army and about all the conspirators. The more vigorously
you act, the weaker will be their courage; if they see you hesitate only a
little, immediately they will be upon us and they will be ferocious.

19   'Do not believe that our ancestors made a small Republic great
20 with military weapons. If that were the case, we would now be in
possession of the most beautiful of all states: we have more allies and
21 citizens than they did, more military weapons and horses. No, other
things made them great, things which we do not have at all: disciplined
energy at home, a just empire abroad, a mind free in deliberation,
22 limited neither by guilt nor craving.* In place of these qualities, we
have extravagance and greed, public poverty and private wealth. We
praise affluence, we pursue idleness. We make no distinction between
23 good and bad men; ambition usurps all the rewards of virtue. And no
wonder: when each man of you takes counsel separately for himself,
when at home you are slaves to bodily pleasures and here you are
slaves to money and influence, this is why the Republic, abandoned
by you, has been attacked.

'But I let these things go. There is a conspiracy, the most noble   24
citizens have conspired to burn down the fatherland; the Gauls have
been provoked to war, the Gauls, Rome's most bitter enemy;* the
enemy leader stands over our head with an army. Do you still hesi-   25
tate and wonder what you should do with an enemy that has been
captured within the city walls? Oh, let's pity them, I say—they have   26
gone astray, young men led by ambition—and let's send them off
with their weapons! No, don't let your compassion and mercy turn, if   27
they take arms, into misery. Of course (you say) the situation itself is
difficult but you are not afraid of it. Not true; you do fear it and fear   28
it most of all. But it is your inability to act and your effeminate heart
that makes you hesitate, everyone waiting for someone else, trusting,
of course, in the gods who have often saved this Republic in times of
great danger. But it is not with prayers and womanly entreaties that   29
we earn the help of the gods; it is by being watchful, taking action,
making good policy, that all things succeed. When you have handed
yourself over to apathy and lethargy, it would be an empty gesture to
call upon the gods; they are angry and hostile.

'Among our forefathers, during the Gallic War A. Manlius Torquatus*   30
ordered his own son killed because he attacked the enemy without
orders. That extraordinary young man paid the penalty for unre-   31
strained courage by his death; you are dealing with the most cruel
murderers, and yet you hesitate about what you should decide? Of
course, their prior life mitigates their crime. Yes, spare Lentulus'   32
eminence, if the man himself ever spared his own sense of decency, if
he spared his reputation, if he spared any god or man. Cethegus is a   33
young man; forgive him, if he has not twice made war on his country.
Why should I talk of Gabinius, Statilius, and Caeparius? They would   34
not have made these plans for the Republic, if anything were of value
to them. Finally, conscript fathers, if there were any room for error,   35
by god I would be happy to let you be chastised by experience itself,
since you hold my words in contempt. But we are hemmed in on all
sides. Catiline and his army are at our throats; others are within the
walls and the enemy is in the heart of Rome. We can neither make
any plans nor have any discussion of policy in secret. Therefore, speed
is all the more necessary.

'And so this is my opinion: whereas the Republic is in very great   36
danger because of the wicked plans of its most criminal citizens, and

whereas they have been convicted by the evidence of T. Volturcius and the Allobrogian legates and have confessed that they have planned slaughter, arson, and other hideous and cruel deeds against their fellow citizens and their country, the punishment for capital crimes that is inflicted upon those caught red-handed* must in the manner of our ancestors be inflicted upon those who have confessed.'

1   **53.** After Cato sat down, all the ex-consuls and a great number of senators approved his proposal; they praised to the skies his strength of mind, they scolded each other and called one another timid. Cato was considered a brilliant and a great man. The Senate's decree accorded with his recommendation.*

2   But, for my part, as I read and heard about the many things that the Roman people have done, the brilliant deeds they accomplished at home and in the military, on sea and on land, it happened to become my passionate desire to work out what especially supported such accom-
3   plishments. I was aware that a small band had often fought against great enemy armies; I knew that despite meagre resources they had waged war with opulent kings; in addition I knew that they had often endured the violence of Fortune, that the Greeks were superior in
4   eloquence and the Gauls in military glory. And as I considered many possibilities, it became apparent that everything we accomplished was due to the extraordinary abilities of a few citizens. This was the reason that our ancestors' poverty overcame wealth, that a few overcame many.
5   But after the state had been corrupted by luxury and self-indulgence, the Republic still could support the vices of its generals and magistrates because of its sheer size, and, just as when a woman is worn out by childbirth, for a long time at Rome there was hardly anyone great in
6   manly virtue. Still, in my memory there were two men of extraordinary virtue, but different character, M. Cato and C. Caesar. And since my discussion has brought them forward, it is not my intention to pass them by without saying something to reveal the nature and character of each, to the extent that my talents allow.

1   **54.** And so I turn to them. They were nearly equal in birth, age, and eloquence; their greatness of soul was similar, likewise their glory;
2   but in other respects they were different. Caesar was considered great for his benevolence and generosity; Cato for integrity of life. The former was made famous by his compassion and mercy; intolerance
3   added to the latter's stature. They both attained glory: Caesar by giving, helping, forgiving; Cato by not bribing.* In one there was

refuge for the wretched, in the other death for the wicked. Caesar's 4
easy disposition was praised, Cato's steadfastness. Finally, Caesar's
heartfelt purpose was to work hard, to be vigilant, to neglect his own
interests while being devoted to his friends', and to deny nothing
that was proper to give; for himself he longed for a great command,
an army, a new war in which his excellence could shine. But Cato's 5
drive was for self-restraint, propriety, moral absolutism. He did not 6
compete with the wealthy in wealth or with the partisans in partisanship; he competed with the fervent in virtue, with the restrained in
moderation, with the blameless in abstinence; he preferred to be good
than to seem good; and so, the less he sought renown, the more it
followed him.

55 After the Senate supported Cato's recommendation, as I men- 1
tioned above, the consul thought it best to take precautions for the
coming night and to prevent any new developments during that
time. He asked three men* to make the necessary preparations for
the execution. Guards were deployed and he himself led Lentulus 2
to prison. For the rest, praetors were responsible. In the prison, 3
when you have gone up a little to the left, there is a place called
the Tullianum* which is a depression of about twelve feet into the
ground. Walls protect it on all sides and above there is a dome made 4
with stone arches, but squalor, murk, and stench make it hideous
and terrible to behold. After Lentulus was sent down into this place, 5
the executioners strangled him with a rope as ordered. Thus that 6
man, an aristocrat from the glorious family of the Cornelii, a man who
had held consular power at Rome, found an end that suited his character and his actions. Cethegus, Statilius, Gabinius, and Caeparius
were executed in the same way.

56. While this was happening at Rome, Catiline formed two 1
legions* from all the forces he had himself brought together and those
that Manlius held. He filled out his cohorts according to the number
of soldiers he had. At first he had no more than two thousand men.
Then, as volunteers or allies came into camp, he distributed them 2
equally, and in a short time he filled the legions with their quota.
Only about one-quarter of the entire army, however, had military 3
weapons; the rest were armed as chance would have it with hunting-
spears and lances, some were carrying sharpened sticks.

But after Antonius began to approach* with his army, Catiline 4
marched through the mountains, moving his camp now toward

Rome, now toward Gaul, and not allowing the enemy any opportunity
to fight. He was hoping soon to have a great number of forces, if his
5 allies at Rome could accomplish their tasks. Meanwhile, he refused
to enlist the slaves who had at first come to him in great numbers.
He relied on the resources of the conspiracy, thinking that it was
incompatible with his plans to appear to make common cause between
fugitive slaves and citizens.

1   **57.** Things changed when news arrived in the camp that the
conspiracy at Rome had been exposed, that Lentulus, Cethegus,
and the rest, whom I mentioned above, had paid the penalty. Then
most of those who had been enticed to war by the hope of plunder or
an interest in revolution slipped away. Catiline led the rest through
difficult mountains* on forced marches into the area around Pistoria.
His plan was to flee unseen down footpaths into Transalpine Gaul.*
2 But Q. Metellus Celer was on watch in the Picene field* with three
legions; from the difficulty of the situation he guessed that Catiline
3 would do just what we said he did above. And so, when he learned
from deserters where they were going, he quickly moved his camp
and took a position in the foothills where that man was to descend
4 in haste into Gaul. Furthermore, Antonius was not far away either,
since he, with a great army, was following on more level ground the
5 light-armed men in flight. But when Catiline saw that his path was
cut off by the mountains and the enemy forces, that things had turned
against him in Rome, and that there was no hope either in flight or
for assistance, he thought it was best in such circumstances to try
the fortunes of war. He decided to engage Antonius first. And so he
called an assembly and delivered a speech like this:

1   **58.** 'I know for a fact, soldiers, that words cannot create manly
virtue and that a general's speech does not make an indolent army
2 energetic or a frightened army brave. Whatever daring has been put
in each man's heart by nature and training, that's what he will show
in war. It is futile to exhort a man who is not stirred by glory or danger.
3 Fear in his soul blocks the ears. Still, I have summoned you to remind
you of a few things and at the same time to disclose the reason for my
strategy.

4   'I'm quite sure that you know, soldiers, what a disaster Lentulus'*
lack of courage and his indolence has brought on us and on himself,
and how I was not able to set off for Gaul while waiting for reinforce-
5 ments from Rome. Now, you know as well as I do what difficulties we

are in. There are two enemy armies, one from Rome, the other from 6
Gaul, which block our way. Our lack of food and other supplies does
not allow us to remain here any longer, even if we really wanted to.
Wherever you choose to go, you must open a path with your sword. 7
And so I warn you to have a brave and ready heart, and, when you 8
enter the battle, to remember that in the strength of your right hand
you carry your wealth, honour, and glory, and even your freedom and
your fatherland. If we win, there will be safety everywhere: resources 9
will abound, towns and colonies will open their doors. But if we are 10
afraid and yield, everything will turn against us. No place or friend
will protect the man who doesn't protect himself with his sword.

'And you must keep this in mind as well: the need that presses 11
on us is not the same as what weighs on them. We are fighting for
our homeland, for freedom, for our lives; theirs is an inane struggle
for the power of a few. And so, it is all the more necessary that you 12
attack with reckless courage, remembering the manly virtue you have
displayed before. We could have spent our lives in exile and in utter 13
shame; some of you, having lost your property, could have waited
at Rome for the help of strangers. But you have decided to follow 14
this course because to real men those alternatives seem hideous and
intolerable. If you want to get free of these things, you will need reck- 15
less courage: only the victor gets peace in return for war. To turn the 16
arms which protect your body away from the enemy and hope to find
safety in flight, that is utter madness. In battle the danger is always 17
the greatest for those who are most afraid. Reckless courage is like a
defensive wall.

'When I think of your abilities, soldiers, and weigh what you have 18
already done, I have great hopes for victory. Your courage, your age, 19
your manly virtue encourage me, as does necessity, which can make
even the timid brave. For the enemy is large in numbers, but the 20
narrow passes prevent them from surrounding us. Still, if Fortune 21
is jealous of your manly virtue, do not lose your life without taking
vengeance. Do not be captured and slaughtered like cattle; rather,
fight like men, and leave for your enemy a victory filled with blood
and grief!'

59. When he said these things, he hesitated briefly, ordered the 1
bugle call, lined up his men in battle order and led them into the plain.
He then removed all the horses; in this way, with all the soldiers facing the same danger, their courage would be greater. He was himself

on foot and drew up his army to suit the place and his resources.

2 There was a plain between the mountains on the left and the sharp rocks on the right; so he put eight cohorts in front, and stationed the

3 standards of the rest of the army more closely together in reserve. From those in reserve, he moved all the centurions and the recalled veterans, also all the best common soldiers to the front of the formation. He put C. Manlius in charge of the right side, a man from Faesulae* in charge of the left. He himself took his position with freedmen and colonists* near the eagle that they said C. Marius* had kept in his army during the Cimbrian war.

4 On the other side, C. Antonius, who had a sore foot, had handed his army over to his legate, M. Petreius,* because he could not enter

5 the battle. Petreius placed the veteran cohorts that he had enlisted to resist the insurgency* in the front, behind them he put the rest of the army in reserve. He himself rode about on horseback, addressing each soldier by name, encouraging him, asking him to remember that he was fighting against unarmed bandits for his homeland, his

6 children, his altars, and his hearth. He had been a military man for more than thirty years as tribune, prefect, legate, or praetor, and had served with great distinction in the army. For this reason he personally knew most of the men and their acts of bravery. He enkindled the soldiers' courage by mentioning these things.

1 60. But, when everything was sorted out and with a bugle Petreius gave the signal, he ordered the cohorts to advance slowly. The enemy

2 army did the same. When they were close enough for the light-armed troops to begin the fight, there was a great shout. They clash with hostile standards.* They hurl their javelins; they fight with swords.

3 The veterans, remembering their long-established virtue, press on fiercely fighting hand to hand; those who resist are unafraid. With

4 great violence they struggle. Meanwhile Catiline with his light troops is moving around the front line of the battle: giving aid to those in trouble, sending in fresh troops for those wounded, overseeing everything, himself often fighting, often killing the enemy. He was performing at the same time the duties of the energetic soldier and

5 the good general. When Petreius, to his surprise, sees Catiline exerting himself with great force, he leads his praetorian cohort* into the middle of the enemy's line; he throws them into confusion and he kills them wherever they resist. Then, he attacks the rest on each

6 flank. Manlius and the Faesulanian are among the first to die fighting.

Catiline sees his troops routed, himself left with a few men; then, think- 7
ing of his family name and his long-established dignity, he charges
into the thick of the enemy and there, fighting, is impaled.

61. But only when the battle was over could you truly measure the 1
daring and the mental toughness of Catiline's army. For nearly every 2
man's body, now dead, covered the very place where living he had
stood fighting. A few from the middle of the line had been scattered 3
by the praetorian cohort and had fallen apart from the rest, but everyone had taken wounds in the chest when they fell. Catiline, in fact, 4
was found far from his own men amidst the corpses of the enemy.
He was still breathing a little and maintained on his face that ferocious courage he had had while living. To summarize: not a single 5
native-born citizen from all his army was captured either in battle or
in flight; that is the degree to which no one spared his own life or the 6
life of his enemy.

Still, the army of the Roman people did not attain a joyful or 7
bloodless victory. The most energetic fighters had either been killed
in the battle or had returned gravely wounded. Furthermore, many 8
came from the camp to visit the field or to plunder; when they rolled
over the enemy corpses they discovered now a friend, now a guest or
a relative; likewise, there were those who recognized political opponents. And so through the entire army men were moved in different 9
ways to joy, sorrow, grief, and happiness.

THE JUGURTHINE WAR

INTRODUCTION

The narrative of *The Jugurthine War* may be divided into three sections. The first (5–40) comprises the African prelude and the period of senatorial mismanagement. The transition to senatorial mismanagement is marked by an ethnographic digression (17–19). What follows is the run-up to the *lex Mamilia* (The Mamilian Law), which in 110 or 109 sought reprisals against those senators who had aided Jugurtha in any way. This section includes Memmius' attack on the oligarchy after Jugurtha's actions at Cirta (31), Jugurtha's trip to Rome, and the defeat of the Roman army by Jugurtha's treachery and Roman naivety. The second section (43–83) is defined by the campaigns run by Metellus. Its beginning is set off by a digression on factionalism at Rome, the causes of that factionalism in the defeat of Carthage, and the actions of the Gracchi (41–2). Before the war grinds to a halt, with Metellus attempting to reach a compromise at Cirta, Sallust interrupts the narrative to tell a story about Carthaginian honour, treachery, and the uncertain boundaries between Egypt and Africa (79). It is, of course, just that boundary that the war will eventually secure. The final phase (84–114) begins with Marius' blistering speech at Rome about the privileges of the aristocratic few and his own non-aristocratic, but traditionally Roman, virtues. The conduct of the war, however, repeats Metellus' strategies, especially as Marius sets out to capture Capsa. Then, immediately after his lucky victory at the mountainous stronghold, immediately after Sallust comments on Marius' luck, he brings on Sulla Felix and offers a brief character sketch (95). While the story remains the story of Marius' victory, and while it ends with Marius' triumph, from this point on Sulla will never be far from the narrative. In the following twenty chapters, his name appears in the Latin thirty-six times. The last we hear of Sulla, Sallust says 'Jugurtha was bound and handed over to Sulla, and by him was conveyed to Marius' (113.7). In a short paragraph, Sallust summarizes the ending of the Jugurthine War in terms of what is just beginning: the Cimbri defeated two Roman armies; Marius was made consul in his absence; he celebrated his triumph on the day that he began his second consulship. Sallust does not say so, but this is the first of five consecutive consulships, a period that will end with Marius turning upon his former ally, the tribune, Saturninus (100 BC). But even that will not be the end. In 88 he and Cinna will attempt to wrest Sulla's command against Mithridates from him and this action will set in motion the first real civil war: Sulla will march on Rome; Cinna and Marius will starve and besiege the city; Sulla will return and institute his deadly proscriptions. Thousands will die.

CHRONOLOGY OF THE WAR

Sallust's chronology is not always accurate or easy to follow. The following outlines the events of the Jugurthine War, as precisely as possible, in relationship to certain important events in Rome.

148 Death of Masinissa (ch. 5).

146 Destruction of Carthage.

134 Jugurtha in Spain with Scipio (to 132) (chs. 7–9).

133 Tribuneship of Ti. Gracchus.

122 Tribuneship of C. Gracchus (to 121).

118 Death of Micipsa (ch. 11).

117 Opimius' legation to divide the kingdom of Micipsa (to 116) (ch. 16).

115 M. Aemilius Scaurus consul; M. Licinius Crassus born.

112 Jugurtha's attack on Cirta (chs. 23–6).

111 L. Calpurnius Bestia, consul, in Africa (chs. 28–9).

110 Murder of Massiva (ch. 35). Albinus returns to Rome (ch. 36). Aulus' defeat by Jugurtha (ch. 37).

109 Q. Caecilius Metellus consul; spring: Metellus in Africa (ch. 44); summer: battle at Vaga and the Muthul (ch. 50); autumn: Zama, winter quarters, treaty with Jugurtha (chs. 61–2); Jugurtha renews the war (chs. 62, 66).

108 Metellus' second campaign (ch. 73); summer: Metellus attacks Thala (chs. 75–6). Marius election to consulship (ch. 73).

107 C. Marius consul; L. Cornelius Sulla quaestor.

107 January: Metellus' command transferred to Marius (ch. 73); spring: Marius arrives in Africa (ch. 86); autumn: Marius takes Capsa (ch. 90).

107 Subjugation of Numidia (to 106) (92.3–4).

106 Cicero born; Cn. Pompeius born.

106 Spring: Marius marches to Muluccha, takes stronghold (92.5–94); Marius in winter quarters (106/5) (chs. 97–103).

105 Truce in Numidia (ch. 104); summer: negotiations with Bocchus (chs. 105–13); 6 October: battle of Arausio (ch. 114). November: Marius elected consul.

104 1 January: Marius celebrates a triumph.

THE JUGURTHINE WAR

1 **1.** It is wrong for humans to complain about human nature, speaking of frailty and saying that their short life is ruled rather by chance than

2 by merit.* For, after careful thought, you will discover that nothing else is greater, nothing more stable, and that it is more often the case that human nature is lacking in determined effort than in strength or

3 time. But the leader and ruler of mortal life is the rational soul. And when it proceeds toward glory down a path of manly virtue, it has more than enough power and potential to win fame and it does not need the help of chance, which cannot grant or steal from anyone hon-

4 esty, diligence, and other excellent qualities. But if the mind is seized by perverse desires and descends into the corruption of sloth and bodily pleasures, then for a brief time it enjoys its cravings, but when indolence has worn away strength, time and talent, then men blame the inherent weakness of human nature; each man shifts the blame for

5 what he has created to his troubles. If, on the other hand, men were as concerned about virtuous ways as they are eager to seek what others have and what will do them no good and is often even dangerous, they would control what happens rather than be controlled by it, and they would advance to that height of greatness where they would no longer be mortals, they would become eternal in glory.

1 **2.** I say this because, just as the human race is composed of body and soul, so all of our accomplishments and pursuits follow either our

2 physical or spiritual nature. And so it is that outstanding beauty, great wealth, even physical strength and other similar things quickly pass away, but the extraordinary deeds of intellectual talent are, just like

3 the soul, immortal. Simply put, just as there is a beginning, so there is an end to the benefits of body and fortune; all that is born dies, all that grows, grows old. But the soul is incorruptible, eternal, the director of the human race; it guides and has power over all things,

4 and is not itself controlled. All the more surprising, then, is the depravity of those who are devoted to bodily pleasures and pass their lives in luxury and idleness, but allow their intellectual talent, which is the best and most noble part of human nature, to grow torpid with neglect and indolence, especially when the rational soul has so many different ways to attain the heights of glory.

3. But of all the paths to glory it seems to me that at the present 1
time political office and military power, indeed all public service, is
utterly undesirable, since the honour of public office is not granted
for virtuous action and those who use fraud to enjoy these offices
are not secure or more honourable because of it. This is because the 2
use of force to rule over one's country and subjects,* even though
you could and might correct abuses, is still a risky thing, especially
when every change of circumstances brings with it slaughter, exile,
and other acts of hostility. On the other hand, it is the height of mad- 3
ness to labour in vain and to acquire from one's efforts nothing but
exhaustion and hatred; unless, of course, one is possessed by some 4
dishonourable and dangerous desire to sacrifice one's self-respect and
freedom to the powerful interests of the few.*

4. But there are other activities that employ one's innate intellec- 1
tual abilities, and pre-eminent among these is the recording of historical events. I think I will be silent about its value because others 2
have written of that and because I do not want anyone to think that
out of vanity I am extolling and praising my own endeavour. I also 3
believe that, although my work is difficult and useful, there will still
be those who will stigmatize it with the name of idleness,* because
I have decided not to participate in politics. These are the men 4
who think that the most important activity is to court and greet the
people and to seek influence through dinner parties.* But I ask them
to reconsider the circumstances in which I attained political office,
the kind of men who could not achieve the same thing, and the class
of men who entered the Senate afterwards. If they do, then I am sure
that they will conclude that I changed my mind for good reason, not
out of idleness, and that the outcome of my retirement will benefit
the state more than the busy participation of others will.

The following supports my claim: I have often heard that in the 5
past Q. Maximus,* P. Scipio,* and other eminent men of our state,
used to say that their soul was most irresistibly fired to accomplish
acts of manly virtue when they gazed upon the wax images of their
ancestors.* To be sure, it was not the wax or the image that had 6
such power in itself but the memory of things done that nourished
the flame in the breast of extraordinary men, and that flame did not
die down until their manly virtue had equalled that fame and glory.
But who is there today with our contemporary morals that would 7
rather compete with his ancestors in moral fibre and hard work than

in wealth and ostentatious consumption? Even the 'new men', who before with their virtuous actions used to surpass the old aristocracy, use underhanded fraud and open violence in their struggle for military power and political offices rather than decent moral practices.

8 It is as if the praetorship and the consulship and all other offices of this kind were in themselves noble and magnificent things, and not things

9 whose value corresponded to the virtue of those who held them. But I have digressed too far and freely in expressing my contempt and disgust for our political morality. I now turn to my project.

1   5. I am going to write about the war which the Roman people waged with the Numidian king Jugurtha, first because it was great and brutal, with victories on both sides, and second because that was the first time there was any opposition to the aristocracy's abuse of power.

2 This struggle confused all things, human and divine, and proceeded to such a pitch of madness that political partisanship had its end

3 in war and the devastation of Italy. But before I begin this narrative, I will review a few earlier events so that all that follows may be clearer and more easily understood.

4   In the Second Punic War,* Hannibal, the leader of the Carthaginians, eroded Italy's power more than anyone since the Roman name became great. During this war, P. Scipio, the man whose manly virtue would later earn him the cognomen 'Africanus', accepted Masinissa, the king of the Numidians, as a friend. Masinissa performed many glorious military deeds, and it was on account of these deeds that, when the Carthaginians were conquered and Syphax*—whose power in Africa was great and broad—was captured, the Roman people gave to the king as gift whatever cities and fields he had himself taken in

5 battle. Consequently our friendship with Masinissa remained strong and honourable. His rule ended with his death.

6   Next, his son Micipsa* succeeded to the throne; he ruled alone since his two brothers, Mastanabal and Gulussa,* had fallen sick and

7 died. Micipsa himself had two sons, Adherbal and Hiempsal. He raised Jugurtha, the son of his brother Mastanabal, in the palace with the same care as his own sons, but he allowed Jugurtha to remain a commoner, because he was the child of a concubine.

1   6. When Jugurtha first reached manhood, he was strong in body, handsome to look at but above all powerful in his intellectual talents. He did not allow himself to be corrupted by extravagance or idleness. Rather, as is the custom with that nation, he rode horses, threw the

javelin, competed with his peers in races and, though he surpassed all in glory, he was still loved by all. In addition, he spent most of his time hunting and was the first or among the first to wound the lion or other beasts. He accomplished the greatest things, but spoke the least about himself.

In the beginning Micipsa was pleased by this conduct, thinking 2 that Jugurtha's manly virtue would be a source of glory for his realm. But then he noticed that the young man's power was growing greater and greater, that his own life was coming to a close and that his sons were still young. He was deeply disturbed by these circumstances and began to think through many things in his mind. He was terrified by 3 human nature, which is greedy for power and heedless in satisfying its inner desires; he was terrified by the opportunity offered by his advanced age and the age of his children: it was an opportunity which could lead even average men astray in their hope for plunder; in addition, the zeal of the Numidians terrified him, they were fired up with enthusiasm for Jugurtha and this made him worry that, if he treacherously killed such a man, some rebellion or war would arise.

7. Constrained by these obstacles, he saw that he could not elimin- 1 ate such a popular man through violence or treachery. He decided that, since Jugurtha was ready for action and eager for military glory, he would expose him to the dangers of war and in this way see what fortune would do. The Roman people were at war with Numantia* 2 and Micipsa was sending them reinforcements of cavalry and foot soldiers. Hoping that Jugurtha would be easily killed either while flaunting his military prowess or because of the enemy's savagery, he put him in charge of the Numidians he was sending to Spain. The result 3 was not at all what he had planned. For Jugurtha had a quick and 4 sharp mind and he soon came to understand the nature of the Roman general, P. Scipio, and the character of the enemy. Then, laboriously and carefully, by modestly accepting orders and frequently meeting dangers, in a short time he attained such a reputation that he came to be greatly admired by our men and to be the greatest terror to the Numantians. In fact, he was both relentless in battle and wise in 5 counsel, something very difficult to accomplish, since prudence tends to create fear and confidence results in recklessness. Consequently, 6 Scipio relied on Jugurtha's help for nearly all difficult tasks, counted him among his friends, and grew more and more fond of him daily because neither his advice nor his actions were fruitless. In addition 7

to this he showed a generous disposition and an ingenious wit, qualities which made him a close friend to many of the Romans.

1   8. At that time there were many in our army, both 'new men' and old aristocracy, who thought wealth preferable to virtue and honour; they were politically factious at home, powerful among the allies, more famous than honourable. Jugurtha's mind was no ordinary mind, and these men kept firing it up with promises that, if King Micipsa should die, he could take sole possession of the kingdom of Numidia: they said that he was superior in military valour, that at Rome everything was for sale. But Scipio offered other advice.

2   After Numantia was destroyed and he had decided to dismiss the reinforcements and to return home himself, he gave Jugurtha gifts and praised him generously before a meeting of the soldiers. Then, he led him into his tent and there privately warned him to cultivate the friendship of the Roman people as a whole rather than through private individuals and not to fall into the habit of bribery: it was dangerous, he said, to purchase from a few what was owned by many. If he would be willing to rely upon his own characteristics and qualities, both glory and power would come to him without effort; but if he proceeded too hastily, his money would bring about his downfall.

1   [9.] So he spoke and dismissed him with a letter for Micipsa. The general sense of the letter was the following:

2   The heroic valour displayed by your nephew Jugurtha in the Numantine War was by far the greatest and I know that this fact will be a joy to you. He is dear to us because of his accomplishments; we will work as hard as we can to make the Senate and the Roman people feel the same. As your friend, I congratulate you. You have a man worthy of yourself and of Masinissa, his grandfather.

3   When the king learned from the letter that the rumours he had heard were true, he was moved both by the Jugurtha's valour and his position of influence and so he changed his mind. He attempted to win over Jugurtha with gifts and immediately adopted him* and in
4   his will made him an heir equal to his sons. Then, after a few years,* when the king, broken by disease and age, knew that the end of his life was at hand, in the presence of friends and relatives, and also his sons Adherbal and Hiempsal, he is said to have spoken as follows:

1   10. 'When your father died, Jugurtha, and you were a young boy without hope, without resources, I took you into my kingdom.

I was thinking that because of my kindnesses I would be no less dear to you than if I had begotten you. And my hopes have not deceived me. For, to say nothing of your other great and extraordinary achieve- 2 ments, most recently your return from Numantia has brought honour and glory to me and my kingdom; and because of your abilities the Romans, once merely friends, are now very close friends. In Spain, our family name has new life.* And finally, what is most difficult among mortals: your glory has overcome envy. Now, as nature puts 3 an end to my life, I urge and beseech you, by this right hand, by the good faith of my realm, that you hold dear these men who are your relatives by birth and your brothers because of my generosity. I ask you not to prefer making new alliances with strangers over maintain- ing these ties of blood. Armies and treasuries are not what protect 4 a kingdom; but friends are, men you can neither coerce with arms nor buy with gold. They are acquired through acts of devotion and loyalty. And what friendship is closer than brother to brother? On the 5 other hand, what stranger will you find loyal, if you are an enemy to your own family?

'I am handing over to you and your brothers my kingdom: if you 6 do right, it will be strong; weak, if you do wrong. For in concord, small things grow; in discord, great things collapse. But it is your 7 duty, Jugurtha, rather than theirs; you are superior to them in age and wisdom; you ought to provide against any other outcome. For in every struggle, the more powerful person, even if he receives an injury, still seems, because of his greater power, to have inflicted the injury. Now, as for you, Adherbal and Hiempsal, you should love and 8 emulate this great man, imitate his virtues, and struggle to show that I have not adopted a son better than those I have begotten.'

11. Although Jugurtha was aware of the pretence in the king's words 1 and was himself making other plans in his mind, still he responded graciously according to the occasion. A few days later Micipsa died. 2 The princes held a magnificent royal funeral and then convened to discuss together the general situation. Hiempsal, who was the young- 3 est of them, was a naturally truculent man. Having previously treated Jugurtha's birth with contempt because he was inferior to them on his mother's side, he took his seat on the right of Adherbal. In this way he prevented Jugurtha from sitting in the middle, the place of honour among the Numidians. But afterwards, when repeatedly 4 asked by his brother to show respect to age, he reluctantly moved to

5 the other side. Then, while they were discussing many details of government, Jugurtha proposed among other things that all the laws and decrees of the past five years be rescinded. He said the reason was that during this time age had impaired Micipsa's mental abilities.

6 Immediately Hiempsal said that he approved the proposal; after all, Jugurtha himself had been adopted and gained a share of the kingdom

7 in the past three years. This statement struck deeper into Jugurtha's

8 heart than anyone thought. And so, from that time on Jugurtha was stirred by anger and fear; he devised and planned and thought only

9 about how he could deceive and trap Hiempsal. And when his plans proceeded too slowly and his ferocious spirit was not soothed, he decided to accomplish his project by whatever means necessary.

1 　12. At the first meeting between the princes, which I mentioned above, they failed to arrive at an agreement and so decided to divide the treasury and the imperial territory among themselves individually.*

2 They set a time for both of these matters, but put the distribution of wealth first. Meanwhile the princes each settled in a different place

3 near the treasury. It happened that Hiempsal stayed in the town of Thirmida* in a house belonging to Jugurtha's closest lictor,* a man who had always been dear and pleasing. Chance had offered an agent, and so Jugurtha piled on the promises. He persuaded him to go to his house as if to inspect it and to make duplicate keys for the door, since the originals were always given to Hiempsal. As for the rest, Jugurtha

4 said he would come with a large force when the time was right. The Numidian quickly did what he was asked and admitted Jugurtha's

5 soldiers at night, as directed. They burst into the house, divided up, and went looking for the king. They killed some as they slept, others as they ran forward; they searched recesses, burst open locked doors, filled everything with noise and confusion. Meanwhile Hiempsal was found hiding in a maidservant's hut, where he had first fled, fright-

6 ened and ignorant of the place. The Numidians, as ordered, brought his head to Jugurtha.

1 　13. News of so fierce a deed soon spread throughout all of Africa. Fear descended upon Adherbal and all who had been subjects of Micipsa. The Numidians divided into two factions: most followed

2 Adherbal, but the better warriors followed his rival. As a result, Jugurtha armed as many troops as he could, brought cities under his command, some by force and others by choice, and made plans to

3 rule all of Numidia. Adherbal had sent legates to Rome to inform the

Senate of his brother's death and his own misfortune. Still, relying on the size of his military, he made preparations for armed combat. But 4 when it came to a struggle he was defeated and fled from the battle into the province* and from there he headed to Rome.

After he gained control of all of Numidia, Jugurtha had accom- 5 plished his goals. It was then that he took the time to think about what he had done. He began to fear the Roman people and to hold that there was no hope against their wrath except in aristocratic greed and his own money. And so within a few days he sent legates to 6 Rome with quantities of gold and silver. He had ordered them first to shower his old friends with presents and then to acquire new friends, and finally not to hesitate in accomplishing anything that lavish generosity could accomplish. But when the legates arrived in Rome 7 and, following the king's orders, sent magnificent gifts to Jugurtha's former hosts* and to others who wielded power in the Senate at that time,* such a change was effected that their very great resentment turned into gratitude and support. Some of these, induced by hope, 8 others by rewards, solicited individual senators, asking them not to pass any serious decrees against Jugurtha. And so, when his legates 9 felt confident enough, a date was set for both parties to come before the Senate. At that point we are told that Adherbal spoke as follows:

14. 'Conscript fathers, my father Micipsa told me as he was dying 1 that I should think that my job was only the administration of the kingdom of Numidia and that the law and the power lay in your hands, that I should strive both at home and in the military to be of the greatest use to the Roman people. He directed me to think of you as my relatives, as my kin. He said that if I did these things, I would have in your friendship an army, wealth, and protection for my realm. And I was following my father's directions when Jugurtha, 2 a man who is the greatest criminal of all those the earth sustains, treated your imperial authority with contempt and drove me, the grandson of Masinissa, your ally by birth and the friend of the Roman people, from my kingdom and from all my fortunes.

'And for my part, conscript fathers, since I was destined, it seems, 3 for this misery, I only wish that I could have sought your help in return for my own services, not for those of my ancestors, and above all I could have wished that the Roman people owed me favours I did not need, or, failing this, that if I did need them, I could accept them as what was due to me. But since righteousness is no protection in 4

itself and since I could not control the kind of man Jugurtha is, I have fled to you, fathers of the Senate. And it is a bitter sorrow to me that
5 I am compelled to be a burden before I have done any service. Other kings have entered into friendship* with you after being defeated in war or they have sought an alliance with you in times of danger. Our family, on the other hand, established friendship with the Roman people during the Carthaginian war, at a time when your word was
6 more to be trusted than your fortune. I am a descendant of that family, the grandson of Masinissa.* Do not, Fathers of the Senate, allow me to seek your aid in vain.

7   'If I had no reason for making my request beyond my wretched fortune—recently a king, powerful in family, reputation, and wealth, now helpless, looking for the aid of others—still it used to be exemplary of Roman majesty to put an end to injustice and to prevent any
8 realm from increasing through crime. But in my case, it is from the very lands that the Roman people gave my ancestors that I have been driven, lands from which my father and grandfather helped you drive Syphax and the Carthaginians. It is your kind gifts that have been stolen away, conscript fathers. When I am injured, you are treated
9 with contempt. Ah, poor me! I ask my father, Micipsa: is this the result of your good deeds? That the one whom you made an equal with your children and to whom you gave a share of the kingdom, that he of all men will destroy your line? And so, is there no rest for our
10 family? Will blood, battle, and flight always be our lot? While Carthaginian power was unbroken, it was expected that we would suffer all sorts of cruelty: the enemy was at our flank; you, our friends, were
11 far away. Our only hope was in our weapons. But, after that plague was removed from Africa, we were happy and pursued peace because we had no enemy, unless it happened that you said the word. But now look, suddenly Jugurtha appears, bearing himself with intolerable arrogance, wickedness, contempt. He kills my brother, his own relative. Then he makes my brother's kingdom the spoils of his crime. Next, since he cannot trap me with the same treachery, he drives me, as you can see, from my country and home, an exile, without aid and drenched in sorrow, just when I thought that your power would protect me from violence or war. As a result, the most dangerous place in the world for me is my own kingdom.

12   'I used to believe, Fathers of the Senate, what I had heard my own father often say, that those who carefully cultivated your friendship

would undertake a great labour, but they would have the greatest security of all. And in every war our family has done everything it 13 could to support you. Now in peacetime our security, conscript fathers, is in your hands. Our father left us, two brothers, and he thought 14 that his acts of kindness would join the third, Jugurtha, to us. Now, one brother has been killed; I myself have barely escaped the hateful hands of the third. What am I to do? Where, given the depths of 15 my misery, am I to find refuge? Every protection my family offered has been destroyed. My father yielded, as we all must, to nature. My brother, who least deserved it, lost his life through the criminal actions of his kinsman. Neighbours, friends, others near to me have each been overwhelmed by one disaster or another. They have been captured by Jugurtha; some nailed to crosses, others hurled to wild beasts; the few who got to live were shut up in darkness where with grief and sorrow they drag out a life that is worse than death.

'But everything was still safe, all that has been lost and all that has 16 turned from familial affection to its opposite, nevertheless, conscript fathers, I would still turn to you, if some unexpected evil occurred. Just as your empire is great, so it is proper that you take care of justice and all injustices. But now, as an exile from my country and 17 my home, alone, with nothing that befits my station, where else can I turn? On whom can I call? Shall I turn to the nations and kings who are all enemies of my family because of our friendship with you? What place can I go to where there are not many hostile reminders of my ancestors? Can anyone who was once an enemy of yours take pity on us? The fact is that Masinissa instructed us, conscript fathers, 18 to make no friends except the Roman people, to accept no new alliances, no treaties: we will have, he said, great and abundant security in our friendship with you; if fortune ever fails this empire, with it we must die. It is your virtue and the favour of the gods that has made 19 you great and prosperous; all things submit and obey; and so it is easy for you to correct the injuries your allies suffer.

'I have only one fear: that private arrangements with Jugurtha, 20 alliances whose character you do not understand, are turning some of you against me. I hear that some people have been working very hard, canvassing you individually, pressuring you not to reach a decision while Jugurtha is absent, before he states his case. They say that I am making things up and pretending to be in flight, that I could have stayed in my kingdom. I only pray that some day I may see him, 21 the man whose impious actions have created my misery, making a pretence like mine, and I pray that at some point either you or the immortal gods may begin to care for the affairs of men. Then, truly, that man, ferocious and famous among his crimes, would be tortured in every evil way and pay a heavy penalty for his impious conduct toward our father, for the murder of my brother and the misery he has caused me.

22 'Now, my brother, most dear to my heart, now, though you have lost your life before your time, killed by one who should have been the last to raise his hand against you, still I think we should rejoice

23 and not grieve for your misfortune. You lost your life, but you did not lose your kingdom; you lost flight, exile, poverty, all the troubles that overwhelm me. I, on the other hand, am cursed, hurled from my father's kingdom down into great troubles, a lesson in the human condition, uncertain what I should do, whether I should avenge your wrongs by myself without help, or try to save my kingdom when the

24 power over my life and death lies in the hands of others. I wish that death were an honourable escape from my misfortunes; I wish that I would not be an object of contempt, if exhausted by my troubles I let injustice win. Now, it is not pleasing to live or possible to die without shame.

25 'Conscript fathers, I ask you in your own name, in the name of your fathers and children, in the name of the majesty of the Roman people: help me in my misery, oppose the wrongs done me; do not allow the kingdom of Numidia, which belongs to you, to be destroyed by bloody crimes against my family.'

1   15. After the king finished speaking, Jugurtha's legates, relying more on their bribes than their arguments, made a brief reply. Hiempsal, they said, had been killed by the Numidians for his cruelty; Adherbal had started the war, and after he had been defeated he was complaining because he could not persist in injustice; Jugurtha was asking the Senate to believe that he was the man they came to know at Numantia and to put his actions before his enemy's words. Both

2 sides then left the Senate house. The Senate immediately took up the matter. Those who favoured the legates and a large number of senators besides whom influence had corrupted contemned Adherbal's speech, lauded Jugurtha's virtue, used influence, words, and every means available, exerting themselves on behalf of another man's crime

3 and shame as if for their own glory. On the other hand, a few who cared

more for justice and goodness than for wealth voted that Adherbal should be helped and that the death of Hiempsal should be severely punished. Of all of these, most noteworthy was Aemilius Scaurus,* 4 an aristocrat, a restless man, a partisan, greedy for power, office, and wealth, but clever in hiding his faults. He saw the king's scandal- 5 ous and shameless bribery and was afraid that the outcome would be the usual one, namely that polluted licence* would create popular resentment. And so he restrained his typical self-indulgence.*

16. Nevertheless, the faction that preferred money or influence 1 prevailed in the Senate. It was decreed that ten legates* should 2 divide the kingdom which had been Micipsa's between Jugurtha and Adherbal. The leader of the commission was L. Opimius,* a distin- guished man. He was at that time powerful in the Senate because of the harshness with which as consul he followed up the aristocratic victory over the plebs when C. Gracchus* and M. Fulvius Flaccus* were killed. Although Jugurtha considered him to be among his 3 opponents at Rome, he received him with the greatest respect. Jugurtha offered him many gifts and many promises, and so he persuaded him to hold the king's pleasure above his own reputa- tion, his own integrity, and eventually all his own real interests. He 4 approached the other legates in the same way and won over most; a few thought integrity more important than money. In the division 5 of the kingdom, the part of Numidia that was adjacent to Mauretania and was richer in land and men was given to Jugurtha;* the other part, more beautiful than useful, arrayed with more ports and build- ings, was made Adherbal's possession.

17. My topic seems to require a brief exposition of the geography 1 of Africa and some mention of those peoples with whom we have fought wars or made alliances. But regarding the places and nations 2 that are scarcely visited because of heat or harsh terrain, and likewise the deserts, I cannot discover or relate much information. The rest I will discuss in as few words as possible.

In their division of the world most people* make Africa the third 3 continent; a few acknowledge only Asia and Europe, and place Africa in Europe. Africa is bounded on the west by the strait between our 4 sea and the Ocean,* on the east by a sloping tract which the natives call Catabathmos.* The sea is rough, without harbours; the land is 5 rich in grain, good for herds, barren of trees. Neither sky nor land provides much water. The natives are healthy, fast runners, hard 6 workers; and most die of old age, except for those killed by weapons or animals. They are not often overcome by illness. In addition, there are many species of dangerous animals.

7   As for the men who originally populated Africa and those who arrived afterwards or how they intermingled, I will speak as briefly as possible. My account is different from what is generally accepted but is in accordance with the Punic books which King Hiempsal* is said to have written, and it agrees with the account given by those who dwell in the land. Still, responsibility for the truth will rest with my authorities.

1   18. Africa was originally inhabited by the Gaetuli* and the Libyans;* they were wild and uncultured people, who fed on the meat of wild
2 animals or, like cattle, on the fodder of the field. They were not governed by customs or by law or by anyone in authority. They lived a nomadic wandering life and made their home wherever nightfall
3 compelled them to stop. But after Hercules died in Spain, as the Africans think, the various peoples who composed his army soon dispersed: they had lost their leader and throughout the army many
4 individuals began to seek power for themselves. From their numbers, the Medes, Persians, and Armenians travelled by ship to Africa
5 and settled on the coast of our sea. The Persians, however, moved closer to the Ocean and they used the inverted hulls of their ships for huts. This was because there was no timber in the fields and they
6 had brought from Spain no resources for buying or trading: the size of the sea and their ignorance of the language made commerce impos-
7 sible. Gradually they intermarried with the Gaetuli and, because they often moved from place to place testing the soil and moving on, they
8 called themselves Nomads.* Still to this day the buildings of Nomad peasants, which they call 'mapalia', are long with curved sides and
9 a roof like the hull of a ship. The Medes and Armenians, on the other hand, were neighbours to the Libyans—for they lived nearer to the African Sea, while the Gaetuli were further south, not far from the tropics—and all three soon built cities. This was possible because they were separated from Spain by only a narrow strait and had insti-
10 tuted a system of barter. Over time the Libyans corrupted the name of the Medes, calling them in their barbaric tongue Mauri.*

11   Still, the Persian state* quickly grew stronger, and afterwards, some left their parents because of overcrowding and under the name of Numidians populated those places near Carthage which are

called Numidia. Thereafter, both populations,* supported by the 12
other, forced their neighbours by arms or fear to accept their authority.
They grew in name and glory, especially those who had settled near
our sea, because the Libyans were less warlike than the Gaetuli. In
the end, the Numidians gained control of most of northern Africa, all
the conquered people were absorbed into the race and name of their
rulers.

19. Later the Phoenicians arrived. Some were trying to relieve 1
overpopulation at home; others wanted more power; they solicited the
common people and others restless for change, and founded Hippo,*
Hadrumetum,* Leptis,* and other cities on the coast. Soon these grew
prosperous, some were a protection for their homelands, others were a
decoration. As to Carthage, however, I think it better to be silent than 2
to say too little, since time tells me to hurry on to other topics.

And so, next to Catabathmos, a place which separates Egypt from 3
Africa, the first city as you follow the sea-coast* is Cyrene,* a colony
of Thera, and then the two Syrtes with Leptis between them, then
the Altars of the Philaeni,* a place which the Carthaginians consider
the boundary of their empire on the Egyptian side. After these there
are the other Punic cities. The rest of the territory as far as Maure- 4
tania is controlled by the Numidians; the Mauri are nearest to the
Spains.* We are told that the Gaetuli live beyond Numidia, some in 5
huts, others in a less civilized fashion as nomads; that the Ethiopians 6
are beyond them; and then there are the places burned by the heat of
the sun. At the time of the Jugurthine War, most of the Punic cities 7
and the territory that the Carthaginians had recently possessed* were
administered by the Roman people through magistrates; Jugurtha
held power over a great part of the land inhabited by the Gaetuli and
most of Numidia all the way to the river Muluccha.* King Bocchus,
a man generally ignorant of the Roman people except by name and
likewise previously unknown to us in either war or peace, ruled all
the Moors. Concerning Africa and its inhabitants, I have said all that 8
my topic requires.

20. After the realm was divided and the legates left Africa, and 1
after Jugurtha saw that contrary to the fears of his heart he had been
rewarded for his crime, he concluded that what he had heard from his
friends in Numantia was true: at Rome everything was for sale. At the
same time, he was further encouraged by the promises of those men
whom he had just before loaded with gifts and so he set his sights on

2 the kingdom of Adherbal. Jugurtha was himself fierce and war-like; but the man he sought was quiet, peaceful, with a calm disposition, a
3 target for injury, more fearful than fearsome. And so, without warning he invaded* his land with a large army. He seized many men together with cattle and other plunder, he burned buildings and maliciously
4 attacked many places with his cavalry. Then, he returned to his own kingdom with all his men, thinking that Adherbal, moved by indignation, would avenge his injuries militarily and that this action would
5 be an excuse for war. But Adherbal realized that he was not Jugurtha's equal in arms and he had more confidence in the friendship of the Roman people than in his Numidians. Therefore, he sent legates to Jugurtha to complain about the damages. All they brought back was insults, but he still decided to put up with it all rather than undertake
6 war, something he had already tried* without success. This, however, did not restrain Jugurtha's ambition: in his mind he had already
7 invaded the entire kingdom. And so he began to wage war and openly to seek supremacy over all of Numidia, not with a band of marauders
8 as before, but with a large army which he had raised. Wherever he went, he was wasting the cities, the fields; driving off booty; courage grew among his men, terror among the enemy.

1   **21.** Adherbal, when he understood that things had reached a point where he had to either give up his kingdom or fight to retain it, had
2 no choice but to enlist troops and proceed to meet Jugurtha. For a time, both armies took a position not far from the sea near the town of Cirta* and, because it was near the end of the day, no battle was engaged. But when most of the night had passed, and twilight was beginning to appear, the signal was given to Jugurtha's soldiers: they invaded the camp, the enemy, some half asleep, others grabbing for their weapons, was routed and put to flight. Adherbal fled to Cirta with a few cavalry, and, if not for the crowd of togas* that prevented the Numidians from entering the walls, in a single day the war
3 between the two kings would have begun and ended. So Jugurtha besieged the town: he attempted to storm it with mantlets and towers and war machinery of every type, being especially eager to pre-empt the legates* whom he had heard Adherbal had sent to Rome before the battle began.

4   The Senate, however, when they heard the kings were at war, dispatched as legates three young men* to Africa. They were to approach

both kings and announce that it was the wish and the decree of the Senate and the Roman people that they put aside their arms, that they decide their dispute by law not by war: this, they said, was in accord with Roman dignity and their own honour. [22.] The leg- 1 ates came quickly to Africa, all the more so because in Rome, as they were getting ready to leave, there was talk about the battle that had taken place and the siege of Cirta. But the rumour was charitable. When Jugurtha heard what the legates had to say, he responded that 2 nothing was more important or more precious to him than the authority of the Senate. He said that since he was a young man he had tried to win the approval of all the best citizens, that he had won the approval of P. Scipio, a very great man, not because of viciousness but because of his virtues; it was on account of these same qualities, not from lack of children, that Micipsa had adopted him as heir to his kingdom. However, he said, the more he acted with moral pur- 3 pose and vigour the less his heart could brook injustice. Adherbal 4 had treacherously plotted against his life; and, when he had discovered this, he confronted the crime. The Roman people would not be acting correctly or for the common good if they denied him rights granted by the law of nations. Finally, he said that he would soon send legates to Rome concerning all these matters. On this under- 5 standing both sides departed. There was no opportunity to speak to Adherbal.

23. When Jugurtha thought the legates had left Africa, he sur- 1 rounded the walls with a rampart and a trench because Cirta's posi- tion* did not allow him to storm the town with his troops. He built towers and fortified them with guards; in addition, he was testing them day and night with open force or by treachery, offering the defenders at one moment rewards, at another terror. Exhorting his men he raised their courage. Everything was readied with unflagging focus.

When Adherbal understood that his future was dire, that the enemy 2 was ferocious, that there was no hope of support, that the war could not be dragged on because he lacked supplies, he selected from those who had fled with him to Cirta two especially rugged individuals; making promises and deploring his own situation, he persuaded them to proceed at night through the enemy fortifications to the nearest sea-coast and from there to Rome. [24.] The Numidians carried out 1 these instructions in a few days. Adherbal's letter was read in the Senate; this is the substance of it.

2 It is not my fault that I have often appealed to you, conscript fathers; but Jugurtha's violence forces me. He is overcome with such a desire to destroy me that he has no thought for you or for the immortal gods. My blood 3 is more important to him than anything. And so for five months now I, a friend and ally of the Roman army, have been held under siege. Neither the good deeds of my father, Micipsa, nor your decrees have been any help. I cannot say whether sword or famine is more fiercely crushing.

4   My misfortune counsels against writing more about Jugurtha. Besides, it has already been my experience before this that men do not put much 5 faith in those who suffer. But I do know that he is aiming at something more than me and that he does not hope for your friendship and my kingdom at the same time. Which weighs more heavily with him is obscure to 6 no one. For, in the beginning he killed my brother, Hiempsal; and then he drove me from my father's kingdom. These personal injuries clearly do 7 not pertain to you. But now he holds your kingdom with his army. You made me ruler of the Numidians but now he blockades and besieges me. 8 My dangers make clear how much he values your legates' words. What is 9 left that can move him except your military strength? As for myself, clearly I would prefer that both this that I am now writing and the complaints I have made before in the Senate were meaningless, I would prefer that my 10 suffering not prove the truth of what I say. But, since I was born to become the ostentatious display of Jugurtha's crimes, I no longer pray to be spared death or tribulation, but only my enemy's unrestricted power and physical torture. Consider as you will the realm of Numidia; it is yours. But by the majesty of your realm, by the loyalty of our friendship, if any memory of my grandfather, Masinissa, remains with you, I ask you to deliver me from impious hands.

1   **25.** When the letter was read, there were some who thought that an army should be sent to Africa and aid should be brought to Adherbal as soon as possible, that, meanwhile, they should take up the matter 2 of Jugurtha since he had not obeyed the legates. On the other hand, the same men* who had favoured the king made every effort to 3 prevent such a decree. And so, as is often the case, the public good 4 was sacrificed to private interests. Legates, nevertheless, were sent to Africa, older aristocrats,* men who had held high offices. Among these was M. Scaurus, whom we mentioned above,* an ex-consul and 5 at that time leader of the Senate.* Because the matter had caused

public indignation and also because of the Numidians' pleas, the commissioners set sail within three days. Shortly they arrived in Utica* and sent a letter to Jugurtha: he should come to the province as quickly as possible; they had been sent to him by the Roman Senate. When he heard that prominent men, whose influence at Rome he had 6 learned was powerful, had come to oppose his undertaking, at first he was agitated, variously moved now by fear and now by greed: he was 7 afraid of the Senate's anger if he did not obey the legates; and yet his heart, blinded by desire, kept driving him to complete his crime. But, 8 in a greedy mind the twisted plan prevails. And so, he surrounded 9 Cirta with his army and used all his force in an effort to break into the town, hoping especially that by dividing the enemy's army he would find a chance for victory either by violence or treachery. But when his plans did not work out and he could not accomplish 10 his intention of getting Adherbal into his power before he met the legates, he came to the province with a few of his cavalry, because he did not want to irritate Scaurus, a man whom he especially feared, by further delays. The legates brought dire warnings in the name of the 11 Senate, concerning the fact that he had not lifted his siege. Nevertheless, they wasted many eloquent words and left frustrated.

26. After this news came to Cirta, the Italians who were coura- 1 geously defending the city walls became confident that the pre-eminence of the Roman people would protect them from harm if they surrendered. Consequently, they persuaded Adherbal to hand himself and his city over to Jugurtha and to bargain only for his life. They said the Senate would take care of the rest. Adherbal was of 2 the opinion that nothing was less important to Jugurtha than good faith, but nevertheless, since these men had the power to force him if he opposed them, he surrendered as the Italians had advised. Jugurtha first of all tortured Adherbal to death, then he killed all who 3 had taken up arms to oppose him, making no distinction between the young Numidian men and the foreign traders.

27. But when this became known in Rome and the matter was 1 taken up by the Senate, the same agents of the king kept trying to mitigate the atrocity of his deed by interrupting debate and delay-ing discussion, often using their influence, sometimes arguing. Then, 2 C. Memmius,* a tribune elect* of the plebs, a fierce man and enemy of aristocratic power, told the Roman people that the king's crime was being condoned because of a few of his supporters. If not for

this, all the public outrage would have dissipated through delays and deliberations: such was the power of the king's influence and money.
3 But the Senate had a guilty conscience and feared the people; so, in accordance with the *lex Sempronia*,* Numidia and Italy were declared
4 the consular provinces for the next consuls. P. Scipio Nasica and L. Bestia Calpurnius were elected.* Numidia fell to Calpurnius, Italy
5 to Scipio. An army was then enlisted* for service in Africa. Pay and other military requirements were decided.

1   **28.** Jugurtha was surprised when he heard the news—of course, he had it stuck in his mind that everything at Rome was for sale. He sent a son* and two family friends as legates to the Senate and directed them, as he had directed the men he sent after killing Hiempsal,* to
2 make an assault on every mortal with money. As they drew near the city of Rome, Bestia consulted the Senate: did they want to receive Jugurtha's legates within the walls? They decided that the legates should leave Italy within the next ten days unless they had come to
3 surrender their kingdom and their leader. The consul ordered an announcement in accordance with the Senate's decree. And so the legates departed for home without accomplishing anything.

4   Meanwhile, Calpurnius levied an army and chose for his staff* partisan aristocrats whose influence, he hoped, would protect him from any misconduct of his own. (Among these was Scaurus, whose nature
5 and character I mentioned above.*) Our consul did this because, though he had many good features of mind and body, all of these were hobbled by his greed: he endured hard labour, had an aggressive mind, could be prudent, was well versed in war, unyielding in the
6 face of danger and personal assaults.* The legions* were transported through Italy to Regium and from there to Sicily, then from Sicily to
7 Africa. At first, Calpernius organized his supply routes and aggressively attacked Numidia; in the fighting he seized many men* and a number of cities.

1   **29.** But when Jugurtha began to use legates to tempt the consul with bribes and to point out the difficulty of the war that he was undertaking, the consul's mind, already sick with greed, was easily changed.
2 Scaurus was taken on, in addition, as an ally and accomplice in all of his plans. Originally Scaurus had very aggressively opposed the king, though most of his faction had already been corrupted; still, he was transformed from a good and honourable man into a crook by the
3 magnitude of the money. Jugurtha, at first, only wanted to purchase

a delay in the war, thinking that in the meantime fee or favour would create some opportunity at Rome. But after he learned that Scaurus was participating, he began to have high hopes of attaining peace and decided to deal in person with the legates about all the conditions. In the meantime, however, the consul, as an act of good faith, sent 4 the quaestor Sextius* to Vaga,* a town controlled by Jugurtha. The apparent purpose was to receive the grain which Calpurnius had publicly demanded of the envoys on the grounds that they were observing an armistice because of a delay in the surrender. And so, 5 the king came into the camp as he had planned and spoke briefly before the Council* about the resentment of others at his action and asked to be received in surrender. The other details he arranged in secret with Bestia and Scaurus. Then, on the next day, votes were solicited for an omnibus bill* and he was received in surrender. In accordance with what was ordered before the Council, thirty 6 elephants, cattle, and many horses were handed over to the quaestor together with a small amount of silver.* Calpurnius set out for Rome 7 to oversee the elections.* Peace* was observed in Numidia and in our army.

30. After rumours about the events in Africa and how they were 1 handled became common, the consul's actions were the topic of conversation everywhere people gathered in Rome. The plebs were indignant, the 'fathers' troubled. There was no agreement as to whether they should endorse such a disgraceful action or invalidate the consul's decree. They were especially deterred from a good and 2 true decision by the powerful influence of Scaurus, because he was said to be the originator and Bestia's ally. Still, while the Senate hesi- 3 tated and delayed, C. Memmius, whose frank character and hatred of aristocratic power we mentioned above,* began to urge the people in assembly to stand up for themselves, he warned them not to abandon the Republic, not to abandon their own freedom; he pointed out the many arrogant and cruel deeds of the aristocracy. In short he was intent on inflaming the passions of the people in every way possible. But since Memmius' eloquence was at that time brilliant and power- 4 ful in Rome, I have decided that from so many speeches it is proper to write out one, and I will recall the one that he spoke in the assembly after Bestia's return. It went like this:

31. 'If my concern for the Republic were not the most important 1 thing, fellow citizens, there would be many reasons to be cautious

about addressing you:* the resources of a faction, your long-suffering
patience, the lack of law, and especially the fact that for innocence
2 there is more danger than honour. Indeed, it is sad to recall how in
these past fifteen years* you have been the plaything of the arrogant
few, how shamefully your defenders have died, and how they have
3 died unavenged. The result is that your spirit has been corrupted by
indolence and apathy, a spirit that even now does not rise up against
a vulnerable enemy. And now you are even afraid of those to whom
4 you ought to be a terror. And yet, in spite of all this, my heart com-
5 pels me to oppose the power of the faction. To be sure, I will use the
liberty I inherited from my father; but it lies in your hands, citizens,
whether my action is futile or to the point.

6   'I do not urge you to take up arms against the injustices you suffer,
· a thing your ancestors often did.* There is no need for violence, no
need for secession. Your oppressors will necessarily ruin themselves
7 in their own way. They killed Ti. Gracchus, said he wanted to be
king; then, they prosecuted the Roman plebs.* After the murder of
C. Gracchus and M. Fulvius,* many men of your order were put in
prison and killed: in neither case did the law end their slaughter; they
8 stopped because they wanted to. But, for the sake of argument, suppose that the restoration of rights to the plebs really was the beginnings of kingship; suppose that whatever cannot be avenged without
9 blood-letting is a legal action. In former years you were silently indignant that the treasury was plundered, that kings and free peoples paid
tribute to a few aristocrats, that the same men held both the highest
10 glory and the greatest wealth. And yet they did not think that doing
such deeds with impunity was enough; and so in the end they have
handed over to your enemies the law, your sovereignty, all things
human and divine. And those who have done these things are neither
ashamed nor sorry. Instead they parade before your eyes, grand men,
displaying priesthoods and consulships, some their triumphs, as if
11 they held these things as an honour, not as plunder. Slaves who are
purchased with money do not endure unjust treatment from their
masters; will you, my citizens, who were born for empire, calmly
accept servitude?*

12   'But who are these men who have taken over the state? They are
the most criminal of men, with bloody hands, savage greed, the most
malignant and yet the most arrogant, for them honesty, propriety,
devotion, in fact everything whether honourable or dishonourable,

serves only for profit. Some of them have murdered the tribunes 13
of the plebs, others created illegal tribunals, many slaughtered you:
this is their protection. And so the most wicked agent is the safest. 14
Their crime should make them afraid, but they transfer that fear to
your indolence. They pull together out of common desires, common
hatreds, common fears. Among good men, this is friendship;* but 15
among wicked men, it is a cabal. And yet if you cared as much for 16
liberty as they yearn for domination, I am sure the state would not be
devastated as it is now, and your favours* would be bestowed on the
best men, not on the most arrogant. Your ancestors twice seceded, 17
took up arms, occupied the Aventine* in order to get justice and
establish their sovereignty. Will you not struggle with every resource
for the liberty that you received from them? And all the more pas-
sionately because it is a greater disgrace to lose what was once won
than not to have won it at all.

'Someone will ask, "What, then, do you advise?" I say punish those 18
who have betrayed the country to the enemy, but do not use force or
violence (that is something more shameful for you to do than for them
to suffer), but use the courts and the evidence of Jugurtha himself.
For if he is under surrender, I'm sure he will obey your demands; but 19
if he holds them in contempt, you will of course be able to judge what
sort of peace or surrender it is from which Jugurtha gets impunity
for his crimes, a few powerful men get great wealth, and the country
comes to ruin and disgrace. The alternative, of course, is that you are 20
not yet tired of their domination and the present opportunity is not
as pleasing to you as those days when everything divine and human—
kingdoms, provinces, laws, justice, the courts, wars and treaties—
was in the power of a few, those days when you, I mean the Roman
people, unconquered by enemies, rulers over all races, thought it was
sufficient just to keep on breathing. I say that because it was slavery
and who of you dared to reject it?

'As for me, although I think it is an utter disgrace for a real man 21
to receive an injury without exacting vengeance, still, since they are
citizens, I would not chafe at your forgiveness of men who are utter
criminals, if your compassion were not to end in your own destruction.*
And it will be your destruction because those men are so insolent 22
that it is not enough for them to do evil with impunity unless they
also take away the privilege of action, and you, you will be left in a
state of eternal anxiety when you understand that you must either

23 be slaves or take up arms to win back your freedom. As for trust and harmony, what hope is there for that? They want to be masters, you want to be free; they want to break the law, you want to stop them;
24 finally, they treat our allies like enemies, our enemies like allies. With such different ideas about the world can there be peace or friendship between you?
25 'And so I warn you and urge you not to let such a crime go unpunished. The treasury was not embezzled; money wasn't violently stolen from allies. These things, although serious, are now common and considered inconsequential. But the authority of the Senate has been betrayed to a most bitter enemy; your power has been betrayed;
26 at home and in the military the Republic is for sale. And if these things are not prosecuted, if the guilty are not punished, what will be left for us except to live in obedience to the perpetrators? Surely this is what it means to be a king: the ability to do with impunity
27 whatever you want. I am not urging you, Romans, to prefer your fellow citizens to have acted wrongly rather than rightly, but do not
28 destroy good men by forgiving wicked men. Besides, in a Republic it is much better to remember injuries than favours; the good man only becomes uninterested when you neglect him, but the bad man
29 becomes worse. Besides, if there were no injustices, you would not need help so often.'

1 32. By saying this and other similar things in public assemblies Memmius persuaded the people to send L. Cassius,* who was then praetor, to Jugurtha and to bring him to Rome under a pledge of public protection, in order that his testimony could make more readily apparent the crimes of Scaurus and the others who were charged with
2 taking bribes. While this was going on at Rome, those whom Bestia had left in Numidia in charge of the army followed their general's example and committed a very large number of very shameful deeds.
3 There were some who, corrupted by gold, returned to Jugurtha his elephants; others offered deserters for sale; some took booty from
4 those who were at peace with us: such was the violence of the greed
5 that invaded their souls like a plague. Still, to the amazement of the entire aristocracy, C. Memmius' bill was passed, and the praetor Cassius set out for Jugurtha. Jugurtha was fearful and from a guilty conscience did not trust his situation. Still, Cassius persuaded him that, since he had handed himself over to the Roman people, he should test their mercy rather than their power. Privately, Cassius

gave him his personal guarantee of protection, a guarantee which Jugurtha considered as important as a public one. Such was Cassius' reputation at that time.

33. As a result, Jugurtha came to Rome with Cassius; he was 1 dressed, contrary to the royal fashion, in the most wretched clothing possible. And, although his self-confidence was powerful and he was 2 reassured by all whose power or crime had helped him accomplish everything I have mentioned above, still for a large price he purchased a shameless tribune of the plebs, C. Baebius,* whose lack of restraint could protect him against all legal proceedings and all personal injury. But when C. Memmius called an assembly, the plebs were hostile 3 to the king and some were calling for him to be put in chains, others for him to be punished like an enemy in the ancestral manner* if he did not disclose his accomplices. Nevertheless, Memmius had more regard for dignity than for anger: he began to quiet their emotions and soothe their hearts, finally he confirmed that as far as was in his power the public pledge of safety would not be violated. Afterwards, 4 when there was silence, Jugurtha was produced. Memmius spoke; he recalled Jugurtha's actions at Rome and in Numidia. He described his crimes against his father and brothers. He said that, although the Roman people knew who had helped him do these things and who were his assistants, still they wanted greater clarity from that man. If he would disclose the truth, he could have great hope in the faith and clemency of the Roman people. If he was silent, on the other hand, there would be no safety for his accomplices, but he would destroy himself and his own hopes.

34. Then, when Memmius finished speaking, Jugurtha was told 1 to respond. C. Baebius, the tribune of the plebs (we noted above that he had been bribed), told the king to be silent. The assembled crowd became violently incensed and tried to terrify him with their shouts, their looks. They made many threatening gestures and everything else that anger loves to do. Nevertheless, victory belonged to Jugurtha's insolence. And so the people were treated with utter contempt, and they left the assembly; the confidence of Jugurtha, Bestia, and the 2 others who had been threatened by the investigation increased.

35. At this time there was at Rome a certain Numidian named 1 Massiva.* He was the son of Gulussa, the grandson of Masinissa. After the surrender of Cirta and the murder of Adherbal, he had left his country in exile because he had opposed Jugurtha during

2 the kings' quarrels. Sp. Albinus,* who held the consulship with Q. Minucius Rufus* in the year after Bestia, persuaded this man to ask the Senate for the kingdom of Numidia, pointing out that he was in the line of Masinissa and that Jugurtha was hated and feared for
3 his crimes. The consul was eager to wage war; he preferred putting everything in motion to letting everything languish. The province of
4 Numidia had gone to him; Macedonia to Minucius. After Massiva began to promote his plan, Jugurtha found little protection among his friends: conscience inhibited some; a bad reputation and fear others. So, Jugurtha ordered Bomilcar,* his closest and most faithful attendant, to purchase for a price—this was the way he had accomplished so much—assassins who would kill the Numidian, preferably in secret,
5 but if that did not work, in whatever way they could. Bomilcar carried out the king's commands in a timely fashion, and, using men who were experienced in such business, he determined Massiva's travel plans and the times of his departures; in short he worked out his position at every time. Then, when the situation required it, he set the
6 trap. Consequently, one of those who had been hired for the murder was not careful enough; Massiva was slaughtered but he was caught. Under pressure from many, but especially the consul, Albinus, he
7 made a full confession. Bomilcar was made defendant more out of an interest in equity and fairness than in accordance with international
8 law, since he had come to Rome under public protection. It was obvious that Jugurtha was guilty of this great crime, but he did not cease denying the truth until it became clear that the resentment for his
9 action was beyond his influence and money. Consequently, although he had earlier handed over fifty of his friends as sureties,* he secretly sent Bomilcar back to Numidia. He was thinking more of his throne than of the sureties, and he was afraid that, if Bomilcar was punished, the rest of his people would hesitate to obey him. Within a few days he himself set off for the same destination under orders from the Sen-
10 ate to leave Italy. It is reported that after he left Rome he often looked back in silence and finally said that it was a city for sale and soon to fall, if it could only find a buyer.*

1   **36.** Meanwhile Albinus renewed his war effort. He hastened to get provisions, pay, and other military supplies shipped to Africa, and he himself set out at once, hoping that by victory, surrender, or in some other way he could bring the war to an end before the elections, which
2 were not far off. But Jugurtha, on the other hand, let everything drag

on, creating now one reason, now another for delay. He promised a surrender, and then pretended to be afraid; he withdrew when attacked and a little later pushed forward so his men would not think he was timid. In this way, he toyed with the consul, now postponing a fight, now postponing the peace. Some people thought that Albinus 3 knew what the king was doing and that it was unbelievable that after so much haste the war would drag on out of incompetence rather than treachery. But as the time slipped away and the day for elec- 4 tions approached, Albinus left his brother Aulus* as propraetor in the camp and set out for Rome.*

37. At this time the state was savagely troubled by tribunician 1 revolts. P. Lucullus and L. Annius,* tribunes of the plebs, were trying 2 to extend their time in office though their colleagues resisted, and this contest prevented elections for an entire year. Because of the 3 delay, Aulus, whom we said above had been left in the camp as a pro-praetor, began to hope that he could either end the war or terrorize Jugurtha with his army and so extort money from him. In January* he summoned soldiers for active duty from their winter camps* and with forced marches arrived despite the severe winter weather* at the town of Suthul* where the king's treasury was kept.* The place could 4 not be taken or besieged because of the severe weather and the town's location: around the walls, built on the edge of a sheer cliff, there was a muddy plain which the winter rains had turned into a swamp. Still, Aulus brought forward the military mantlets; he did this either as a pretence designed to frighten the king or because he was blinded by his desire to possess the town and its treasury. He hurried to raise a mound and to prepare the other things which suited his purpose.

38. Jugurtha, on the other hand, knowing of the legate's* narcis- 1 sism and ignorance, cunningly encouraged his irrational behaviour: he kept sending legates* as suppliants; he himself led his army down footpaths through wooded places as if evading conflict. Finally, with 2 hope of a treaty he drove Aulus to drop the siege of Suthul and to follow him, as if retreating, into the interior. [Thus the legate's dere-liction of duty was more hidden.] Meanwhile, he employed skilful 3 agents day and night to test the army: bribing the centurions and cavalry officers so that some would desert and others would abandon their posts when the signal was given.

All this was done according to his instructions. Then, unexpect- 4 edly, in the dead of night he surrounded Aulus' camp with a number

5 of Numidians. The Roman soldiers were bewildered by the unusual
commotion, some grabbed their weapons, others tried to hide, a few
encouraged the terrified. Fear was everywhere. The enemy force was
great; the sky dark with night and clouds; danger on both sides. Was
6 it safer to flee or wait? Unclear. But then from among those whom
we said above* had been bribed, one cohort of Ligurians* and two
squadrons of Thracian cavalry* and a few ordinary soldiers joined
the king. The centurion of the first rank* of the third legion gave
the enemy a point of entry through the fortifications which he had
7 been assigned to defend. Here all the Numidians burst in. Our men
in shameful flight occupied a hill nearby; many had thrown away
8 their weapons. The enemy was stopped from pursuing their victory
9 by night and the plunder they found in the camp. Then on the next
day Jugurtha had a conference with Aulus: Aulus and his army
were surrounded by starvation and swords, he said; nevertheless, he
was mindful of the human condition; and, if Aulus would make a
treaty with him, he would send all under the yoke and let them go
unharmed. Another condition was that he had to leave Numidia in
10 ten days. These terms were severe and deeply humiliating. But they
were offered in exchange for their fear of death.* And so, the peace
was concluded in a way that pleased the king.

1   **39.** But when people heard about this at Rome, fear and sorrow
overwhelmed the state: some grieved for the glory of the empire,
others who did not understand war feared for their freedom. Everyone resented Aulus, and especially those who had frequently distinguished themselves in war because Aulus had been armed but had
2 sought safety in disgrace rather than in combat. For these reasons the
consul Albinus, fearing the hatred that arose against his brother from
his dereliction and the subsequent danger to himself, consulted the
Senate about the treaty. In the meantime he nevertheless conscripted
reinforcements for the army; he summoned aid from the allies and
the Latins;* in short, he hurried to make all kinds of preparations.
3 The Senate decided, as was fair, that no treaty could be made with-
4 out their consent and that of the people. The consul was prevented
by the tribune of the plebs from taking with him the troops he had
raised. Since the entire army had been removed from Numidia, as
agreed, and was wintering in Africa, he set out in a few days for that
5 province. Upon his arrival he was at heart eager to pursue Jugurtha
and to repair the hatred that had arisen against his brother, but when

he saw his soldiers demoralized, apart from their flight, by the licence and depravity of neglected discipline, given the range of choices he decided that there was nothing for him to do.

40. Meanwhile at Rome C. Mamilius Limetanus,* tribune of the 1 plebs, proposed to the people a bill to investigate those who had advised Jugurtha* to neglect the Senate's decrees, those who had received money from him while on embassies or holding military commands, those who had returned his elephants and deserters,* and also those who had reached agreements with the enemy concerning peace or war.* Some senators, conscious of their complicity, created obstacles 2 to the bill. Others were afraid of the dangers arising from partisan hatred, but they could not resist openly without confessing their approval of such actions. So they worked against the bill secretly through their friends* and especially through the Latins* and the Italian allies. But it is incredible to note how determined the plebs 3 were and with what vehemence they insisted on its passage. This was more out of hatred for the aristocracy, for whom these investigations would be real trouble, than out of a concern for the Republic; such were the passions of partisanship. And so, while the rest were 4 panic-stricken, M. Scaurus, who we said above* had been Bestia's legate, amid the people's joy and the flight of his friends, with the city still in a state of confusion, managed to get himself elected as one of the three commissioners* authorized by the Mamilian bill. Still, 5 the investigation was carried out with bitterness and violence, on the basis of rumour and the people's caprice: just as often before the arrogance of success had seized the aristocracy, so this time it seized the plebs.

41. But the pattern of routine partisanship and factionalism, and, 1 as a result, of all other vicious practices, had arisen in Rome a few years earlier.* It was the result of peace and an abundance of those things that mortals consider most important. I say this because, before the 2 destruction of Carthage, mutual consideration and restraint between the people and the Roman Senate characterized the government. Among the citizens, there was no struggle for glory or domination. Fear of a foreign enemy preserved good political practices. But when 3 that fear was no longer on their minds, self-indulgence and arrogance, attitudes that prosperity loves, took over. As a result the tranquillity 4 they had longed for in difficult times proved, when they got it, to be more cruel and bitter than adversity. For the aristocracy twisted 5

their 'dignity' and the people twisted 'liberty'* towards their desires;
every man acted on his own behalf, stealing, robbing, plundering. In
this way all political life was torn apart between two parties, and the
Republic, which had been our common ground, was mutilated.

6   But the aristocracy, as a faction, had more power;* less potent,
the people's strength was dissipated and dispersed among the
7 multitude.* A few men controlled military and domestic affairs; the
same men held the treasury, the provinces, political offices, honours
and triumphs.* The people were oppressed by military service and
8 by poverty.* The spoils of war were ravaged by the generals and
their friends. Meanwhile, if soldiers' parents or their little children
were neighbours to one of the more powerful, they were driven
9 from their homes. And so, joined with power, greed without moderation or measure invaded, polluted, and devastated everything,
considered nothing valuable or sacred, until it brought about its own
10 collapse. For as soon as men were found* among the aristocracy who
put true glory above unjust power, the state began to tremble and
civil strife began to rise up like an earthquake.

1   **42.** I say this because of Ti. and C. Gracchus.* They had ancestors*
who had done much for the Republic during the Punic and other
wars. But after they began to assert the freedom of the plebs and
expose the crimes of the oligarchy, the aristocracy, which was guilty
and therefore frightened, opposed their actions, now using the allies
and the Latins, occasionally using the Roman *equites*, whom they
seduced away from supporting the plebs with the hope of a coalition.*
First it was Tiberius they murdered, then Gaius, as he was pursuing the same policies a few years later, the one a tribune, the other
a member of the triumvirate for founding colonies; they killed
2 M. Fulvius Flaccus along with him. Admittedly, the Gracchi were
3 not sufficiently moderate in their passion for victory; but it is better
for the good to be conquered than to overcome injury in a vicious
manner.* The aristocracy enjoyed their victory and gratified their
passions; they eradicated many men either by killing them or sending
4 them into exile. And in this way, for the future they increased their
fears more than their power. In general, this is what destroys great
states: one group wants to overcome the other in any possible way
5 and then to take a bitter vengeance on the defeated. But if I were to
discuss in detail partisan passions and the general character of the
state or treat this subject in accordance with its importance, I would

sooner run out of time than material. Therefore, I am returning to my initial topic.*

43. After Aulus' agreement and the egregious flight* of our army, 1 Metellus and Silanus,* the consuls designate,* divided the provinces between themselves. Numidia fell to Metellus, a fiercely energetic man, and, although he was opposed to the popular party, still he had a consistently unassailable reputation. As soon as he entered his 2 term of office,* he turned his attention to the war, thinking that he and his colleague had a common interest in everything else.* And so, 3 distrusting the old army he began to enrol soldiers, to summon auxiliaries from everywhere, to gather together arms, weapons, horses, and other military material, and, in addition, to requisition sufficient supplies and everything else that is typically needed for a war that is complex and requires many resources. Furthermore, the Senate 4 aided these preparations with its authority; the allies, the Latins, and subject kings by taking the initiative in sending reinforcements. In short, the whole state worked with great enthusiasm. And so when 5 all was ready and ordered to the consul's satisfaction he set out for Numidia. The citizens had high hopes because of his good character and especially because his mind was invincible to wealth. Before this time the greed of our magistrates in Numidia had broken our power and increased that of our enemies.

44. But when he came into Africa, the army he received from 1 Sp. Albinus, the proconsul, was lazy and cowardly, unable to endure danger or labour, more glib than capable, predatory with our allies and itself preyed upon by our enemies, restrained neither by authority nor by shame. And so the army's corrupted character gave the 2 general more reason for fear than its size gave reason for relief or hope. The delay in the elections* had shortened the time for a summer campaign and he was aware that the citizens were eagerly awaiting an outcome. Nevertheless, Metellus decided not to touch the war 3 before traditional discipline had forced the soldiers to endure military hardships. The reason for this deterioration was that Albinus, 4 shaken by the disaster that befell his brother Aulus and his army, had decided not to leave the province during that part of the summer campaign season in which he was in command. After that, he held his soldiers in a standing camp, except when the stench or the lack of food forced them to change location. Still, there were no forti- 5 fications, no night watches kept in military fashion: each man left his post when he wanted; camp-followers mingled and walked about with the soldiers day and night; wandering around they wasted the fields, attacked farmhouses, held contests in carrying off slaves and cattle as booty, and exchanged them with traders for imported wine and such things. Further, they sold the grain they were given from the public stores, traded it daily for bread. In short, whatever vices of laziness and luxury can be mentioned or invented, they were all present in that army and more besides.

1   **45.** But in those difficulties just as in military action it is my asssessment that Metellus was a great and wise man: he managed with great restraint a course between charming ambition and cruel discipline.

2 In the first place, he removed by edict the practices that encourage laziness: no one, he decreed, could sell bread or any other prepared food in camp; no followers could attend the army; no special forces or regular troops could have a slave or a pack animal in camp or on the march. In other matters he established strict regulations. Next, he moved the camp daily with transverse marches,* built fortifications with a rampart and trench just as if the enemy were nearby, imposed sentry posts at short intervals and inspected them himself with his legates. Likewise, on marches he was present now in the vanguard, now in the rear, now in the middle, to see that no one fell out of order, that they marched close together near the standards, that each soldier carried his food and armour. In this way, by preventing

3 derelictions rather than punishing them, in a short time he toughened up his army.

1   **46.** Meanwhile, Jugurtha learned about Metellus' actions from messengers and at the same time was informed from Rome of his integrity. He began to distrust his position and then for the first time

2 attempted a real surrender. Accordingly, he sent to the consul legates with suppliant offerings, asking only for the life of Jugurtha* and his children, saying they would give everything else to the Roman

3 people. But Metellus had already come to know through prior experiences* that the Numidian people had a fickle temperament and were not to be trusted, that they were always eager for change.

4 And so he approached the legates, each individually apart from the others, testing them little by little, and, after he learned that they could be useful to him, he persuaded them with many promises to hand Jugurtha over to him, preferably alive, but if that did not work out, then dead. Publicly, however, he told them to take back a

reply that would suit the king's desires. Then in a few days Metellus 5
himself proceeded into Numidia with an army eager and ready for
battle. There, instead of the face of war, he found huts filled with
men, herds and farmers in the field. From the towns and mapalia*
officials of the king came forward to meet him prepared to offer grain,
to carry supplies, in short to do all that they were told to do. But for 6
all of this, as Metellus proceeded he kept his battle line protected, just
as if the enemy were present. He spied on all the territory around him.
He believed that those signs of surrender were a ruse and that they
were trying to find an opportunity for treachery. And so he him- 7
self marched at the head with his light-armed infantry and a selected
group of slingers and archers; in the rear his legate C. Marius*
was in charge of the cavalry; on both flanks he had distributed the
auxiliary cavalry* and put the legionary tribunes and the prefects of
the cohorts in charge. The light-armed troops were mixed with these
so as to repel the enemy's cavalry wherever they might attack. For 8
Jugurtha was so treacherous, had such knowledge of the place and
of warfare, that it was unclear whether absent or present, whether
waging peace or war he was more dangerous.

47. Not far from the route Metellus was taking there was a Numid- 1
ian town named Vaga,* the busiest market for selling goods in the
entire kingdom. Many men of Italian descent had become accustomed
to living and trading there. Here the consul stationed a garrison, in 2
order to see if they would allow it, and simultaneously to take advantage of the position. He further ordered that grain and other provisions for war be brought, thinking, as the circumstances suggested,
that the number of merchants would both help the army with supplies and even serve to protect what they had already gathered. While 3
these negotiations were going on, Jugurtha was more serious about
sending envoys as suppliants, begging for peace, granting Metellus
everything except his own life and that of his children. As before, 4
the consul again lured the legates into his plan for betrayal and sent
them home. He neither denied nor promised the king the peace he
was asking for, and during these delays he waited for the envoys to do
what they had promised.

48. Jugurtha compared Metellus' words with his actions and 1
discovered that he was being attacked with his own methods.* He
was offered peace in words, but in fact a war was going on and it was
deadly; his greatest city had been taken; his country was familiar to

2 the enemy; the affections of his people were tested. And so he examined the enemy's route. Since the territory had advantages for him,
he began to hope for victory: he readied as many troops as he could of
every type and through hidden footpaths he moved into a position in
advance of Metellus' army.

3   In the part of Numidia which had been allotted to Adherbal
there was a river called Muthul* which flows from the south; about
†twenty†* miles away and parallel to it was a mountain range,
naturally barren and uncultivated. But in the middle* there arose
something like a hill, extending for a very long distance, covered with
wild olives and myrtles and other types of trees that grow in dry and
4 sandy soil. Because of the lack of water, the intervening plain was
barren, except for the places near the river. This was planted with
bushes and frequented by herds and farmers.

1   **49.** And so it was on this hill, which we described as extended on
a transverse course,* that Jugurtha drew out his battle line and took
a position. He gave Bomilcar his orders and put him in charge of the
elephants and part of the foot soldiers. He himself positioned his men
nearer the mountain range with all the cavalry and special infantry.
2 Then he went about to the individual squadrons and companies and
warned and begged them to remember their former virtue and prior
victory and to defend him and his kingdom from the greed of the
Romans. He said that the struggle would be with men they had already
defeated and sent under the yoke, men who had changed their leader,
he said, but not their spirit. He said that he had provided for his
own men everything that a general should provide, that they had the
superior position; they should fight like skilled warriors with novices,
not like few against the many or like the ignorant against superiors.
3 Consequently, when the signal was given, they should be ready and
focused on attacking the Romans: that day would be the confirmation
of all their labours and victories or it would be the beginning of their
4 greatest suffering. Then he went to each man whom he had honoured
with money or status for some military action and reminded him of
his fine deed and presented him as an example to the others. Finally,
he inspired each man according to his character by promising, threatening, entreating.

    In the meantime, Metellus was seen coming down the mountain,
5 unaware of the enemy. At first, he was unsure what the unusual sight
might mean. For the Numidians and their horses stood among the

bushes and, though they were not completely hidden because the bushes were low, still it was unclear what was there, since the men and their military standards were obscured by the surroundings and by camouflage. Soon the trap was recognized and the consul halted his march briefly and changed his formation: he arranged his battle 6 line with the threefold protection on the right side, which was closest to the enemy; he distributed slingers and archers among the companies; he put all the cavalry on the wings. After a brief address, all that the time allowed, he turned his front line at right angles and led the army down into the plain in its new formation.*

50. But when he saw that the Numidians did not respond or leave 1 the hill, he became afraid that his army would succumb to thirst because of the season and the lack of water. So he sent ahead the legate Rutilius* with the light-armoured cohorts and part of the cavalry to the river to anticipate Jugurtha and seize a place for a camp. He was thinking that the enemy would try to delay his march with continuous skirmishes and assaults on his flank and, since they would not trust their arms, they would try to wear his men down with fatigue and thirst. Then he himself moved forward slowly, in the same for- 2 mation in which he had descended from the mountains, taking into account the circumstances and the place. He kept Marius behind the front line;* he himself was with the cavalry on the left wing which had become the front of the marching line.

But when Jugurtha saw that the end of Metellus' line had passed 3 the beginning of his own, he occupied the mountain, where Metellus had descended, with a garrison of about two thousand foot soldiers, lest his adversaries should have a refuge when they retreated and, thereafter, protection. Then, suddenly, the signal was given; the 4 enemy attacked. Some Numidians killed the rearguard, some attacked from the left and the right. They were present everywhere, hostile and menacing; Roman order was thrown into turmoil. Even those who had, with stauncher hearts, met the enemy in the past were baffled by the unfamiliar fighting; they were being wounded only from a distance and given no chance of striking back or engaging in hand-to-hand combat. Jugurtha had previously instructed his cavalry not to 5 come together as a body when a squadron of Romans began to pursue, or to gather in one place, but to spread out as much as possible here and there. Thus, if they could not prevent the enemy from pur- 6 suing, they could with their superior numbers cut off the stragglers from behind or on the sides; if, on the other hand, it seemed better to retreat to the hill than to stay on the plain, the Numidian horses, who were accustomed to these places, could easily move among the thickets, while our cavalry were being hampered by their ignorance and the harsh terrain.

1   **51.** The entire encounter had the face of confusion, uncertainty, shame, and misery. Some, separated from their comrades, gave way; others attacked; they neither kept near the standards nor held their ranks; where danger found each man, there he stood and fought; armour and weapons, horses and men, enemies and citizens intermingled. Nothing was done by plan or order; chance ruled everywhere.
2   And so it was already late in the day, when the outcome was still
3   unsure. Everyone was weak from exhaustion and heat. Then, finally, Metellus noticed that the Numidians were attacking less vigorously. He drew his soldiers together in one place, restored their ranks and opposed four legionary cohorts to the enemy's infantry, a large number
4   of whom had sat down exhausted on the higher ground. At the same time he pleaded and exhorted his soldiers not to weaken and not to allow the fleeing enemy to win: they had neither a camp nor any forti-
5   fications to go to if they yielded; all depended on their arms. Meanwhile, Jugurtha was not resting either: he did the rounds, exhorted his men, renewed the battle, and with select troops made every effort. He brought aid to his men, attacked the enemy if they hesitated; if they stood firm, he held them off by fighting from a distance.

1   **52.** In this way these two generals, both extraordinary men, continued to fight. They were themselves equals, but their resources
2   were unequal. Metellus enjoyed the courage of his soldiers, but his position worked against him; for Jugurtha everything except his
3   soldiers was to his advantage. In the course of the fighting, the Romans realized that retreat was impossible but that the enemy would not give them a chance to fight. And now it was evening. As ordered, they
4   turned towards the hill and attacked. The Numidians gave up their position, were routed and fled. A few were killed; most were saved by their agility and the enemy's ignorance of the terrain.
5   Meanwhile, Rutilius moved past Bomilcar, whom, as we noted above,* Jugurtha had placed in charge of the elephants and some of the infantry. Bomilcar slowly brought his men into the plain but took no action, while the legate continued hurrying to the river where he had been sent. He drew up his battle line as the circumstances

suggested but continued to scout out everything that the enemy was
doing. When he heard that Rutilius had made camp and was begin- 6
ning to relax, and when at the same time he heard the clamour from
Jugurtha's battle growing louder,* he became afraid that the legate
Rutilius would bring aid to his struggling comrades if he knew what
was going on. The battle line, which he had arranged in tight order,
distrusting his men's courage, he now extended more loosely, hoping
to block the enemy's path, and in this formation proceeded toward
Rutilius' camp.

53. Unexpectedly the Romans suddenly noticed a great cloud of 1
dust. This was because the field, overgrown with shrubbery, had
blocked their view. At first they thought that a windstorm was blow-
ing up the dry earth. But when the cloud did not change and they saw
it come closer and closer, moving like a battle line, they understood
what was happening and quickly seized their arms and took their
positions, as ordered, in front of the camp. Then, when the army drew 2
near, both sides attacked with a great shout. The Numidians stayed 3
in the fight only as long as they thought the elephants could help
them; after the elephants became entangled in tree branches, were
separated from each other, and surrounded, they fled. Most threw
away their arms, found protection in the hill and the night that was
upon them, and got away safely. Four elephants were captured; all 4
the rest, forty in number, were killed. The Romans were exhausted; 5
the march, the work of making camp, and the battle had worn them
out. Still, when Metellus was later than expected, they took their
formations and marched forth to meet him. They remained vigi- 6
lant because Numidian treachery did not allow for any relaxation or
carelessness. The night was dark, and, at first, when the two armies 7
were not far apart, the noise from both sides, like that of an enemy
approaching, frightened the other side and at the same time created
some confusion. Ignorance would have caused a dreadful outcome,
if the cavalry of both armies had not been sent ahead and discovered the truth. And so, joy suddenly replaced fear: the soldiers hap- 8
pily called to each other; they told and listened to stories, each man
extolled to the skies his brave deeds. To be sure, that is the way
human affairs are: in victory, the coward is allowed to boast; failure
discredits even the brave.

54. Metellus remained in the same camp for four days. He care- 1
fully tended the wounded, granted military honours to those who

had earned them in battle; he praised and thanked all in a public address, and urged them to take care of the details that remained with equal energy: the fight for victory is complete, he said; further
2 efforts would be for the spoils of war. Nevertheless, in the meantime he sent deserters and others who seemed suitable to find out where Jugurtha was and what he was doing, whether he was with a few men
3 or had an army, and how he was acting in defeat. Jugurtha on the other hand had retreated to a wooded area, a place with natural fortifications, and was there putting together an army larger in numbers,* but timid and weak, more experienced with the farm and animals
4 than with war. This happened because after the rout only the royal cavalry followed the king. The Numidian soldiers ran off wherever they pleased, and this is not considered a disgrace for the military. Such is their custom.

5   Metellus saw that the king's spirit was still ferocious and that a war was resuming that could only be fought on Jugurtha's terms. Moreover, he saw that Jugurtha had an unfair advantage: the Numidian defeat cost less than his victory. Therefore, he decided that he ought
6 not to fight in pitched battles, but in some other fashion. And so he headed to the richest areas of Numidia. He laid waste the fields, he captured and burned many fortresses and towns that had been hastily fortified or lacked any protection, he ordered the adults killed and let everything else become booty for his soldiers. The people became so terrified that many men were handed over to the Romans as hostages; grain and other necessities were supplied to their satisfaction;
7 wherever the circumstances demanded, a garrison was imposed. All these operations frightened the king more than the battle his soldiers
8 had lost. And reasonably so: he, the man who had put all his hope in flight, was now being forced to pursue, he, who had not been able to defend the territory he controlled, now had to wage war in territory
9 controlled by others. Nevertheless, given his resources he chose what seemed the best course: he ordered most of his army to wait where they were and with a special force of cavalry he himself went after Metellus. Travelling at night and avoiding the usual routes, he was
10 not noticed. Suddenly, he attacked some Roman stragglers. Most of them were killed unarmed; many were captured; none fled without wounds. Before help could arrive, the Numidians scattered, as he had ordered, into the nearby hills.

55. Meanwhile there was great joy in Rome when they heard of 1
Metellus' accomplishments:* he had handled himself and his army
in the ancestral fashion; in adverse circumstances his virtuous character had brought him victory; he controlled enemy territory; he had
forced Jugurtha, a man made arrogant by Albinus' incompetence, to
take refuge in flight and in the desert. The Senate decreed a thanks- 2
giving to the immortal gods* for these successes; the citizens, who had
before been fearful and anxious about the war, were joyful. Metellus'
fame was brilliant. As a result, he worked all the more eagerly for 3
victory. At every opportunity, he moved quickly, but was careful not
to give the enemy any opening. He remembered that resentment follows fame. And so, the brighter his reputation, the more concerned 4
he was. After Jugurtha's surprise attack, he stopped plundering the
countryside with an army out of formation.* When he needed grain
or fodder, the infantry stood on guard together with all the cavalry.
But they usually destroyed the fields with fire rather than by plundering them. Metellus himself led part of the army; Marius led the rest.* 5
They made camp in two places not far apart. When force was needed, 6
they joined together; otherwise, they acted separately so that flight 7
and devastation would be more widespread.

All this time, Jugurtha kept up with them, following through the 8
hills, seeking a time and a place for a battle. When he heard where the
enemy was headed, he would spoil the fodder and the springs, which
were scarce resources. At one moment, he would let Metellus see
him; then, Marius. He attacked those at the end of the column and
immediately returned into the hills. He attacked again, one group,
then another. He neither offered battle nor allowed the enemy to rest;
he only prevented them from doing what they set out to do.

56. When the Roman general saw that he was being worn down 1
by this clever strategy and that the enemy offered no opportunity
for a fight, he decided to attack Zama,* a great city and the bulwark
of the realm in the area where it was located. He thought that
Jugurtha would have to come to the aid of his people if they were
in trouble and that then a battle would ensue. But Jugurtha learned 2
from deserters what was in store and with forced marches arrived
ahead of Metellus. He urged the people of the town to defend their
walls. Deserters were used as reinforcements—they were the most
reliable part of the king's forces because they could not change their

minds again. He also promised that he and his army would arrive at
3 the right time. Thus, after he made these arrangements, he withdrew
to the most secluded places he could find and a little later he learned
that Marius had been sent to Sicca* with a few cohorts to gather
corn. This town had been the first to defect from the king after his
4 defeat, and so Jugurtha proceeded there at night with his special
cavalry. He attacked the Romans at the gate as they were leaving.
At the same time, with a loud voice he urged the people of Sicca to
surround the cohorts from behind: Fortune, he said, offered them
a chance for a noble deed; if they took advantage of it, afterwards
he would live in his kingdom and they would live in freedom without
5 fear. Surely, all or most of the people of Sicca would have changed
their allegiance—so fickle are the Numidians—if Marius had not
hurried to bring forward his standards and move his troops out of the
6 town. As it happened, Jugurtha was able to hold his soldiers in order
for only a short while; when the enemy pressed forward with greater
force, they scattered and fled with a few losses.

1	57. Marius arrived at Zama. That town, located on the plain
and protected more by man than by nature, lacked no useful resource
2 and was rich in arms and men. Consequently, Metellus, making
preparations to suit the circumstances, surrounded all the walls with
3 his army, put each officer in charge of a particular position. Then,
at his signal, a great shout arose simultaneously from everywhere.
But this did not frighten the Numidians: hostile, focused, without
4 commotion, they waited. The battle began. The Romans fought in
accordance with their individual talents: some from afar with slings
or stones; others, eager to fight in close combat, advanced and either
5 undermined the wall or attacked from ladders. In response, the townspeople rolled stones on those close to the walls; they hurled stakes,
6 javelins, even torches covered with burning pitch and sulphur. No
one was protected, not even those whose timidity kept them at a distance. The javelins hurled by machine* or by hand wounded many.
The danger was the same for the courageous and the cowardly, but
the glory was different.

1	58. At Zama the fight was continuing like this, when Jugurtha
unexpectedly attacked the enemy camp with a great force.* The
sentries were relaxed and not at all expecting a battle, when Jugurtha
2 burst through the gate. Terror-stricken, our men took care of themselves according to their individual character: some fled, others seized

their arms; a great number were wounded or killed. But from the 3
entire army, no more than forty kept in mind the fact that they were
Romans: they formed a unit and seized a position a little higher than
the rest. Despite the enemy's greatest efforts, they could not be
dislodged from this place; rather, they hurled back the weapons that
were thrown at them from afar. A few men taking aim at so many
seldom missed. But it was when the Numidians came too close
that they really showed their military virtue: they slaughtered with
extraordinary violence, scattering and routing.

Meanwhile, as Metellus was most fiercely carrying on his siege, he 4
heard a hostile uproar behind him. He turned his horse and saw men
in flight coming toward him, an indication that they were Romans.
He therefore quickly dispatched the entire cavalry toward the camp 5
and ordered C. Marius to follow immediately with cohorts of allies.
Weeping, he begged Marius in the name of their friendship and the
Republic* to prevent any disgrace from coming upon his victorious
army and to allow no enemy to depart unpunished. Marius promptly 6
carried out his orders. Jugurtha, on the other hand, was impeded
by the camp's fortifications: some of his men fell headlong over the
ramparts, others ran into each other as they hurried through narrow
places. After suffering many losses, he withdrew to safety. Metellus 7
did not complete his assault, but, when night came on, he returned
to camp with his army.

59. And so, on the next day, before he left to assault the town, 1
he ordered all the cavalry to patrol in front of the camp where the
king had approached. He assigned the gates and neighbouring places
to the tribunes. Then he himself went to the town and attacked the
wall as on the day before. At the same time Jugurtha suddenly from 2
an ambush attacked our men. At first, those closest to the attack
were terrified and confused, but only for a while; the others quickly
came to help. Nor would they have been able to resist the Numidian 3
longer, if the infantry and the cavalry had not joined forces and in the
conflict together created great slaughter. They did not pursue and
then withdraw, as is typical in a cavalry battle; instead, relying on the
infantry, they turned their horses, rushed ahead, engaged and routed
the battle line. In this way,* they presented their light-armed infantry
with an enemy nearly conquered.

60. At the same time the struggle for Zama was continuing with 1
great violence. Wherever a legate or tribune was in charge, there the

struggle raged most fiercely and no one trusted another more than himself. The townspeople fought equally hard: attacks and preparations everywhere. On each side men were more eager to wound 2 others than to protect themselves. A roar mixed with encouragement; joy with groaning; likewise, the din of armour rose to the skies; weap- 3 ons flew from both sides. But those who were defending the walls, whenever their enemy relaxed the attack only a bit, gazed intently at the cavalry battle. You would have seen them* now happy, now 4 frightened, depending on how things went for Jugurtha. And, as if they could be heard or seen by their comrades, some gave warnings, others encouragement or they signalled with their hands or strained with their bodies, and moved here or there as if avoiding or hurling a 5 spear. But, when Marius, who was in charge of this area, noticed this, he purposefully began to attack less fiercely and to pretend that he distrusted his position, to allow the Numidians to watch their king's 6 battle undisturbed. So, when their attention was fixed on their comrades, suddenly he made a violent attack on the wall. His soldiers were climbing up the ladders; they had now already nearly seized the top of the wall when the townspeople came running: they hurled 7 down stones, fire, and other missiles. At first our men resisted; then, when ladder after ladder was shattered, and those who had mounted them were dashed to the ground, the rest retreated in whatever way 8 they could, a few unharmed, many weakened by wounds. Finally, on both sides night broke off the fighting.

1	**61.** Metellus saw that his plan was frustrated, that the town was not falling, that Jugurtha was not fighting except from ambush or on his own ground, that the summer was already over. Accordingly, he left Zama and placed garrisons in the cities that had defected to his side 2 and were well fortified by their position or their walls. He stationed the rest of his army in winter quarters* in the province which borders 3 Numidia. But during this time he did not yield as others usually do to rest and pleasure. Rather, since the war was not proceeding well through force of arms, he began to lay traps for the king by using 4 his friends and their treachery in place of weapons. Therefore with many promises he approached Bomilcar, who had been at Rome with Jugurtha and, after paying bail, had secretly fled to avoid trial for the murder of Massiva.* A great friendship provided a great opportunity 5 for duplicity.* First, he got the Numidian to come to him in secret for a conference; then, he gave his word that, if he handed over Jugurtha dead or alive, the Senate would grant him impunity and restore all his property. He was easily persuaded, since he was treacherous by nature and at that time was afraid that, if there was peace with the Romans, he would himself be handed over for execution as one of the conditions.

62. Meanwhile, Jugurtha was worried and bemoaning his fate.* As soon as there was an opportunity, Bomilcar went to him. He gave warnings and in tears asked him to take thought at last for himself and his children, for the Numidian race that had served him so well: they had been defeated in every battle,* he said; the fields were wasted; many men were captured or killed; the resources of the realm were shattered; fate and the military virtue of his soldiers had already been tested often enough. He should be careful, he said, lest the Numidians make their own plans while he hesitated. Using these and other such arguments he inclined the king's mind toward surrender.

Legates were sent to the Roman general to announce that Jugurtha would do as he was ordered and would hand himself and his kingdom over to the general's good faith without any conditions. Metellus quickly ordered all men of senatorial rank to be summoned from their winter quarters. He held a council with them and with others he thought appropriate. Then, by decree of the council and in the manner of our ancestors,* he sent legates to order Jugurtha to hand over two hundred thousand pounds of silver, all his elephants, and a considerable quantity of horses and arms. This was done without delay. Then he ordered all the deserters to be brought to him in chains. Most were brought as ordered; a few had fled to King Bocchus* in Mauretania* as soon as the surrender began. And so Jugurtha, stripped of arms, men, and money, was himself summoned to Tisidium* to receive his orders. But once again his heart began to waver and from a guilty conscience he began to fear the punishment he deserved. He consumed several days in hesitation, at one moment, tired of adversity, he thought that anything was better than war; sometimes he reconsidered how grave it was to fall from kingship into slavery. Finally, though he had lost many great resources and had accomplished nothing by it, he took up the war again. At Rome the Senate deliberated about the provinces and assigned Numidia to Metellus.*

63. During this period* Marius was by chance offering sacrificial animals to the gods at Utica.* The soothsayer told him that great and marvellous things were portended for him, and, relying on the gods,

he should do exactly what he had in mind, that he should test his
2 fortune* as often as possible; all would turn out well. Now for a long
time he had been unsettled by a great craving for the consulship* and,
except for his lineage,* he was more than qualified in other respects:
he was hard-working, honest, had great knowledge of the military;
his spirit was prodigious in war but moderate at home; he was not a
victim of lust or wealth,* all he really longed for was glory.

3   But he had been born and raised throughout his youth in Arpinum.*
There, as soon as he was of military age, he devoted himself to earning a military stipend, not to Greek eloquence or urban polish.* His
unspoiled nature quickly matured in the midst of wholesome influ-
4 ences. And so, when he first ran for the office of military tribune,*
though most of the people did not recognize his face, he was known
5 for his actions and was easily elected by all the tribes. Thereafter, he
received one magistracy after another, and he always held office in
such a way that he was thought to be worthy of a higher office than
6 the one he held.* Nevertheless, this man, up to that time such a fine
man—I say this because afterwards he was precipitously destroyed
by ambition*—did not dare to seek the consulship. For even at that
time, while the people bestowed other offices, it was the aristocracy
that passed on the consulship from hand to hand among themselves.*
7 No 'new man' was so famous or so accomplished in action that he
was considered worthy of that honour; the 'new man' was treated as
unclean.*

1   **64.** Therefore, when Marius saw that the soothsayer's words
pointed to the very thing his internal cravings urged him to seek,
he asked Metellus for a furlough* in order to become a candidate.
Now Metellus abounded in manly courage and love of fame and the
other things good men desire, but still his spirit was contemptuous
2 and haughty, a common flaw among the aristocracy. And so he was
at first unsettled by the unexpected plan; he expressed his surprise
and cautioned Marius, as if through friendship, not to make wayward
plans and not to reach beyond his station in life. Everything is not for
everyone, he said; a man ought to be well enough pleased with what
is his. Finally, he warned him not to seek from the Roman people
3 what could be justifiably denied him. When these and other similar
arguments failed to change Marius' mind, he said that he would do
4 what Marius asked as soon as his public duties allowed. It is said
that later when Marius kept making the same request, he told him

not to be in a hurry to leave; that it would be time enough to seek the consulship when his son did. Metellus' son,* at that time, was about twenty years old and serving in Africa in his father's regiment.* This exchange greatly inflamed Marius' passions both for the office he wanted and against Metellus. His mind was ravaged by craving and rage, the worst advisers. There was nothing he would not do 5 or say to further his ambitions. The soldiers under his command in winter quarters enjoyed a looser discipline than before.* Traders* were found in great numbers in Utica and he talked with them about the war, alleging crimes and bragging: if he were given half of the army, Jugurtha would be in chains in a few days. He said that the general dragged on the war* purposely, because he was an inane and proudly tyrannical man who took too much pleasure in his power. All this seemed very likely to the traders because the duration of the 6 war had damaged their personal profits and nothing happens fast enough when the soul is filled with desire.

65. Furthermore, there was in our army a certain Numidian named 1 Gauda,* the son of Mastanabal, the grandson of Masinissa, whom Micipsa had made his second heir. He was weakened by diseases and as a result not fully competent mentally. When he asked Metellus 2 for a seat next to the consul, in the royal manner, and again later for a squadron of Roman cavalry for protection, Metellus denied both requests. The honour, because it should belong only to those whom the Roman people had given the title, King; the guard, because it would be an insult to the cavalry if they were made attendants of a Numidian. Gauda was galled; Marius approached him and offered 3 his help in seeking vengeance for the general's insults. The man was not very strong-minded because of his diseases and Marius bolstered him further with encouraging talk. He was a king, he said; a prodigious hero, the grandson of Masinissa; if Jugurtha were captured or killed, he would immediately gain control of Numidia; in fact, this could happen soon, if Marius himself were made consul and put in charge of the war. And so both Gauda and the Roman *equites*, who 4 were serving as soldiers and traders, were prompted—Marius himself persuaded some, most were persuaded by their hopes for peace—to write to their friends in Rome bitterly attacking Metellus' handling of the war and asking that Marius be made general. In this way the 5 consulship was sought for Marius with the most honourable support of many men. At the same time the plebs had just overwhelmed the

aristocracy in passing the *lex Mamilia** and they were promoting 'new men'. Thus, everything was going Marius' way.

1   66. Meanwhile,* Jugurtha had abandoned the surrender and begun to make war. He was very careful in all his preparations; he acted quickly. He gathered an army. He tried with threats and promises to win over the states that had defected from him. He fortified the places he held, repaired or repurchased arms, weapons and other things he had lost in his hope for peace. He enticed Roman slaves and even tried to bribe the men who were in the Roman garrisons. In short, he left nothing untouched, nothing undisturbed, agitation
2   everywhere. As a result, the king's entreaties prevailed upon the people of Vaga, a town where Metellus had originally stationed a garrison when Jugurtha sued for peace. Before, they had not voluntarily turned against their king; now the leaders of the state conspired together.* The lower classes, as is typical and particularly true of the Numidians, had a fickle disposition, were rebellious and seditious, eager for revolution, opposed to peace and quiet. Then, when everything was arranged, they made their plans for the third day because it was a festival day* celebrated throughout Africa, a day that prom-
3   ised games and licentiousness rather than any reason for fear. When the time arrived, the centurions and military tribunes and even the prefect of the city, T. Turpilius Silanus,* were invited by different townspeople to their various homes. While they were feasting, they were butchered, all except Turpilius. Next, the conspirators attacked the soldiers, who were wandering about unarmed because it was a
4   holiday and they were off duty. The plebs joined in, some under instructions from the aristocracy, others excited and eager for such activities—they did not understand the plan of action; the turbulence itself and revolution was pleasure enough.

1   67. The Roman soldiers were confused by the unforeseen danger and had no idea what to do. They were in a panic. The town's citadel, where their standards and shields were, was cut off by the enemy guard; the gates, already shut, prevented their flight. In addition, women and boys, perched on the rooftops, competed in hurling
2   down stones and whatever else their position offered. There was no protection from the double danger and the bravest could not fight back against the weakest types. Side by side, the good and the bad, the warlike and the weak, were slaughtered without retaliation.
3   It was gruelling and the Numidians were savage. Though the town

was completely locked up, Turpilius the praetor escaped unscathed and was the only Italian to do so. We have not discovered whether this happened because of the compassion of his host or because of some agreement, or just by chance. In any case, in the midst of great danger he preferred a life of turpitude* to an unsullied reputation. He seems to have been wretched and despicable.*

68. When Metellus learned about what had happened at Vaga, he 1 disappeared from sight for a while in grief. Then, as rage and sorrow mingled, he hurried to take a most careful vengeance for the outrage. At sunset he made ready the expedition and led forth the legion with 2 which he was wintering and as many Numidian cavalry* as he could muster. On the next day at about the third hour he arrived at a plain surrounded by slightly higher ground. His soldiers were exhausted by 3 the long march and were at the point of rejecting any further orders; he told them that the town of Vaga was no more than a mile away and that they ought to be patient and endure the toil that remained so that they could avenge their fellow citizens, men most courageous and most wretched. He also made a generous offer of booty. In this 4 way he roused their spirits and ordered the cavalry to proceed in an open formation in front, the infantry to follow in as tight a formation as possible and to hide their standards.

69. When the people of Vaga noticed an army coming their way, at 1 first they concluded rightly that it was Metellus and they shut their gates. Then, when they saw that their fields were not being devastated and that the cavalry in front was Numidian, they reconsidered and concluded that it was Jugurtha. With great joy they came forth to meet the army. Suddenly the signal was given. The cavalry and 2 the soldiers acted: some slaughtered the crowd that had poured out of the town; others hurried to the gates; others seized the towers: wrath and the hope for booty overcame their exhaustion. Thus, the 3 people of Vaga enjoyed their treachery for only two days. Their great and opulent city became nothing but vengeance and plunder. Turpilius, whom we mentioned above as the prefect of the town, the only man to escape, was ordered by Metellus to explain himself. When he could not adequately justify his actions, he was condemned, beaten, and put to death. He paid the penalty because he was a citizen from Latium.*

70. During this period, Jugurtha became suspicious of Bomil- 1 car, who had prompted him to begin the peace talks he had in

fear abandoned. And Bomilcar was suspicious of Jugurtha. He wanted a change of government and he began to plot the king's destruction;

2 day and night he wracked his brains. Finally, leaving nothing untried, he made Nabdalsa* his ally, an aristocrat, very wealthy, well known and popular with his people. This man usually led an army separate from the king's and managed everything that Jugurtha overlooked when he was exhausted or occupied with more important matters.

3 This was the source of his fame and wealth. And so the two of them decided on a day for their treachery; the details they chose to extem-

4 porize according to the circumstances. Nabdalsa set out for his army. It had been stationed as ordered between the Roman winter camps so as to prevent the enemy from devastating the fields with impunity.

5 But then Nabdalsa began to be troubled by the enormity of his actions. He did not appear at the agreed time; his fears began to thwart the enterprise. Bomilcar was both eager to bring his own plans to fruition and worried about his ally's timidity. To prevent him from abandoning the original plan and adopting some new strategy, he used men he trusted to get a letter to Nabdalsa in which he reprimanded the man's weakness and cowardice, called upon the gods by whom they had sworn, and warned him not to convert the rewards of Metellus into his own destruction: Jugurtha's end, he said, was near; the only question was: would he die through their valour or Metellus'; accordingly, he should reconsider whether he preferred rewards or torture.

1   71. But, when this letter arrived, Nabdalsa happened to be
2 exhausted from exercise and was resting in bed. At first, he read Bomilcar's words and was concerned; then, as is typical for a wor-
3 ried mind, he fell asleep. He had a secretary, a certain Numidian, a man he trusted, respected and made privy to all his plans except this
4 most recent one. When the secretary heard that a letter had arrived, he thought that his services or advice would be needed, as usual. He entered the tent and, since Nabdalsa was sleeping, he picked up the letter that lay carelessly on the pillow above his head and read it.
5 Then, having discovered the plot, he hurried to the king. Nabdalsa awoke a little later and, when he could not find the letter, he understood all that had happened. At first, he tried to pursue the informer. When that failed, he went to Jugurtha to appease him. He said that he had been prevented from doing what he had already decided to do by his dependant's disloyalty; weeping he called upon their friendship

and his own many faithful actions and he asked Jugurtha not to hold him suspect of such a crime.

72. To this Jugurtha responded benignly, which was not what he 1 felt at heart. Bomilcar and many others he discovered were involved in the plot were put to death. Then he suppressed his wrath lest a rebellion arise from this business. But after this event, Jugurtha 2 never enjoyed a peaceful day or night: he did not fully trust any place, any mortal or any time; he feared citizens and enemies alike; he was always wary; startled at every sound; he rested at night in different places, places often unworthy of the dignity of a king; occasionally he would awaken from sleep, grab his armour, and create an uproar: the fear that hounded him was like madness.

73. Metellus heard from deserters about the death of Bomilcar 1 and how the evidence came to light. Consequently, as if beginning the war anew, he quickly readied and hurried along everything. Marius kept pestering him about a leave and so he was dismissed to 2 go home.* His thought was that Marius, discontent and angry, would not be very useful. At Rome the plebs willingly accepted what they 3 had heard about both men from the letters that had been sent concerning Metellus and Marius. For the general, the noble birth that 4 had previously been an honour became a source of resentment. But for the other, his humble origins added to his appeal.* In both cases, however, partisanship was more of a factor than personal advantages or disadvantages. Furthermore, seditious magistrates* stirred up 5 the common people, accused Metellus of capital offences in every public assembly, and exaggerated the virtues of Marius. In the end, 6 the plebs* were so enraged that the craftsmen and farmers, all those whose success and credit depended on their hands, dropped their own work and crowded about Marius. They put their own needs second to his advancement. In this way the aristocracy was beaten down 7 and the consulship was given for the first time in many years to a 'new man'. When the people were asked by the tribune of the plebs, T. Manlius Mancinus,* whom they wanted to carry on the war with Jugurtha, they voted* in a block for Marius. A little before the Senate had given the province of Numidia to Metellus;* but that decree was for nothing.

74. At the same time Jugurtha lost his friends: he had killed most 1 of them, the rest fled in fear, some to the Romans, others to the king, Bocchus. Since he was unable to wage war without assistants and considered it dangerous to try the trust of new friends after such treachery from old ones, he became inconsistent and confused. No action or plan or any human being was wholly satisfactory: he changed his marching orders and his officers daily; at one moment he set out for the enemy, sometimes he retreated to the desert; often he put his trust in flight and a little later in war. He was not certain whether his people's courage or their good faith was less to be trusted. And so, wherever he turned, he met with opposition.

2   But in the midst of all this hesitation suddenly Metellus appeared* with his army. Jugurtha readied his Numidians and put them in for-
3 mation as time allowed. Then the battle began. Most of his soldiers were beaten back and routed at the first charge, but, where the king took part in the fighting, the struggle lasted for a while. The Romans gained possession of a significant number of standards and weapons, but few enemy soldiers. That is because in nearly all their battles the Numidians save their feet sooner than their weapons.

1   **75.** This rout made Jugurtha distrust his situation even more unstintingly. He went into the desert with the deserters and some of his cavalry, and then to Thala,* a town that was large and wealthy, where most of his treasure was placed, and where there were many
2 opportunities to educate his children. When Metellus found out, he began to hope he could end the war by gaining possession of the town. He knew that there were fifty miles of arid desert between Thala and the nearest river; nevertheless, he resolved to overcome every
3 obstacle and even to defeat nature in pursuing his hope. Consequently, he ordered all the pack animals to be relieved of their baggage except for ten days' supply of grain; only skins and other containers for
4 water were to be carried. Furthermore, he acquired from the fields as many domestic cattle as possible and loaded them with contain-ers of any kind, but generally of wood, which he gathered from the
5 Numidian huts. In addition, he ordered the neighbouring people (they had surrendered to Metellus after their king fled) to bring as much water as they could, specifying the day and place where they
6 were to meet him. He himself loaded the animals from the stream which above we noted was the water closest to the town. Supplied in this way he set off towards Thala.

7   Then, when he arrived at the place he had specified to the Numidians, he pitched and fortified his camp. Suddenly, such a force of water is said to have been sent down from the heavens that

this alone was more than enough for the army. Moreover, the sup- 8
plies were greater than they hoped because the Numidians, like most
men right after a surrender, were intent on doing their duty. But 9
the soldiers for religious reasons preferred to use the rainwater and
this greatly improved their spirits because they thought that they
were under the special care of the immortal gods. Then on the next
day they arrived at Thala, much to Jugurtha's surprise. The towns- 10
people, who had believed that they were protected by the difficulties
of their location, were terrified by this great and unprecedented feat.
Still, they eagerly got ready for battle; our men did the same.

76. But now the king believed that Metellus could do anything. 1
His energy had overcome everything: arms and weapons, places and
circumstances, finally even nature herself, who gives orders to everyone else. So he fled from the town at night with his children and a
great part of his wealth. And afterwards he never delayed in any place
for more than one day or one night. He would pretend that he was
hurrying off on business, but treachery is what he feared, and he was
thinking he could avoid it by rapid movement: for plans like that, he
thought, require leisure and opportunity.

But when Metellus saw that the townspeople were eager for battle 2
and that the town was protected by fortifications and by its position, he surrounded the walls with a stockade and a trench. Then 3
in the two most suitable places he put up mantlets and pitched up a
mound and on the mound he placed towers to protect the mantlets
and the workers. On the other side the townspeople were quick to
act and make preparations. In fact, nothing was omitted by either 4
side. Finally the Romans, exhausted by all their labours and battles, 5
forty days after they had arrived, took possession of the city, but only
the city: all the booty had been destroyed by the deserters. When 6
they saw the wall being shaken by the ram and their own situation in
ruins, they had carried the gold and the silver and other valuables to
the king's palace. There, they stuffed themselves with wine and food,
and then destroyed in a fire the booty and the palace and themselves.
They willingly exacted from themselves the penalty that they feared
from the enemy if they were conquered.

77. Now, at the same time that Thala was captured, legates from 1
the town of Leptis came to Metellus begging him to send them a garrison and a prefect. They said that a certain Hamilcar,* a combative
partisan aristocrat, wanted things to change. Neither the authority of

the magistrates nor the laws made any difference to him; if Metellus did not hurry, their safety and Roman allies would be in the greatest

2 danger. In fact, already at the beginning of the war with Jugurtha* the people of Leptis had sent an embassy to the consul Bestia and

3 afterwards to Rome to seek friendship and alliance. Then, when they got their request, they had always remained true and faithful and energetically accomplished everything asked by Bestia, Albinus, and

4 Metellus. For this reason the general readily granted their petition. Four Ligurian cohorts were sent there and C. Annius* as prefect.

1   78. The city was founded by the Sidonians,* who we understand came by boat as exiles into that territory because of civil discord. It was situated between the two Syrtes, who get their name from the

2 following fact. There are two bays near the edge of Africa, differing in size, but similar in nature. Where they are near the land, they are very deep; elsewhere, as chance determines, some places are deep,

3 others are full of shoals in a storm. For when the sea begins to swell and grow savage with the winds, the tide drags up dirt and sand and huge rocks. The bays are called the 'Syrtes' because of this

4 'dragging'.* Intermarriage with the Numidians changed only the language of that community; the laws and culture are generally Sidonian, and they retain this character because they live far from

5 the Numidian king's authority. There are many vast deserts between them and the populated areas of Numidia.

1   79. But since our discussion of the problems of Leptis has brought us into these regions, I think I should relate the extraordinary and marvellous deed* of two Carthaginians, which the place calls to mind.

2 At the time when the Carthaginians ruled most of Africa, the people

3 of Cyrene were also strong and wealthy. The land between them was sandy, undifferentiated, without river or mountain to mark their boundaries. This circumstance kept the people engaged in a bitter

4 and protracted war. After legions and fleets had been routed and put to flight many times on both sides, and each side had done significant damage to the other, they became afraid that soon someone else would attack them. Both the conquered and the victorious were worn out by their war. So they made a truce through a treaty and agreed that on a specific day legates from both cities would set out from their homes: the common boundary for both people would be determined

5 by where they met in the middle. Consequently, two brothers, named the Philaeni, were sent from Carthage and they hurried to complete

their journey. The men from Cyrene were slower. I do not know whether this was caused by laziness or by chance, but it is true that in 6 that country storms can impede travel as much as they do on the sea. When the wind rises on ground that is level and bare of trees, it blows the sand up from the ground and, driven with great force, it is wont to fill the mouth and eyes. The result is that men cannot see where they are going and they delay their journeys. The men of Cyrene, 7 when they saw that they were outdistanced, became afraid that they would be punished for having botched things. They charged the Carthaginians with having left their home before the time; they tried to confuse the issue; in short they preferred anything over leaving in defeat. The Phoenicians then asked the Greeks to offer any other 8 terms, provided they were fair. The Greeks offered a choice: either the Carthaginians would be buried alive in the place they claimed as the boundary of their state or the Greeks would proceed under the same condition to wherever they wanted. The Philaeni agreed to the 9 terms and gave themselves and their life to the republic. And so they were buried alive. On that spot, the Carthaginians consecrated altars 10 to the Philaeni brothers. Other honours were granted them at home. Now, I will return to my topic.

80. After Jugurtha lost Thala he began to think that nothing was 1 sufficiently secure against Metellus. He travelled through great deserts with a few men and came to the Gaetuli, a wild and uncivilized race that at that time had not heard of the Roman people. He brought 2 a great number of them together and gradually trained them to hold rank, follow standards, observe orders, and do other things required of a soldier. In addition, he used lavish gifts and more lavish promises 3 to persuade the close friends of King Bocchus* to be devoted to his cause. Then, with the help of these men he prompted the king to begin a war against the Romans. This required less effort and was 4 all the easier because at the beginning of the war Bocchus had sent legates to Rome to seek a treaty and an alliance, which would have 5 been advantageous to the war effort, but a few men, blinded by greed, men whose custom is to put a price on everything, honourable or dishonourable, blocked the petition. Furthermore, already before this a 6 daughter of Bocchus was married to Jugurtha. But this is considered an insignificant connection among the Numidians and the Moors, because each individual has as many wives as he can afford, some ten, others more, and kings proportionately more. In this way affection is 7

dispersed across the group: none is held as a consort, all are equally unimportant.

1 **81.** And so the two armies met in a place that suited both kings. There they exchanged oaths of loyalty and Jugurtha inflamed Bocchus' heart with a speech: the Romans are unjust, he said, suffering from profound greed, the common enemy of all people. He said that they had the same reason for war with Bocchus, with himself, and with all others: lust for empire. And for this reason all kingdoms were their enemy. At the moment, he said, he was the Roman enemy; a little bit earlier, it was the Carthaginians and King Perseus;* and it will be the same thing in the future: to the extent that anyone appears wealthy,

2 so he will be the enemy of Rome. When he had said this and similar things, they marched toward Cirta* because Metellus had placed

3 his plunder there with his captives and baggage. Jugurtha had the following thought: either it would be worth while to capture the city or, if the Roman came to help his men, he would engage him in battle.

4 For it was just this that he cleverly hurried on: a reduction in the chances of peace for Bocchus. He was afraid that continuing delays might make him prefer something other than war.

1 **82.** The general found out about the alliance between the kings, but did not act rashly, nor did he offer an opportunity for a fight everywhere, as he had often done before when Jugurtha was defeated. Rather, he fortified camps not far from Cirta and waited for the kings. He thought that, since he was engaging a new enemy, it was better to fight at his convenience after he saw what kind of fighters

2 the Moors were. Meanwhile, he learned through letters from Rome that Numidia had been given to Marius. He had already heard that Marius had been elected consul. This circumstance shook him more than was good or honourable: he neither held back his tears nor watched his tongue. He was an extraordinary man in other ways, but

3 endured disappointment like a woman. Some interpreted his response as arrogance, others said that his noble nature had been provoked by indignity; many thought that it was because a victory already won was being ripped from his hands. We think the evidence suggests that he was tortured more by Marius' advancement than by his own humiliation, and that he would not have been so resentful if the province had been taken and given to anyone other than Marius.

1 **83.** As a result, hampered by his heartbreak and because it seemed to him stupid to expose himself to danger while taking care of another

man's interests, he sent legates to Bocchus to petition him not to become an enemy of the Roman people without cause: he had, he said, at this time a great opportunity for cementing an alliance of friendship, and that would be better than war; although he was confident in his resources, still he ought not to trade a sure thing for an unsure thing; warfare is always easily taken up, but brought to an end with great difficulty; the beginning and the end of war were not in the same person's power; anyone can begin a war, even a coward, but the fighting only stops when the winner stops. And so, Metellus said, he should think about himself and his kingdom, and he should not mingle his flourishing state with Jugurtha's hopeless prospects. To these 2 words the king replied in a conciliatory way: he wanted peace, but he pitied Jugurtha's misfortune; if the same opportunity were offered to Jugurtha, there would be total agreement. Again the general sent 3 messengers in response to Bocchus' demands; Bocchus accepted some, rejected others. And so the time passed while messengers were sent back and forth from each side, and the war, untried, dragged on as Metellus desired.

84. But Marius, as we said above, was made consul with the eager 1 support of the plebs. He had long before been hostile to the aristocracy, but, after the people assigned him the province of Numidia, he attacked the nobles frequently and fiercely. Sometimes he slashed at individuals, other times at the group; he said that he had seized the consulship from them as spoils from the conquered; and he said other things that glorified himself and caused them pain. Meanwhile, he 2 gave first priority to the needs of war: he asked for reinforcements for his legions, he called for auxiliaries from foreign peoples and kings; furthermore, from the Latins and the allies he drafted the bravest men, most known to him personally for their military service, a few only by reputation, and by personal canvassing he compelled men who had earned their stipends to march forward with him. The 3 Senate was opposed to him, but they did not dare to deny him in regard to any business. In fact, they were even pleased to authorize supplementary troops, thinking that the plebs were not eager soldiers and that Marius would consequently lose either military resources or the people's support. But this was a vain hope: so great a desire to go with Marius had overwhelmed most. Each man obsessed over 4 the thought that he would be rich with booty, that he would return home victorious, and so on. And Marius provoked them not a little

5 with a speech. After all his demands were met and it was time to enrol
the soldiers, he called a public assembly, both for the purpose of encouraging the enlisted men and, as was his custom, baiting the aristocracy.
He discussed things as follows:

1   85. 'Citizens, I know that many do not show the same character
when they are seeking power from you as when they exercise it: at
first, they are industrious, suppliant, moderate; afterwards, they pass
2 their time in idleness and arrogance. But the opposite seems right to
me: for, inasmuch as the whole state is more valuable than the consulship or the praetorship, so it ought to be governed with more careful
3 attention than its offices are sought. I am not unaware of the burden
your extraordinary kindness places upon me. It is more difficult than
you imagine, citizens, to prepare for war and spare the treasury at
the same time, to force into military service men whom you do not
want to offend, to take care of all domestic and foreign business and
4 to do so surrounded by jealousy, opposition, and partisanship. Furthermore, when others fail, they are protected by old family name,
the deeds of their ancestors, the wealth of relatives and in-laws, their
many dependants. For me, all hope lies in myself, and I must protect
those hopes by manly virtue and innocence; for other things are fee-
5 ble. I also understand this, citizens: that all eyes are turned upon me,
that fair and good men value me because my deeds have benefited
the Republic, but that the aristocracy is looking for an opportunity to
6 attack. And so I must struggle all the harder that you are not deceived
7 and that they do not succeed. I have lived my life since childhood
8 in such a way that I consider all labours and dangers familiar. It is
not my plan now, citizens, to accept my reward and abandon what
9 I did without reward before your kindness to me. It is difficult for
men who have pretended excellence in order to win elections to be
moderate when they gain power. But I have spent my entire life as an
exercise in moral character and now from habit it has become natural
for me to do the right thing.

10   'You have ordered me to wage war against Jugurtha, and this has
greatly distressed the aristocrats. I am asking you to reconsider in
your hearts whether it is better to change your decision: should you
send to this or some other great task some member of the aristocratic
horde, a man of ancient lineage and many family images and no real
military experience? Of course, in such an important task, wholly
ignorant of what to do, he will hustle and bustle; he will run about

and find some commoner to remind him of his duty. So it generally 11
happens that the man you order to take command requires someone else to command him. I even know, citizens, of men who, after 12
they were made consuls, began to read about the deeds of our ancestors and to peruse Greek military treatises. Preposterous men; for
action follows election in terms of time, but in fact and in experience
it comes first. Compare, now, citizens, those men, their arrogance, 13
with me, a "new man". The things that they heard or read about,
some of them were things I saw, the rest were things I did. What they
learned from books, I learned being a soldier. Now you must judge 14
whether deeds or words are of more value. They scorn my status as
a "new man", I scorn their cowardice; I am taunted for my station
in life, they for their shameful activities. I believe that we all have a 15
single common nature, but that the bravest man is the most noble.
And, if the fathers of Albinus or Bestia could be asked whether they 16
would rather have a son like me or like the nobles, what do you think
they would say except that they wanted the best possible children?
On the other hand, if it is right for them to look down on me, they 17
should look down on their own ancestors too, men whose nobility,
like mine, began in manly virtue. They are jealous of my office; there- 18
fore, let them be jealous of my hard work, my integrity, even the
dangers I have faced, since it was through these that I have gained
that office. But these men, vitiated by arrogance, pass their lives as 19
if they despised the honours you can give, but seek those honours as
if they had lived an honourable life. Surely they are deceived if they 20
expect to enjoy the pleasures of indolence and the rewards of manliness, two contradictory things. Furthermore, when they speak before 21
you or in the Senate, most of their speech is taken up with praising
their ancestors: they think that by recalling those brave deeds they
themselves become more glorious. But the converse is true. For the 22
more glorious the life of their ancestors is, the more shameful their
own cowardice becomes. Certainly this is the truth of the matter: 23
the glory of their ancestors is like a light which does not allow their
virtues or faults to be hidden. I confess, citizens, that I have no 24
advantages of this kind, but I have that which is much more glorious: I can talk about my own deeds. Now consider how unfair they 25
are. They do not grant to me from my own virtue the very thing
they arrogate to themselves from the virtue of others—of course
it is because I do not have family portraits and my nobility is recent.

But surely it is better to have created nobility than to have received and corrupted it.

26 'I am fully aware that if they wanted to respond to me now, they would deliver a very eloquent and crafted oration. But on the occasion of the very great kindness you have bestowed, since they cut me and you at every opportunity with insults, I did not want to be silent. I did not want modesty to be construed as a guilty conscience.

27 In fact, it is my heartfelt opinion that no speech can damage me: the truth necessarily speaks well for me; lies are refuted by my life and

28 character. But it is your judgement that is denounced, you who gave me the greatest office and the most important mission, and so you must consider again and again whether your action is to be regretted.

29 I cannot justify your confidence by bringing forth the portraits or triumphs or consulships of my ancestors; but, if circumstances demand, I can bring forth spears, a banner, medallions, other military hon-

30 ours, and in addition the scars on the front of my body. These are my family portraits, my nobility, not an inheritance bequeathed to me, as theirs is, but won by my own many labours and dangers.

31 'My words are not well crafted; I care little for that. Manly virtue can present itself well enough; they are the ones who need artifice

32 to hide their shameful deeds with a speech. And I have not learned Greek: I had no desire to learn that which of course was of no help

33 in teaching the teachers virtue. But I have learned those things that are most important to the state: to strike the enemy, to defend a position, to fear nothing but a disgraceful report, to endure alike the cold of winter and the heat of summer, to sleep on the ground, to sustain

34 hunger and hard work at the same time. These are the lessons I urge upon my soldiers. And I am not stingy with them while being lavish with myself; I do not give them the labour and take glory for myself.

35 This is effective, this is civic command. For when you live a soft life of safety, but coerce an army with threats of punishment, that is to

36 be a slave-owner, not a commander. It was by doing these and other similar things that your ancestors glorified themselves and their state.

37 But the aristocrats, relying on that glory, while being themselves of a very different character, hold us in contempt, though we emulate their ancestors. And then they seek from you all the political offices, not because they deserve them, but as if they were entitled to them.

38 But these men are filled with arrogance and they are very wrong.

Their ancestors left them all that they could leave: wealth, family portraits, the glorious memory of their own actions; they did not leave them virtue, nor could they. That is the only thing that cannot be given or received as a gift. They say I am vulgar and uneducated 39 because I do know how to set an elegant dinner table and I do not have an actor or a cook worth more than my foreman. But I'm pleased 40 to confess that this is true, citizens. For I have learned from my parents and other righteous men that elegance is for women, labour is for men; that good men ought to have more glory than wealth; that armour is the true ornament, not furniture.

'Well, then, let them always do what they enjoy, what they con- 41 sider valuable: let them fall in love, get drunk, continue to do in old age what they did as young men—attend banquets, remain dedicated to their belly and the shameful parts of their body. Let them leave to us the sweat and the dust and other such things; to us these things are sweeter than banquets. But, it doesn't happen like that. For when 42 these most disgraceful men have debased themselves with their own dereliction, they set out to steal the rewards due to good men. And so 43 it is most unjust that these most wicked practices, extravagant waste-fulness and cowardly indolence, do no damage to those who adopt them, but they are the ruin of the innocent Republic.

'Now, since I have responded to the aristocrats as far as my charac- 44 ter, but not their wicked deeds, demand, I will say a few things about the Republic. First of all, citizens, be confident about Numidia. You 45 have removed everything that up until now has protected Jugurtha: greed, inexperience, and arrogance. Second, you have an army there 46 that knows the terrain, though (good lord!) they have been more intrepid than fortunate. For a great part of the army has been depleted by the greed and recklessness of its leaders. And so I ask all of you 47 who are of military age to work with me and serve your country. No one should become afraid because of the misfortunes of others or the arrogance of the generals. I will be there with you on the march and in the battle, both as your adviser and your companion amid dangers. In all circumstances, I will treat you and myself alike. And I declare 48 that with the gods' help all is ready: victory, plunder, praise. But if these things were dubious or out of reach, still all good men ought to come to the aid of their country. You know that cowardice does 49 not make anyone immortal, and that no parent would pray that his

children live for ever rather than that they live a good and honourable
50 life. I would say more, citizens, if words could make the timid manly.
For the intrepid, I think I have said quite enough.'

1   86. Such was the speech Marius delivered. When he saw that
he had aroused the enthusiasm of the plebs, he quickly loaded his
ships with supplies, money, arms, and other necessities. He ordered
2 his legate, A. Manlius, to set sail.* Meanwhile, he himself enlisted
soldiers, not in the traditional way from the propertied classes, but
accepting whoever volunteered, generally from the headcount.*
3 Some said this was done because there was a lack of good men, others
attributed it to the consul's ambition, because his glory and success
came from that class and, when a man seeks power, the most needy
men are the most useful: their own possessions are not dear to them,
because they have none, and anything that entails a profit seems to
them honourable.
4   As a result, Marius set out for Africa with a force significantly
larger than decreed by the Senate.* In a few days he arrived at Utica.
5 The army was handed over to him by the legate, P. Rutilius, since
Metellus avoided a face-to-face meeting with Marius, not wanting to
see what his heart could barely endure to hear about.

1   87. After bringing his legions* and auxiliary cohorts up to full
strength,* he marched into an area of the country that was fertile and
rich in booty. He gave to his soldiers everything that they captured
there. Then he attacked some fortresses and towns that were poorly
2 protected by nature and manpower. There were many battles in
different places, but they were not very demanding. Meanwhile, the
new recruits began to enter battle without fear. They saw runaways
captured or killed, and that the bravest were the safest. Weapons
protected freedom, fatherland, parents, and all else;* weapons won
3 glory and wealth. Thus, in a short while the new recruits and the
4 veterans were assimilated; manly courage made them all equals. But
when the African kings heard that Marius had arrived, they separated
and went into difficult terrain. This was Jugurtha's idea. He hoped
that the enemy, divided in pursuit, could soon be attacked and that
the Romans, like most men, would have less discipline and greater
licence when there was no immediate cause of fear.

1   88. Meanwhile, Metellus set off for Rome, where contrary to his
expectations he was welcomed with the greatest rejoicing.* Once
ill will subsided, he was equally dear to the people and to the senators.

Marius, on the other hand, attended to the situation of his own men 2
and that of the enemy with equal energy and prudence. He looked
for the good points on both sides and the opposite on both sides, he
scouted out the kings' movements, he pre-empted their plans and
traps, and he allowed nothing remiss in his army, nothing safe in
theirs. And so he often attacked and routed the Gaetuli and Jugurtha 3
while they were plundering our allies, and not far from the town
Cirta he forced the king himself to flee without his arms. But when 4
he noticed that these actions only brought glory, not an end to the
war, he decided to besiege the individual cities that were most advantageous to the enemy and most detrimental to himself, either because
of their manpower or their location. In this way, Jugurtha would
either be stripped of his fortresses, if he allowed Marius to proceed,
or he would have to engage in a battle. Now Bocchus had often sent 5
messengers to Marius, saying that he wanted friendship with the
Roman people, that Marius should not fear any hostile action from
him. It is not clear whether he was dissembling in order to strike 6
unexpectedly a more deadly blow, or whether his fickle disposition
typically wavered between peace and war.

89. Still, the consul approached the fortified towns and strong- 1
holds as he had planned. Some he turned against the enemy by violence, others by fear or by offering bribes. At first he proceeded with 2
some moderation, thinking that Jugurtha would come within his
reach in order to protect his people. But when he heard that Jugurtha 3
was far away and engaged in other business, he thought the time was
right for undertaking greater and harsher things.

In the midst of the large desert there was a great and powerful town 4
named Capsa.* Its founder is recorded as being the Libyan Hercules.
The citizens of this town were free from taxation under Jugurtha; he
exercised his power lightly and for this reason they were very faithful to him. They were protected from enemies not only by walls and
arms and men, but much more effectively by the difficulties of the
location. For, except for the area near the town, all else was desolate, 5
uncultivated, lacking water, but infested with snakes whose power,
like that of other wild animals, was made all the greater by the lack
of food. In addition to this, it is the nature of serpents, in themselves
deadly, to be provoked by thirst more than anything else. Marius was 6
very eager to take possession of this town, both because of its strategic
usefulness and because it was a difficult task. Metellus had gained

great glory by taking the town Thala, which was situated and fortified in a similar way, except that at Thala there were some springs not far from the walls. The people of Capsa enjoyed a single unfailing spring

7 within the town, otherwise they made do with rainwater. This condition is more easily tolerated there and in the uncultivated African interior because the Numidians fed on milk and the meat of wild animals and they did not use salt or whet the appetite in other ways.

8 For them, food staved off hunger and thirst; it was not an object of indulgence or great expense.

1 　**90.** And so the consul examined all aspects of the situation and, I think, put his trust in the gods. It is, after all, not possible in planning against such great dangers to provide sufficiently for every contingency. In fact, he was already troubled by insufficient grain, since the Numidians are more interested in pasturage for their animals than in cultivated fields and whatever had been grown had been taken into the fortresses by command of the king. In addition, the field was dry and barren of crops at that time, since it was the end of summer. Nevertheless, Marius made provisions as prudently as

2 the situation allowed. All the cattle which had been the booty of the previous days were given to the auxiliary cavalry to drive forward; he ordered the legate A. Manlius to go with his light infantry to the town Lares* where money and supplies were located. And he said that in a few days he would come to the same place on a plundering

3 expedition. In this way he hid his real intention and set off for the river Tanais.*

1 　**91.** Daily during the march he distributed cattle to the army, to the men of each century and likewise to the cavalry squadrons, and he ordered them to make sacks from the hides. He was making up for the lack of grain and, at the same time, preparing what would soon be useful to all, though they did not know it. When they arrived at the river on the sixth day, they had created a large supply of sacks.

2 There he set up camp with a few fortifications and ordered his men to take their dinner and be ready to leave camp at sunset; they were to abandon their packs and load themselves and their animals only

3 with water. Then, when the time seemed right, he broke camp and they marched the entire night before stopping. He did the same thing on the next day. Then on the third day, long before dawn arrived, he came to a hilly area not more than two miles from Capsa. There he waited with all his troops, keeping them as hidden as he could.

When day began and the Numidians, fearing nothing hostile, left 4 the city in a crowd, Marius suddenly ordered all his cavalry and with them the fastest foot soldiers to make for Capsa and besiege the gates. Then he himself followed quickly and eagerly, and he did not allow his soldiers to plunder. When the townspeople saw what was hap- 5 pening, the alarming situation, great panic, unforeseen evil, and in addition part of the citizen body outside the city walls in the enemy's power, everything compelled them to offer surrender. Still, the city 6 was set on fire; the adult Numidian men were killed; all the others were sold; booty was divided among the soldiers. This action, contrary 7 to the laws of war,* was caused not by greed or the consul's wickedness, but because the place was advantageous to Jugurtha, difficult for us to reach, the race of men fickle and faithless, previously controlled neither by kindness nor fear.

92. Marius was already regarded as great and glorious, but, after he 1 accomplished such a great victory without any losses to his own men, he began to be considered even greater and more glorious. Every 2 poorly planned action was treated as a sign of courage: the soldiers, restrained with a gentle discipline and at the same time enriched, praised him to the heavens; the Numidians feared him more than any mortal; in short, all men, allies and enemies alike, believed either that he had divine insight or that all was revealed with the gods' approval. But when this event turned out well, the consul proceeded to other 3 towns. He captured a few when the Numidians put up a fight. Many, deserted because of the wretched fate of Capsa, he destroyed with fire. All of Numidia was filled with grief and slaughter. Finally, after 4 capturing many places,* most without his army shedding a drop of blood, he undertook a new project, not with the some severity as the Capsian project, but no less difficult.

Not far from the river Muluccha,* which separated Jugurtha's and 5 Bocchus' kingdoms, there was a rocky mountain in the middle of a plain, broad enough for a moderate fortress, reaching to the heights, leaving a single narrow path of approach. Everywhere it was sheer 6 by nature, as if strategically built that way. Since the king's treasury was here, Marius intended to use all his force to capture the place. His success was more a matter of luck than design. The fortress had 7 a reasonable number of men and arms, a great supply of grain, and a spring of water. It was not well suited to embankments and towers and other siege-works. The path that the occupants of the fortress

8 used was very narrow and steep on both sides. It was very dangerous
to bring forward the mantlets and it did no good. For as soon as they
9 moved forwards a bit, they were destroyed by fire or stones. Because
of the slope of the land the soldiers could not hold their position in
front of the siege-works, nor could they act without danger under the
mantlets: the best soldiers were killed or wounded, among the rest
fear was growing.

1   93. Marius spent many days and consumed much labour on this
project. Then he became worried and debated with himself whether
he should abandon his plan, since it was a failure, or wait for fortune,
2 which he had often enjoyed to his advantage. While he passed many
days and nights distressed over this, it happened by chance that a
certain Ligurian, a common soldier from the auxiliary cohorts, left
camp to look for water. Not far from the side of the fortress which
was furthest from the fighting* he noticed among the stones some
snails crawling along. He reached for one, then another and then
many, and in his eagerness to collect them he gradually ascended to
3 near the top of the mountain. When he noticed that he was alone,
his desire to accomplish something difficult, a human tendency,
4 turned his attention away from the snails. And it happened that in
that place a large oak had grown between the rocks, at first a little
downwards, and then bending up and rising into the air. Such is the
nature of all growing plants. Using now the branches of the tree,
now the jutting rocks, the Ligurian climbed to the level plain where
the fortress stood. The Numidians were all focused on the battle, so
5 he noted all that he thought would be of some use in the future, and
returned by the same path, not thoughtlessly as he had ascended, but
6 testing and examining everything. Then he went quickly to Marius,
told him what had happened, urged him to try the fortress where
he had climbed up, promised to take the lead in showing the way
7 and meeting the danger. Marius sent some of those present with the
Ligurian to evaluate his proposal. They reported back, according to
their character, that it would be difficult or easy. Still, the consul's
8 interest was piqued. And so from his trumpeters and horn-blowers
he selected the five quickest men and he sent with them four centurions to act as guards; he told them all to follow the Ligurian's orders
and he set the next day for the operation.

1   94. When the time seemed right according to his order, the
Ligurian arrived at the place with all preparations completed.

Those who were to climb with him had changed their armour and equipment as instructed by their guide: their heads and feet were uncovered so they could see better and climb more easily over the rocks; swords and shields were on their backs, but they were Numidian shields made of leather, both because they were lighter and because they would make less noise when struck. The Ligurian went 2 ahead, tying ropes to the rocks and to any roots projecting because of age. Lifting themselves with these ropes, the soldiers ascended more easily; occasionally he gave a helping hand to those who were nervous because of the unusual path. When the ascent became more difficult, he sent the men unarmed ahead of him in single file, then he himself followed with their armour. Where it seemed that the ground might not support them, he was the first to test it; he helped encourage the rest by going frequently up and down in the same place, and then quickly moving aside. And so after a great effort they 3 finally arrived, exhausted, at the fortress. It was deserted on that side because everyone was, as on other days, face to face with the enemy. Marius had kept the Numidians intent on battle for the entire day, but when he heard from his messengers what the Ligurian had accomplished, he began to urge on his soldiers. He himself left the mantlets, formed a 'tortoise' and advanced to the wall while at the same time his catapults, archers, and slingers were terrifying the enemy from a distance. The Numidians did not keep themselves 4 safely within the fortress's walls because they had many times before overturned or burned the mantlets. Rather they moved about day and night in front of the walls, maligning the Romans and accusing Marius of madness, they threatened our soldiers with slavery at the hands of Jugurtha. Success had made them fearless. Meanwhile, 5 everyone, Roman and enemy alike, was intent on the battle. They fought with enormous force on both sides, one for glory and empire, the other for safety. Suddenly, a trumpet sounded from the rear. The first to flee were the women and children, who had come out to watch; then, anyone who was near the wall; finally, everyone, armed or not. When this happened, the Romans pushed forward more fiercely, 6 they routed the enemy but only wounded most of them. Then they made their way over the corpses of the dead, and greedy for glory they competed to reach the wall. No one stopped for booty. In this 7 way Marius' recklessness was amended by chance, and in place of blame he found glory.

1   **95.** While this was going on, however, L. Sulla,* a quaestor, arrived
in the camp. He brought the large cavalry unit which he had been left
in Rome to raise from the Latins and the allies.

2   But since our discussion has brought this great man to our attention, it is appropriate to speak briefly about his nature and character.
I say this for two reasons: we will not speak about Sulla's affairs elsewhere and L. Sisenna,* who has written the best and most accurate

3   account, does not seem to have spoken with sufficient frankness. And
so to Sulla: he was a noble of patrician descent, but from a family
that was nearly reduced to oblivion because of his idle ancestors.
He was educated alike in both Greek and Latin; he had enormous
ambitions, craved pleasure, craved glory more. He spent his leisure
time extravagantly, and yet was never distracted from business by
pleasure, except for the fact that his attitude concerning his wife*
could have been more honourable. He was well spoken, clever and
easygoing as a friend. He had an incredible depth of talent when it
came to disguising his activities, but he was generous in many ways,

4   especially with money. Before his victory in the civil war he was the
most fortunate* of all men, but his good fortune did not exceed his
efforts. As for what he did afterwards, I do not know whether one
should feel more shame or disgust in talking of it.

1   **96.** And so Sulla, as I said, came to Africa and to Marius' camp
with the cavalry. Previously inexperienced and ignorant of war, in a

2   short time he became the most astute of all. In addition, he was courteous in talking with the soldiers; he granted favours to many who
asked and to others on his own initiative. He did not like to accept
favours, but repaid them more quickly than a loan. He never asked
for repayment from others, rather he laboured to have as many as

3   possible in his debt. He could joke or be serious with the humblest,
and often joined them at work, on the march or on night watch. In
the meantime he did not undermine the reputation of the consul or
any good man—as men of twisted ambition usually do. He was only
concerned that no other be superior in counsel or in action; and he

4   surpassed most. Because of these characteristics and conduct he
became very dear to Marius and the soldiers in a short time.

1   **97.** Now, after Jugurtha had lost the town of Capsa and other
fortified places that were useful to him and a large amount of money
as well, he sent messengers to Bocchus. He asked him to bring his
troops to Numidia as soon as possible. The time for war was at hand,

he said. When he heard that Bocchus was hesitant and vacillating, 2
considering the advantages of war and peace, Jugurtha acted as he
did before. He bribed the king's closest associates and promised
one-third of Numidia to the Moor himself, provided that either the
Romans were driven from Africa or the war ended without any loss
to his territory. Lured by this reward, Bocchus joined Jugurtha with 3
a large army.

The kings united their two armies and attacked Marius an hour
before sunset as he was heading for his winter camps.* They thought
that the night which was upon them would benefit them if they were
defeated, and, if they won the victory, it would be no impediment
because they were familiar with the location; on the other hand, the
darkness would make either outcome more difficult for the Romans.
And so the consul heard about the arrival of the enemy from many of 4
his men at the same time as the enemy were themselves present. And
before the army was either put in formation or their baggage gathered
together, in fact, before any signal or order was given, the Moorish and Gaetulian cavalry charged upon our men, not in formation
or with any military deployment, but in groups formed by chance.
All our men, trembling at the unforeseen danger, were nonetheless 5
mindful of their courage. They began seizing their weapons or holding the enemy off from others who were arming. Some mounted
their horses, turned against the enemy. The fighting was more like an
attack of robbers than a battle. Without signals, without formations,
the cavalry and infantry were mixed together. Some gave ground,
others were butchered, many were surrounded from behind while
fighting fiercely the enemy in front of them. Neither manly courage nor weapons offered sufficient protection because the enemy was
superior in numbers and poured in upon them from all sides. Finally
the Romans, veterans and for that reason savvy about war, whoever
had been brought together by chance or place, created circular formations, and in this way, both protected and organized on all sides,
they withstood the enemy's attack.

98. Even in the midst of this dangerous operation, however, Mar- 1
ius was not frightened or any more disheartened than before, but
with his squadron, which he had formed from the bravest soldiers
rather than from personal friends, he traversed the battlefield and
now brought help to his men in trouble, now attacked the enemy
where they stood thickest. He commanded his men with his hands

2 since he was not able to give orders in the general confusion. Soon daylight was gone, but the barbarians did not slacken at all; they attacked more fiercely, thinking that the night would help them,

3 as the kings had said. Then Marius took counsel according to the opportunities available and occupied two hills that were close to each other so that his men would have a place for retreat. One hill, too small for a camp, had a large spring of water; the other was well positioned because being for the most part high and sheer it needed little

4 fortification. He ordered Sulla and his cavalry to spend the night on the hill that had the water; he himself gradually brought together his soldiers, who were scattered across the field—the enemy being in equal disorder. Then he led them all at a rapid pace to the hill.

5 Thus, the strength of the Roman position prevented the kings from continuing to fight. Still, they did not allow their men to wander afar; instead, they surrounded both hills with a large force, and made

6 camp in loose order. Next, they built many fires and rejoiced most of the night as barbarians will, they exulted and shouted aloud; even their leaders were ferocious: because they had not been routed, they

7 acted like victors. But in the darkness and from their elevated position the Romans could easily see all these activities and they were greatly encouraged.

1   99. Marius was especially reassured by the enemy's lack of experience and ordered his men to be as quiet as possible, not even to sound the trumpet as usual at the change of watch. Then, when dawn was approaching, the enemy was now exhausted and had just a little earlier fallen asleep. Suddenly Marius ordered the sentinels, likewise the trumpeters of the cohorts, squadrons, and legions, all to sound the signal at the same time. He ordered the soldiers to raise a shout

2 and break through the gates. The Moors and the Gaetuli were suddenly awakened by an unfamiliar and horrible sound. They were not able to flee or to seize their arms; they could not do anything or make

3 any plan. And so amid the shouting and the clamour, the lack of help and the attack of our men, the confusion, fear, terror, all were overwhelmed with despair. In the end all were routed and put to flight, a large number of weapons and military standards were captured. More men were killed in that battle than in all the former ones. Sleep and sudden terror had hampered their ability to flee.

1   100. Marius then proceeded to his winter camp, as he had started to do. He had decided to winter in the maritime towns because of

their provisions.* The victory had not made him careless or arrogant; rather he advanced in a squared line* just as if the enemy were watching. He placed Sulla on the right with the cavalry, on the left Manlius 2 was in charge of the slingers and archers, also the Ligurian cohorts. He located tribunes front and rear with the light-armed infantry. Deserters, who had the least value and knew the territory best, spied 3 on the enemy's march. At the same time the consul, as if he had no subordinates, took care of all provisions, appeared everywhere, praised and chastised as was deserved. He was himself armed and 4 active; he compelled his soldiers to do likewise. They fortified their camp in the same way they had marched: he sent legionary cohorts to guard the gates, auxiliary cavalry to patrol outside the camp. He put some men above the ramparts on the fortifications. He personally went around the night watches, not from any fear that his orders would not be followed, but to make the soldiers more willing when they saw that their general worked as hard as they did. Clearly, Mar- 5 ius at that time and at others during the war with Jugurtha controlled his army more with shame than with threats. Many said that he did this to win popularity; others said that the hardship he had known since childhood and the other things that the rest of the world considers suffering he regarded as pleasure. However that may be, the state was served as well and honourably as it would have been by the severest discipline.

101. Finally on the fourth day, when they were not very far from 1 the town of Cirta, the scouts appeared quickly and simultaneously on all sides. This meant that the enemy was near. But the consul 2 was uncertain about how to draw up his men, since all the scouts made the same report even though they were returning by different paths from different directions. So he waited where he was, changing nothing, prepared for any attack. This frustrated Jugurtha's plans, 3 since he had divided his troops into four parts, thinking that if he attacked equally from all directions some of his men would meet the enemy from behind. Meanwhile, Sulla, who engaged with the 4 enemy first, encouraged his men squadron by squadron. With the horses in as tight a formation as possible he and others attacked the Moors; the rest remained in place protecting their bodies from the long-range javelins and slaughtering anyone who came within reach. While the cavalry were fighting in this manner, Bocchus, who 5 had not participated in the earlier battle because he had been delayed

in transit, attacked the rear line of the Roman army with the foot
6 soldiers whom his son Volux led. At that time, Marius was fighting
among those in the vanguard because Jugurtha was there with most
of his men. But when the Numidian heard of Bocchus' arrival, with
a few men he secretly wheeled towards the infantry.* Then in Latin,
which he had learned to speak in Numidia,* he shouted out that our
men were fighting in vain, that just now he had killed Marius with
his own hand, and at the same time he held out a sword smeared
with blood, which he had covered with gore by killing with some
7 vigour a foot soldier of ours.* When the soldiers heard this, they
were horrified, more by the cruel deed* than because they trusted
the news; but, at the same time, the barbarians' spirits rose and they
8 attacked more fiercely the shocked Romans. And now they were close
to being routed, when Sulla, having crushed those who opposed him,
returned and attacked the Moorish flank. Bocchus immediately ran
9 away. But Jugurtha, while eager to support his own men and to hold
on to the victory he had already nearly won, was surrounded by the
cavalry. Men died on his left and on his right, all of them; he alone
10 escaped the enemy's weapons and fled. Meanwhile Marius had put
the cavalry to flight and rushed to the aid of his men, whom he had
11 heard were being beaten. Finally, the enemy was now routed everywhere. The open field was a ghastly spectacle: pursuit, flight; death,
capture; horses and men suffering; and many, who could neither flee
because of their wounds nor endure to be still, now struggled to rise
and immediately collapsed. In the end, everything, everywhere you
looked, was strewn with weapons, armour, corpses, and between
them the ground drenched in blood.*

1   **102.** After this cirumstance, the consul, now the undisputed
2 victor, proceeded to Cirta, his original destination. There, on the
fifth day after the barbarian's second defeat, legates came from Bocchus who asked Marius in the words of the king to send him two of
his most faithful officers: he wanted to discuss matters of interest to
himself and the Roman people.* Marius immediately sent L. Sulla
3 and A. Manlius. It was decided that these men, although sent at the
king's invitation, would address the king and attempt to change his
mind, if he was hostile, or, if he wanted peace, to fire up that desire.
4 Manlius, the older man, yielded to Sulla's eloquence;* Sulla spoke a
few words to this effect.

'King Bocchus, we are delighted that the gods have finally admon- 5
ished a man such as yourself to prefer peace to war and not to corrupt
your own excellence by association with Jugurtha's utter depravity.
At the same time you have removed from us the bitter necessity of
equally prosecuting you in your errors and that most criminal man. In 6
addition, the Roman people have always thought it better, since they
founded their empire, to seek out friends rather than slaves, thinking
it was safer to give orders to the willing than to the coerced. And for 7
you no friendship is more advantageous than ours, first, because we
are far away, a circumstance that produces minimal friction, but the
same advantages as if we were near at hand; second, we have many
subjects but neither we nor anyone else has enough friends. We only 8
wish you had reached this decision at the beginning. Certainly, you
would have received many more benefits by now than the losses you
have suffered. But since Fortune* generally governs human affairs 9
and it was her pleasure that you know both our power and our goodwill, you should now hurry, since Fortune approves, to accomplish
what you have started. You have many opportunities to overcome 10
your errors by accepting your duty. And, finally, put this thought 11
deep in your breast: the Roman people have never been outdone in
generosity. Of course you know what they can do in war.'

Bocchus made a temperate and courteous reply, saying a few words 12
about his own shortcomings. He had not taken up arms, he said, with
a hostile spirit, but to protect his kingdom. For the part of Numidia 13
from which he had forcefully expelled Jugurtha* had become his by
right of war. He could not allow Marius to devastate that territory.
Further, he had sent legates before to Rome, but an alliance had been
rejected.* But he would say no more of the past; and, if Marius would 14
let him, he would send legates to the Senate. Permission was granted. 15
Then friends changed the barbarian's mind. Jugurtha had bribed
them when he had heard of Sulla's and Manlius' embassy, fearing
what was in fact their purpose.

103. Meanwhile, Marius put his army in winter camps* and set off 1
with his light-armed infantry and some of his cavalry into the desert
to attack a regal fortress where Jugurtha had put all the deserters
under guard. Yet again Bocchus selected five men from those depend- 2
ent upon him, men of proven loyalty and strong character. Either
he was reconsidering what had happened to him in two battles or he

had been warned by other friends whom Jugurtha had left unbribed.
3 He ordered these men to go as legates to Marius and then, if Marius
agreed,* to go on to Rome. He granted them licence to act on his
4 behalf and to settle the war in any way possible. They set out quickly
for the Roman winter camps, but on the way they were surrounded
and robbed by Gaetulian marauders. In terror and disgrace they fled
to Sulla whom the consul had left as propraetor when he set out on
5 his expedition. Sulla treated them, not like faithless enemies, as they
deserved, but carefully and generously. And so the barbarians came
to believe that the Roman reputation for avarice was false and that
6 Sulla was, given his munificence, a friend. Clearly, at that time many
men did not understand the purpose of largesse: no one was thought
to be generous with an ulterior purpose; all gifts were accepted
7 as signs of goodwill.* Then the legates revealed to the quaestor
Bocchus' commission. At the same time they asked him to help them
with his favour and advice. In a speech they extolled their troops,
the good faith, the greatness of their king, and spoke of other things
that they believed would be useful or would promote goodwill. Then,
when Sulla promised to do all they asked, after being instructed on
how to speak to Marius and again on how to address the Senate, they
waited there for about forty days.

1   104. After Marius accomplished the purpose of his expedition, he
returned to Cirta. Advised about the arrival of the legates, he summoned them and Sulla as well as L. Bellienus* the praetor in Utica and
everyone anywhere else who was of the senatorial order. In their pres-
2 ence he heard Bocchus' proposal. The legates were given permission to
go to Rome and they asked the consul for a temporary armistice. Sulla
and most of the others agreed; a few wanted a more punitive response.
They, of course, were ignorant of human affairs, how fluid and unstable
3 they are, always turning into their opposite. But the Moors got
what they asked for and three set out to Rome with Cn. Octavius
Ruso* as their leader, the quaestor who had brought the soldiers' pay
to Africa;* the other two returned to the king. Bocchus was delighted
with everything, but especially pleased to hear of Sulla's generosity and
4 support. At Rome, his legates sought pardon for the king's mistakes,
misled as he was by Jugurtha's criminal designs, and they asked for a
treaty of friendship. They received this reply:
5   'It is the custom of the Senate and the Roman people to be always
mindful of kindness and injury. But since Bocchus repents, they

forgive him his derelictions. A treaty and friendship will be granted when he has earned it.'

105. When Bocchus heard this, he asked Marius in a letter to send 1 Sulla to him so that at his discretion they could take up their common concerns. Sulla was sent with an escort of cavalry and Balearic slingers.* Archers came and a Paelignian cohort* in light armour,* 2 which allowed them to march quickly and was as good a defence against the enemy's light weapons as other armour would have been. On the fifth day of their march, Volux, Bocchus' son, suddenly 3 appeared on the open plains with no more than a thousand soldiers. They were moving randomly and were diffusely spread out, and so Sulla and the others thought they were more numerous than they were and became afraid of an attack. Consequently, everyone got 4 ready, tested his armour and weapons, was alert. There was some fear, but greater hope, since they were victors and these were the men they had often conquered. Meanwhile, the cavalry that had been sent 5 ahead to scout out the situation announced that there was no sign of hostilities, as was in fact the case. [**106.**] Volux came forward and 1 called out to the praetor, saying that he had been sent by his father, Bocchus, to meet them and to provide them with protection. Then they joined forces and proceeded without any reason for fear that day and the next.

When they had encamped and it was the evening of the day, sud- 2 denly the Moor, frightened, uncertainty on his face, ran to Sulla, and said that he had learned from his scouts that Jugurtha was not far away. At the same time he asked and urged Sulla to flee with him secretly at night. Sulla rejected the idea with ferocious pride: He did 3 not fear, he said, a Numidian whom he had so often sent into flight; he trusted well enough the virtue of his men; even if certain destruction were at hand, he would rather wait for it than betray the men he was leading; shameful flight would spare a life that was uncertain and perhaps soon destined to die from disease. But warned by the same 4 man to escape during the night, he approved the plan. Immediately he ordered the soldiers to eat dinner in camp and to light as many fires as possible; then, at the first watch, he told them to leave in silence.

All the soldiers were exhausted by the night march. At dawn Sulla 5 was beginning to measure out a campground when the Moorish cavalry brought news that Jugurtha had made camp about two miles in front of them. When our men heard this, they were overcome by 6

an extraordinary fear: they believed that Volux had betrayed them
and that they were trapped by his treachery. There were some who
said he should be physically punished and that with him such a crime
1 must not remain unavenged. [**107.**] Sulla had similar thoughts, but
still he ordered them not to injure the Moor. He urged his men to keep
a brave heart: often in the past, he said, a few good men had fought
successfully against a great multitude; the less cautious they were
about their safety, the safer they would be; and it suited no one to
seek the help of unarmed feet when you had weapons in your hands,
to turn your naked and blind side to the enemy when you are most
2 afraid. Then, he called upon Jupiter the Greatest as witness to the
crime and infidelity of Bocchus and ordered Volux to leave the
3 camp. Volux was in tears; he begged him not to believe it: he had laid
no trap, he said, rather it was Jugurtha's cleverness; of course, he had
4 discovered their path by using spies. Further, he said that Jugurtha
did not have a large force; and, since his hopes and resources depended
upon his own father, he was sure that Jugurtha would not dare to
try anything openly when the son was himself present to witness it.
5 And so he thought that the best plan was to pass openly through
Jugurtha's camp.* He would himself go alone with Sulla, and the
6 Moors could be either sent ahead or left where they were. Given
the situation, this seemed the best plan; and they set out right away.
Their arrival was a complete surprise. Jugurtha was unsure of what
to do and he hesitated. They passed through his camp unharmed.
7 A few days later, they reached their intended destination.
1   **108.** At this time there was with Bocchus a certain Numidian
named Aspar* who spent much time with him as a friend. Jugurtha
had sent him ahead, when he heard that Sulla had been summoned,
to plead his case and to use his cleverness to discover Bocchus' plans.
There was also with him Dabar,* the son of Massugrada, a descendant of Masinissa, but not of equal lineage on his mother's side—her
father was the child of a concubine. Dabar was dear to the Moor and
2 loved by him for his many excellences of character. On many earlier
occasions, Bocchus had found Dabar to be faithful to the Romans and
so he at once sent him to Sulla to announce that he was prepared to
do what the Roman people wanted. He said that Sulla should himself
select the day, place, and time for their discussion, he should not fear
Jugurtha's legate;* he had purposely maintained good relations with
that man so that they could more freely discuss their own common

interests; there was no other way to protect against his treachery. But I find that Bocchus offered both the Romans and the Numidian 3 hope of peace, not for the reasons he alleged but because he had the fidelity of a Carthaginian, and that he often mulled over in his mind whether to hand over Jugurtha to the Romans or Sulla to Jugurtha. Desire turned him against us; fear was persuasive for our cause.

109. And so Sulla replied to Bocchus that he would say a few things 1 openly to Aspar, the rest he would communicate to him in secret with no one else or as few as possible present. He also gave instructions as to what Bocchus should say to him. When they had gathered as he 2 wished, Sulla said that he had been sent by the consul to ask whether Bocchus wanted peace or war. The king followed his instructions and 3 told Sulla to return in ten days; he said that even now nothing was decided but on that day he would respond. Then both separated and 4 went to their own camps. But early in the morning Bocchus secretly summoned Sulla. Only the most trustworthy interpreters were present on both sides; Dabar was also there as mediator, acceptable to both sides for his pious character. Without delay the king began as follows:

110. 'I never thought that I, the greatest king in this land and of all 1 whom I know, would be indebted to a private citizen. Before I knew 2 you, Sulla, I swear by Hercules that I brought help to many who asked it, in some cases I myself took the initiative. I required help 3 from no one. This has been dismantled, a circumstance that others would grieve at, but in which I rejoice. The price of your friendship is that now I stand in need. Let it be. Nothing is more valuable to my heart. And to that end it is possible to test this. Arms, men, money, 4 whatever pleases your heart, take it and use it and never think as long as you live that I have repaid my debt of gratitude to you. It will always be an unpaid debt. And you will never want in vain, as long 5 as I know anything about it. For it is my opinion that it is more disgraceful to fail in generosity than to fail in war.

'But hear a few words about your state, since you have been sent 6 here as its caretaker. I never made war on the Roman people nor did I want it once it came about. But I have protected my borders with arms against armed men. I drop that, since it does not please you. 7 Wage the war you want with Jugurtha. I will not pass beyond the 8 river Muluccha, which was the boundary between me and Micipsa, and I will not allow Jugurtha to pass within. If you shall ask for

anything else that is worthy of me and you, you will not go away with
a refusal.'

1   111. Sulla replied to this, insofar as it concerned him, briefly and
modestly; concerning peace and other common interests he had much
to say. Finally, he made it clear to the king that the Senate and the
Roman people would not be grateful for his promises, since they had
defeated him in war; that he must do something which seemed more
in their interests than in his own. In fact, there was an opportunity at
hand, since he had access to Jugurtha. If he handed over that man to
the Romans, they would be greatly indebted to him; the friendship,
the treaty, the portion of Numidia that he was now seeking would
2 all come to him without asking. At first the king refused: kinship,
marriage, even a treaty interfered; furthermore, he was afraid that
the experience of broken trust would turn his people against him
3 since they liked Jugurtha and hated the Romans. In the end, after
frequent efforts to persuade him, he yielded and promised to do every-
4 thing Sulla wanted. Then they decided on what would seem useful
for the pretend peace they were making, a peace that the Numidian
Jugurtha, exhausted by war, desperately wanted. In this way, the trap
was laid and they departed.

1   112. On the following day the king summoned Aspar, Jugurtha's
legate, and told him that he had learned from Sulla through Dabar
that terms for an end to war were possible: for this reason he should
2 discover his king's opinion. Aspar happily set off to Jugurtha's camp.
Then, receiving complete instruction from Jugurtha, he hurried back
to Bocchus on the eighth day and told him that Jugurtha was happy
to do all that was asked of him, but that he did not trust Marius.
Often in the past a peace treaty with Roman generals had been agreed
3 to in vain. But if Bocchus wanted to take both men's interests into
account and to secure a ratified peace treaty, he should attempt to get
everyone together as if for a discussion of the terms and there to hand
Sulla over to him. When he had such a great man in his power, then
a treaty would be ratified by order of either the Senate or the people.
A noble man, he said, who fell into the power of the enemy not
because of his own indolence but for the sake of the Republic would
not be abandoned.

1   113. For a long time the Moor thought this over and at length
agreed. I have not been able to discover whether his hesitation was
part of a trap or real. But it is generally the case that the desires of

kings are as passionate as they are fickle; often they turn against themselves. After the time and the place were settled, all arrived at 2 the conference as if to discuss peace. Bocchus summoned now Sulla, now Jugurtha's legate; he was kind and made the same promises to both. They were equally pleased and full of good hope.

But on the night that preceded the day determined for the con- 3 ference, it is said that the Moor summoned his friends; then he immediately changed his mind and sent them away. He struggled with himself; his face, his colour, the movement of his body were as variable as his mind, and this of course made clear the secrets of his heart although he himself remained silent. At length he summoned 4 Sulla and laid a trap for the Numidian as suited Sulla's wishes. Then, 5 when the day arrived and he was told that Jugurtha was not far away, he took a few friends and our quaestor, as if to meet him as a mark of honour, and proceeded to a hill that was in full sight of those lying in ambush. The Numidian came to the same place with a large 6 entourage of his people, unarmed as had been agreed. Immediately, the signal was given; he was attacked simultaneously from all sides. Everyone else was slaughtered. Jugurtha was bound and handed over 7 to Sulla, and by him was conveyed to Marius.

114. During the same period our commanders, Q. Caepio and 1 Cn. Manlius,* were defeated by the Gauls.* All of Italy trembled 2 with fear at this. From that time to our times the Romans have held the belief that all else cowered before their manly courage, but the Gauls fought for safety not for glory. But after the war in Numidia 3 was concluded and it was announced that Jugurtha was being brought to Rome in chains, Marius was made consul in his absence and was given the province of Gaul. On 1 January* the consul had a glorious triumph. At that time the hopes and resources of the state were in 4 his hands.

HISTORIES

INTRODUCTION

Sallust's third historiographical project deals with the period between the Jugurthine War and Catiline's conspiracy. Sallust does not, however, begin with Marius' second consulship, the event with which *The Jugurthine War* ends, nor does he make it as far as Catiline. He skips over the Social Wars, during which time Sulla grew in strength and prestige; he passes over Sulla's consulship and his first march on Rome, the first time any Roman general had decided to defeat political opposition with an army; and he overlooks both Cinna's brutal return to Rome with Marius and Sulla's return from Asia, his dictatorship and proscriptions. In other words, he chose not to write of Sulla and Cinna. He had already passed his verdict on Sulla in *The Jugurthine War*: 'Before his victory in the civil war he was the most fortunate of all men, but his good fortune did not exceed his efforts. As for what he did afterwards, I do not know whether one should feel more shame or disgust in talking of it' (*J* 95.4). And so Sallust does not talk of it. Sulla had set aside his dictatorship in 79 and retired from public life. He died early in 78. Sallust's *Histories* begin in 78; he got as far as 67 before he died.

The *Histories* exist today only as fragments: four speeches (Macer, Philippus, Cotta, and Macer), two letters (Pompey and Mithridates), and numerous bits that come from other authors, commentators, and grammarians, each of whom has his own reason for quoting or referring to what Sallust said. I have included the longer fragments here and a few shorter fragments whose content and relevance to Sallust's thought seems clear. The sources for the shorter fragments frequently do not tell us where the word or sentence comes from. As a result, reference or relevance is often uncertain and the sequence of the fragments is itself often the construct of scholars based on probability and guesswork. The notes occasionally refer to short fragments (e.g. at 1.55.14) that did not themselves seem worth translating. Even in dealing with the longer passages, we do not have the full context in which speeches or events are set. As a result, we cannot draw any firm conclusions about the most important aspects of the work: Sallust's understanding either of the broader political relationships between factions or of the inner workings of particular disputes. And without his preface we cannot relate his moral, political, and philosophical view of this history to the trajectory of the events.

The *Histories* begin with the year 78, when Q. Lutatius Catulus and M. Aemilius Lepidus entered upon the consulship. Catulus had been a supporter of Sulla; Lepidus was both a friend of Marius and a man who had benefited from Sulla's brutal proscriptions. The first major fragment is Lepidus' speech to the Roman people, an attack on Sulla and an appeal to the people to reclaim their freedom. Later that year Lepidus would be sent with a consular army to Etruria to deal with men who had been evicted from their land by Sulla's colonists. When Lepidus seemed to be taking their side, he was summoned to Rome; he marched on the city instead. The Senate responded by empowering Catulus and Pompey with their 'final decree'; Sallust records the speech of L. Marcius Philippus who as 'leader of the Senate' proposed the decree. Pompey defeated Lepidus and was rewarded with the command against Sertorius in Spain.

Pompey had already been an important military figure. At the age of 23 he had supported Sulla with three veteran legions when he returned to Italy in 83. Sulla apparently nicknamed him 'The Great', It was a joking reference to his ambitions to become another Alexander the Great. The name would stick with him the rest of his life. His military career would proceed from the command against Sertorius, who was defeated in 73 (when he was assassinated by his own men), to the command against Spartacus in 71 (for whose defeat Pompey appears to have taken more credit than he deserved), to the extraordinary command against the pirates in 67–66 and the command against Mithridates, which he took up in 65. He returned to Rome in 61. The military history of this period is dominated by Pompey, and this is reflected in Sallust's *Histories*. The result of Philippus' speech, the second speech of the surviving *Histories*, was that Pompey was sent against Lepidus. The third speech, by the consul Cotta in 75, refers to the need for funding for the armies in Spain. The fourth major fragment is Pompey's own letter addressing the same need. In the fourth speech, Licinius Macer, tribune of the plebs in 73, declares that Pompey will restore the tribunician rights that Sulla took away. In fact, Pompey and Crassus in their consulship in 70 did just that. And in the letter of Mithridates, probably written in 69, the king is seeking an alliance with Phraates III of Parthia against Rome, which means against Pompey. It is, of course, impossible to tell what thematic role Pompey played in Sallust's narrative. He is mentioned early in the first book and given a character sketch in the second. The fact that he is in some way implicated in so many fragments is suggestive.

Sallust completed four books of his *Histories* and began a fifth. So far as we can tell, they follow the annalistic tradition, covering the events of each year, and do not follow any individual event in a continuous narrative. The following summarizes the content of each of the books, following the reconstruction of McGushin:

Book I: 78–77 BC

Preface and introduction.

Lepidus and his opposition to Sulla.

Sertorius and the early stages of the war against him.

Book II: late 77–early 74 BC

Lepidus' end.

Command against Sertorius transferred to Pompey.

Sertorian War in 76 and 75.

Urban affairs in 76, 75, and early 74.

Pompey's letter.

Book III: 74–72 BC

Urban affairs of 74.

Third Mithridatic War (74–73).

Urban affairs of 73.

  Licinius Macer.

Spartacus (73).

End of Sertorian War (72).

Book IV: 72–68 BC

Urban affairs of 72, 71, 70, 69, 68.

Mithridatic War, 72–68.

  Lucullus' campaigns.

End of Spartacus (71).

Book V: 68–67 BC

Lucullus' final campaigns.

The pirates and the *lex Gabinia* (67).

The fragments are numbered according to the Oxford Classical Text, edited by L. D. Reynolds (who follows B. Maurenbrecher's text (Stuttgart, 1983)). Alternative numbering in parentheses refers to the edition by P. McGushin (Oxford, 1994).

HISTORIES

BOOK I

[Sallust began his *Histories*, as he began his other works, with a preface that reflected on the progress and decline of Rome. He apparently followed this with a more detailed narrative of the events immediately preceding the beginning of his own historical material.]

1. I have composed a military and domestic history of the Roman people during and following the consular year of M. Lepidus and Q. Catulus.*

7 (8). Among us the first disputes arose from a vice of human nature* which, restless and indomitable, is always engaging in contests over liberty or glory or domination.*

11 (9). In its exercise of power the Roman state was at its height in the consulship of Servius Sulpicius and Marcus Marcellus:* all Gaul this side of the Rhine* and between the Mediterranean and the Ocean, with the exception of inaccessible swamps, had been subjugated. On the other hand, the highest moral standards and the greatest harmony were displayed between the second and the last Punic war* . . . [(10).] But it was after the destruction of Carthage* that discord and greed and ambition and the other evils that usually arise during prosperity increased to their greatest extent. For the injustices of the stronger and the secessions of the plebs* from the fathers in reaction to these injustices and other domestic disputes were already there from the beginning; and, after the expulsion of the kings,* a fair and restrained exercise of law lasted only until fear of Tarquin* and a serious war from Etruria was put aside. Then the fathers exercised over the plebs a power fit for slaves: deciding in regal manner about life and flogging; expelling them from their fields; acting alone with sovereign power; the rest disenfranchised. The plebs, taking up the burden of taxes and military service in continual wars, were crushed by these cruelties and especially by debt. They armed themselves and occupied the Mons Sacer and the

Aventine; it was then that they acquired for themselves tribunes of the plebs* and other rights. On both sides the Second Punic War* was the end of discord and struggle.

12. After fear of Carthage had been removed, and there was space to exercise enmity, many mob actions, acts of sedition, and in the end civil wars arose, while the few who had power, and to whose influence most had yielded, aspired to domination under the honourable pretexts of 'the Senate' or 'the people', and men were called* good and bad citizens not for their services to the Republic—all had been equally corrupted—but, as each was one of the wealthiest or more powerful from his injustices, so he was regarded as good because he defended the status quo.

13 (14). The honour of all parties had been corrupted into something of exchange value.*

16 (13). And after that time the moral character of our ancestors collapsed, not gradually as before, but like a rushing torrent. The young men were so corrupted by luxury and greed that it could be rightly said that men had been born who could neither hold on to their family wealth themselves nor allow others to.

[After a preface on Roman history and a review of events in the preceding decades, the *Histories* begin their narrative with the year 78 and the consul, Lepidus, agitating against Sulla's settlement. Although he had joined Sulla during Sulla's civil war and had enriched himself during the proscriptions, he opposed Sulla. He was elected with Pompey's support and against Sulla's wishes. Sulla had resigned his dictatorship three years earlier and may already have been dead. The reason for the speech is not clear without its narrative context, and without any clear indication of when in 78 it was delivered. Still, it is clear that Sallust uses this speech to introduce his theme, the moral and political degeneration of the Republic. The 'Domination of Sulla' (*dominatio* = exercising the power of a master) has reduced the sovereignty of the Roman people to a form of slavery (*servitium*). The other side of the conflict is represented by the speech of L. Marcius Philippus (below, 1.77).]

47. On both sides they were competing with great violence about the prefecture of the city* as if it were about the possession of the Republic.

55 (48). Lepidus,* consul, to the Roman people.

'Your mercy and morality, citizens, which has made you powerful 1 and famous throughout the world, causes me the greatest fear when I think of L. Sulla's tyranny. I am afraid that you will not believe others are capable of what you yourselves consider unspeakable, and so you will be outwitted—especially since that man puts all his hopes in crime and treachery and thinks that he can only be safe if he is more wicked and more detestable than your worst fears; thus, misery removes the concern for liberty from the captive—alternatively, I am afraid that, if you do see what is coming, you will spend your time avoiding danger, not seeking vengeance.

'Consider his followers: men having the greatest names, with the 2 best ancestral examples, I am utterly amazed that they offer their own slavery as the price for enslaving you and prefer a life without equity for both sides to a free life with the best principles of justice. The 3 glorious descendants of the Bruti* and the Aemilii* and the Lutatii,* men born to destroy what the manly courage of their own ancestors created! For what else did we defend against Pyrrhus,* Hannibal,* 4 and Philip and Antiochus,* if not liberty and each man's own home and the right not to obey anyone but the law? But all this is held by 5 this perverted Romulus* as if he had stolen them from foreigners.* He is not satisfied by the slaughter of so many armies and consuls* and other leaders* whom the fortunes of war have destroyed; but he grows more cruel at the very time when success generally turns most men from wrath toward compassion. In fact, he alone of all within 6 the memory of humankind has created punishments for those who are yet to be born, for whom injustice is certain before life is certain,* and the most wicked thing is that the monstrosity of his crimes has kept him safe, while fear of worse slavery frightens you from winning back your freedom.

'You must act and resist, citizens; your spoils must not be in the 7 power of those men. You must not delay or seek help from prayers; unless you happen to expect that Sulla is now bored with or ashamed

of his tyranny and that to his own greater danger he will relinquish
8 what he criminally seized. But he has gone so far that he thinks nothing glorious except safety, and that everything is honourable that
9 bolsters his tyranny. And so there no longer exists that life of peace
and leisure with freedom,* things that many good men were trying
10 to attain in place of hard work with honours, they no longer exist; at
this time one must be a slave or give the orders; one must be afraid
11 or make others afraid, citizens. What else is there? What aspect of
humanity or of divinity survives unpolluted? The Roman people, just
recently the rulers of the world, have been stripped of empire, glory,
law;* incapable of action and despised, they do not even have a slave's
12 rations* left to them. Your grant of citizenship* to a great force of
allies and Latins in return for many extraordinary deeds is forbidden by one man, and the ancestral homes of the innocent plebs have
been occupied by a few of his followers:* it is their reward for their
13 crimes. The laws, the courts, the treasury, provinces, and kings are
in the hands of one man; even the power over the life and death of
14 citizens. At the same time you have seen human sacrifices and tombs
15 stained with civil blood.* Is there anything left for manly men to do
but undo injustice or to die with manly courage? After all nature has
decreed a single end for all, even those protected by plates of iron,
and no one waits for the last necessity while daring nothing, unless
he has a woman's heart.
16   'Now, Sulla says* that I, who complain about the rewards of revolution, am "seditious"; and that I, who demand back the laws of
17 peace, am a "warmonger". But, of course he says this, since under
tyranny you cannot be safe and fully protected unless Vettius Picens*
and the secretary Cornelius* squander the goods that others have
well earned, unless every one of you approves of the proscription of
innocent men for their wealth, the torture of distinguished men, the
devastation of the city by flight or slaughter, the goods of wretched
18 citizens sold like Cimbrian booty* or given away as gifts. But then
he charges me with possessing the property of the proscribed. And
this in fact is the very greatest of that man's crimes: that neither
I nor anyone else was at all safe if we did the right thing. And yet
the things I purchased at that time out of fear, price legally paid,
I nevertheless restore to their owners, nor is it my plan to allow any
19 booty to be taken from citizens. Let those things that we endured
when we contracted madness be enough: Roman armies grappling

with each other in hand-to-hand combat and weapons turned away from the enemy against ourselves. Let there be an end to crimes and outrages, all of them; things which Sulla still does not regret, so much so that he counts them among his acts of glory and, if allowed, would have done them even more eagerly.

'I no longer have qualms about your opinion of him, but I do about 20 your degree of daring. I am afraid that you will be captured while you are each waiting for a different leader, captured not by his resources, which are worthless and corrupted, but by your own lack of courage, which allows plunder and allows him to seem as "Fortunate"* as he dares to be. For who wants what he wants, except his criminal 21 cronies? Who doesn't want everything changed except the victory?* The soldiers, of course, by whose blood Tarula and Scirtus,* most wicked slaves, became wealthy? Or those who lost to Fufidius* in the elections, a shameless working girl,* the dishonour of every honour? And so the victorious army gives me the greatest confidence, an army 22 which got from its wounds and labours nothing but a tyrant, unless 23 they actually marched out to overthrow by arms the tribunician powers which had been established by their own ancestors and to twist from their own hands their legal rights and law courts. An extraordinary exchange to be sure: they are banished to swamps and forests, they know that indignity and hatred is theirs, the rewards are in the hands of a few.

'Why then does he march about with such a following and such 24 arrogance? Because success is a wonderful cloak for vice—but, when it all collapses, fear turns to contempt—unless it is to give the appearance of "peace and harmony",* the names he gives to his crimes and slaughter. He claims that we cannot otherwise have a Republic and an end to war unless the plebs remain driven from their fields—a most cruel civil plunder—unless the law and jurisdiction in all matters, things that were the possession of the Roman people, are in his hands. But if you think this is peace and order, then support the complete 25 chaos and destruction of the state, approve the laws he has imposed, accept peace and slavery, and give posterity a lesson in how to ruin the Republic and pay for it with their own blood.

'As for me, although attaining this high command means meeting 26 the demands of my ancestors' name, of dignity and of safety, still it was not my plan to become privately wealthy; rather, I preferred a dangerous freedom to a peaceful slavery. And, if you approve 27

of this, citizens, lend a hand and with the aid of the gods follow
M. Aemilius, the consul, your leader and champion for recovering
your freedom.'

77 (67). Philippus* to the Senate.

[This speech may seem to be paired with that of Lepidus, giving
both sides of an issue, in the manner of Thucydidean speeches, a
manner which Sallust adopts in *Catiline's Conspiracy* when he gives
paired speeches to Caesar and Cato. There is, however, an important difference: they were not formally paired in the *Histories*, since
Lepidus attacks Sulla at the beginning of his consulship, while
Philippus attacks Lepidus after that consulship. Philippus is arguing
that the Senate's 'final decree' should be declared against Lepidus
because of his recent actions.]

1   'My greatest wish, conscript fathers, would be that the Republic enjoy peace or that it be defended by those most ready and able
in times of danger, and, finally, that twisted plans do harm to their
advisers. But it doesn't work that way: in times of rebellion everything is thrown into turmoil and this is done by those who ought
rather to prevent it. In the end, it is the good and wise who must carry
2   out the decrees of the worst and most stupid. For war and weapons,
though they are hateful to you, still, because they please Lepidus,
must be taken up. Unless, perhaps,* it is someone's policy to offer
peace and endure war.
3   'O you blessed gods, who still protect this city while we have given
up caring! M. Aemilius, the worst of all the criminals—no one can
determine whether he is more vicious or more cowardly—has an
army for the destruction of freedom!* He was once despicable, but
now he's made himself fearful. You mutter and withdraw; with words
and the incantations* of priests you hope for peace rather than protect
it. And you don't understand that your spineless decrees diminish
4   your dignity and diminish his fear. And he's justified: from plunder, he got the consulship;* from rebellion, he got a command with
an army.* What would he have got for patriotic actions, when you
5   reward his crimes so well? But, of course, those who decreed legates,*
peace, harmony, and so on up to the end, they have his gratitude.
Not really. They are despised and thought unworthy to govern, and

they are considered no more than his plunder, because the fear that made them seek peace lost them the peace they had.

'For my part, at the beginning when I saw Etruria conspiring, the 6 proscribed recalled,* the state cut to shreds by bribery, I thought there was no time to hesitate and with a few others I followed Catulus' plans. But there were those who kept praising the good deeds of the Aemilian family,* and claiming that forgiveness had made the Republic great. They were saying that Lepidus had taken no steps at the very time when he had seized a private army to destroy liberty.* By seeking assets or protection for themselves, they corrupted public policy.

'But at that time Lepidus was just a thief* with some drudges 7 and a few thugs whose life no one would exchange for a day's wage; now he is a proconsul* with a military command, one given by you, not purchased by him, with legates who still obey him according to the law; and the most corrupt men of all the orders* flock to him; men blazing with poverty and passions, agitated by their guilty consciences, they find repose in rebellion, and in peace they find turmoil. These men sow revolt after revolt, war upon war. Once they followed Saturninus,* then Sulpicius,* afterwards Marius* and Damasippus.* Now they follow Lepidus. Moreover, Etruria and all the other relics 8 of war are roused; Spain is stirred to arms;* Mithridates* at the borders* of the tax-paying provinces that still sustain us, is looking for an opportunity for war. Nothing is missing for the destruction of our empire except the right leader. And so I pray and beg you, conscript 9 fathers, pay attention; do not allow this criminal licence to spread like an infectious plague to those who are healthy. For when rewards follow the wicked, no one finds it easy to be gratuitously good.

'Or are you waiting for him to bring up his army and invade the city 10 with sword and fire? In his current posture of agitation he is much closer to invasion than peace and harmony* are to his civil arms, arms which he has taken up in defiance of all things human and divine, not to remedy injuries to himself or to those whom he pretends to represent, but to destroy our laws and freedom. For he is troubled and 11 torn by the cravings of his soul and his fear of harm; he has no plan, restless he tries now this, now that; he fears peace, hates war; there must be an end to luxury and licence, he sees that, but meanwhile he abuses your lack of courage. And I myself do not have enough wisdom 12 to work out if I should call this fear or laziness or madness, when it seems that each of you pray that these evils—which threaten like thunderbolts—not touch you, but you don't even try to stop them.

13 'And so I ask you to consider how the natural order has been perverted. In the past, threats to the state were created secretly, aid was brought openly: in this way, good men easily surpassed the wicked. Now, peace and harmony is openly disrupted, defended secretly. The men who are pleased by this are in arms, you are afraid.

14 What are you waiting for, unless you are shamed or disgusted by doing the right thing? Or have Lepidus' pronouncements influenced you? He says he is pleased to render to each his own and he holds on to the property of others;* he wants to rescind the laws established by war when he himself uses armed coercion, he wants to confirm the citizenship of those he denies have lost it, to restore for the sake of harmony the tribunician power by which all our civil discord* has been enkindled.

15 'O you, the most traitorous and shameless of all, do you care about the poverty and grief of the citizens? You who have nothing at home except what you got by violence or injustice. You are asking for a second consulship* as if you had returned the first;* you seek harmony through a war which disrupts the harmony we had acquired; you are a traitor to us, treacherous to your own men; the enemy of all good citizens. Are you not ashamed before the men and gods whom

16 you have violated by oaths or perjury?* But since you are such as you are, don't change your mind, hold on to your weapons, I urge you, and do not, by postponing your revolt, keep yourself ill at ease, or keep us anxious. Neither the provinces nor the laws nor the household gods accept you as a citizen. Complete your plans, so that you may swiftly get what you deserve.

17 'But you, conscript fathers, how long will we delay* and allow the Republic to be endangered and how long will you attack weapons with words? Troops have been levied against you, money has been extorted publicly and privately, garrisons have been moved out and put in place: when they want, they obey the law; and you in the meantime are finding legates and writing decrees. By the gods, since he knows that fear sustains him *more than* good and fair action, the more

18 eagerly you seek peace, the more cruelly the war will be fought. For whoever says that he hates turmoil and the slaughter of citizens and for this reason keeps you unarmed while Lepidus is armed, he has decided that you must suffer what the conquered must endure when

you could be inflicting those very things. He persuades you to make peace with that man, persuades that man to make war on you. If this 19 pleases you, if your spirit is so sunk in torpor that you have forgotten the crimes of Cinna,* whose return to the city destroyed the glory of this order, if you are nevertheless about to hand over yourselves, your wives and children to Lepidus, what need is there for decrees, for the help of Catulus? Surely the care of this man and the other good 20 men for the Republic is a meaningless gesture. Do what you want. Secure for yourself the protection of Cethegus* and other protections from the traitors who want to renew the rape and arson and again arm themselves against our household gods. But if you find freedom and truth pleasing, make decisions worthy of your name and encourage bravery in men of character. A new army is at hand, in addition 21 there are colonies of military veterans, all the nobility, the best leaders: Fortune follows the better men. Soon those dangers which our lack of courage has allowed to gather will dissipate.

'And so, since M. Lepidus has collected an army for his private 22 purposes and leads it toward the city in defiance of the authority of this order and in complicity with the worst enemies of the state, it is my opinion that Ap. Claudius as *interrex** together with Q. Catulus, the proconsul, and others who have military commands should come to the defence of the city and make sure that the Republic is not damaged in any way.'*

[Sertorius, a Sabine general, had supported Cinna against Sulla. He retired to Spain when Sulla returned from the east and there held an army for six years (83–77). Both Pompey and Metellus were sent to regain control of Spain, but Sertorius won significant victories against them. He was not defeated, but assassinated by one of his own men.]

88. As military tribune under the general T. Didius,* he served with great distinction; and he was very useful during the Marsic War.* Many accomplishments under his leadership have not been celebrated, first because he was not an aristocrat, then because writers were envious. While he lived, he displayed a certain number of these accomplishments on the front of his body in scars and an empty eye socket. But he was not troubled by these; in fact, he used to take the greatest delight in the disfigurements of his body because the rest was retained to his greater glory.

BOOK II

[The events of late 77–early 74.]

[We do not have a full portrait of Pompey from Sallust's *Histories*, but fragments 16–19 suggest something of Sallust's perspective.]

16 (17). [Lenaeus, Pompey's freedman, so loved him that he ripped into Sallust with a very bitter satire because Sallust had written of Pompey's] excellent looks, shameless character.

17 (18). . . . moderate in all else, except domination.*

19 (20). . . . he used to compete in jumping with the agile, in running with the swift, in using a crowbar with the muscular.*

(19). And yet beginning in his youth he* had insulted many good men . . .

47 (44). C. Aurelius Cotta,* consul in 75, to the Roman people.

[A shortage of corn created a severe backlash against the consuls in 75. The causes probably included pirates, neglect, and delayed deliveries. Here Cotta attempts to exonerate himself and to appeal to the people's patriotism.]

A few days later with a change of clothing Cotta appeared in mourning* because he had become estranged from the plebs when he desired their goodwill. He spoke in an assembly of the people like this:

1   'Citizens, I have known many dangers at home and on military service; there have been many hardships. Some of these I endured, others I removed with the aid of the gods and by my own mettle. In all of these circumstances there was never any lack of courage in the midst of trouble or of energy for my decisions. Failure and success

2   change my resources, not my character. But in these present miseries it's not like that: everything including fortune has deserted me. Furthermore, old age,* in itself a problem, doubles my concern: with my life almost over I am wretched and I cannot even hope for an

honourable death. For if I am your parricide,* if I, though given a 3
second birth,* place no value on my household gods and my fatherland and its highest office, then what torture would be satisfactory
while I lived or what punishment after I'm dead? Surely my crime has
exceeded all the punishments they say take place in the underworld.

'Since my earliest adolescence, both as a private citizen and when 4
holding office, I have acted in the public eye. Those who wanted my
speech, my ideas, my money, have had them, and I have not exercised a clever eloquence or used my talents for doing evil. Though
I hungered most for private friendships, I have made the greatest
enemies on behalf of the Republic. When those enemies defeated
me and the country at the same time, when I needed the help of
others and expected more troubles, you, citizens, gave me back again*
my fatherland and my household gods along with extraordinary
distinction. In return for these kindnesses I could scarcely seem 5
grateful enough if I gave my life for each of you individually. But
I cannot do that, since life and death are laws of nature; to live without dishonour among my citizens with fame and fortune intact, this
can be given and received as a gift.

'You have made us your consuls, citizens, at a time when the 6
Republic is struggling at home and in war. Our generals in Spain*
require money, soldiers, arms, and grain; and circumstances compel
this since the defection of allies* and the flight of Sertorius through
the mountains* makes it impossible to engage in a battle or to gather
supplies. Armies in Asia and Cilicia* are maintained against the 7
enormous resources of Mithridates;* Macedonia* is full of enemies,
as are the shores of Italy and the provinces,* while the tributary taxes
are small and uncertain due to the war and can only sustain part of
the expenses. And so the fleet we sail with, that used to protect commerce, is smaller than before. If our treachery or apathy has brought 8
this about, do as your anger urges you and inflict punishment; but if
it is our common fortune that has been too harsh, why are you trying
to do what is unworthy of yourselves or us or the Republic?

'If I can diminish any of your problems with my death, I don't 9
object, since my age is closer to death; nor given the nature of the
body could I anytime soon bring my life to a more honourable end
than on behalf of your safety. Here I am, C. Cotta, the consul. I am 10
doing what our ancestors have often done in bitter wars: I am vowing
and dedicating my life to the Republic.* But look around for the man 11

to whom you will next give the Republic. No patriotic man will want such an honour, when either he must give an explanation for acts of fortune and the sea, and for a war that others started, or he must die
12 an ugly death. Only keep in mind that I was not slaughtered for criminal activity or greed, but willingly gave my life as a gift in return for
13 your very great kindnesses. For your own sake, citizens, and for the glory of our ancestors, endure hardships and consider what is best for
14 the Republic. A great empire entails many cares, many great labours, and you cannot refuse them and ask for the prosperity of peace at a time when all the provinces and kingdoms, the seas and the lands, are savage or exhausted by wars.'

[The following passage comes almost entirely from Macrobius' *Saturnalia*. It describes Metellus' conduct after the campaigning season of 74 in the war against Sertorius. Where other sources preserve bits of this description, they sometimes offer different readings. The passage is included here as an example of the luxury that, according to Sallust, characterized much of Roman culture at the time.]

70 (59). But Metellus returned to Further Spain after a year. He was viewed with great glory by all, they ran together from every direction, male and female sex, through the streets and homes. The quaestor, C. Urbinus, and others who understood his desires invited him to a meal. They showed a concern for him that exceeded the Roman norm, and even that of mortal men. The house was adorned with tapestries and decorations; stages were constructed for the display of actors; at the same time the ground was strewn with saffron and other things as if it were a celebrated temple. In addition, when he was sitting, an image of the goddess Victory, let down in a sling* and accompanied by the manufactured sound of thunder, used to place a crown on his head; when he was arriving, he was worshipped like a god with incense. While reclining at a meal, he usually wore an embroidered toga* for his cloak. The banquet was truly the most exquisite, with many types of bird and beast previously unknown not only from throughout the province but from Mauretania across the sea. He detracted a bit from his glory by these actions, especially among the older generation and the pious men who thought that these things were arrogant, serious, and unworthy of a Roman.

98 (82). Pompey's letter to the Senate.

[Pompey was sent to Spain in 77 to help Metellus in the war against Sertorius. This letter is from the narrative of the year 75. Sertorius, after his defeat at Segontia on the river Salo, dispersed his men with orders to meet him at a stronghold in the mountains, where he fortified the walls as if to prepare for a siege. Pompey and Metellus followed him and, assuming he would hole up in this town, invested it. This allowed Sertorius and his troops to escape to Celtiberia, where the rest of the Sertorian War took place. Sertorius used guerrilla tactics to harass the Roman armies on land and to interrupt or destroy their supplies. He used similar tactics by sea. By the end of 75 Pompey needed reinforcement, supplies, and funds for military pay.]

'If it had been to make war against you and the fatherland and our 1 household gods that I undertook so many dangers and troubles in the past when, from the time I was a young man, armies under my command routed the enemy and guaranteed your safety, then you could have done nothing worse against me in my absence than what you are now doing, conscript fathers. Despite my age, you have hurled me into a most savage war and to the extent that you were able you have destroyed me and a most deserving army by starvation, the most miserable of all deaths. Was this what the Roman people expected 2 when they sent their children off to war? Is this the reward for wounds and blood so often spilled for the Republic? I am exhausted with writing letters and sending legates; I have used up all my personal resources and hopes; while in the meantime you have granted barely one year's expenses during this three-year period. By the immortal 3 gods, do you believe that I can fulfil the function of a treasury or do you think it possible to keep an army without food or pay?

'For my part, I acknowledge that I set out for this war with more 4 enthusiasm than strategy,* for after I received from you what was only a titular command,* within forty days* I gathered an army, and I forced the enemy who was already at the throat of Italy from the Alps into Spain. Through these mountains I opened a path which was different from Hannibal's path,* and one better suited to us. I recovered Gaul,* 5 the Pyrenees, Lacetania, the Indigetes,* and withstood the first attack of the victorious Sertorius* though my soldiers were new* and far fewer. I placed my winter camps in the midst of a most savage enemy,

6 not in the towns and not pursuing popularity.* Why should I enumer-
   ate the battles and winter expeditions, the towns that were razed or
   captured, when actions mean more than words? The capture of enemy
   camps at Sucro,* the battle at the river Turia,* the destruction of
   C. Herennius,* leader of the enemy, with the city of Valentia and with
   his army, these things are well known to you. And in return for them,
   O grateful senators, you have given me poverty and starvation.

7   'And so the terms are the same for my army and the enemy's army:
8 neither gets paid by Rome; either could win and enter Italy. But
   I warn you of this and ask you to take heed and not to force me to
9 take care of necessities in private. Nearer Spain, which is not held by
   the enemy, has been devastated to the point of extermination by us
   or by Sertorius, except for the coastal cities. Besides, the latter are an
   expense and burden to us. Last year Gaul supplied Metellus' army*
   with pay and food and now she scarcely keeps herself alive after a
   crop failure. I have exhausted not only my own resources but even
10 my credit. You are what is left. If you do not help, unwillingly but
   as I predict, my army will cross from here into Italy and with it will
   come the entire Spanish war.'

   This letter was read in the Senate at the beginning of the following year.* The consuls* distributed among themselves the provinces
   decreed by the Senate: Cotta got Cisalpine Gaul, Octavius Cilicia.
   Then the consuls for the next year, L. Lucullus and M. Cotta, deeply
   disturbed by the letters and the messages from Pompey, did all they
   could to provide money and supplies. They did so both because the
   matter was very important and because there would be no praise and
   no dignity in an army being brought back to Italy. The aristocracy
   was especially helpful. Most of them were already giving tongue to
   their ferocious spirit and following words with actions.

BOOK III

[The events of 74–72.]

48 (34). C. Licinius Macer,* tribune of the plebs for 73, to the plebs.

[The right of the plebs to protection by their tribunes had been
damaged by Sulla's laws. Every year from 76 to 70 the restoration of

tribunician rights figured in urban politics. In 70 the consuls Pompey and Crassus restored the powers of the tribunate. C. Licinius Macer was an orator of some ability and also a historian who appears to have given some prominence to the struggle between the orders.]

'If you, citizens, could not assess the difference between the rule 1 of law that you have inherited from your ancestors and this slavery that Sulla has created, I would have to expound at length and explain to you how often and for what injustices the plebs took up arms and seceded* from the patricians and how they created the tribunes of the plebs as the defenders of all their rights. But now it is left for me 2 only to urge you on and be first to take the path which, in my opinion, must be taken to recover your freedom.* But it does not escape me 3 what great resources the aristocracy has while I, alone, powerless, and with only the empty appearance of a magistracy,* am setting out to drive them from despotism, and how much more safely a faction of malicious men can act than innocent men acting alone.* But in addi- 4 tion to the good hope that I have, a hope that quiets my fear, I have decided that the hardships of a struggle for freedom are for a brave man preferable to not struggling at all.

'And yet all the others who have been elected to protect your rights 5 have been led by prestige or hope or rewards to turn their whole power and authority against you. They think it is better to be paid for dereliction of duty than to do the right thing without payment. And so all have now yielded to the tyranny of the few, men who have 6 taken control of the treasury, the army, kingdoms, and provinces in the name of military necessity; they have plundered you and made a stronghold of the spoils. In the meantime you hand yourselves over like cattle, a herd of men to be owned and enjoyed by individual mas- ters, stripped of all that your ancestors left you, except that through the ballot now you yourselves choose your own masters, as before you chose your defenders. And so all have moved to their side; but, if you 7 will reclaim what is yours, soon most will move towards you. This is because few men have the courage to defend what they want; the rest are just the possessions of the more powerful.

'Or do you wonder if something can hinder you when you strive 8 with one mind, you whom they feared while you were spineless and faint-hearted? Perhaps you think that Cotta,* a consul from the heart of their faction, restored certain tribunician rights for some reason other than fear? In fact, although you muttered and L. Sicinius was silenced* when he dared to be the first to speak about tribunician power, nevertheless they became afraid of your angry response before you grew tired of their injustice.

9   'And I cannot stop wondering at your attitude, citizens. You understood that your hopes had been dashed. When Sulla died, the man who imposed this criminal servitude, you began to believe your troubles were over. Along comes Catulus,* a man much more
10 savage. A revolt intervened* when Brutus and Mamercus* were consuls. Then, C. Curio* was your master all the way to the death of the
11 innocent tribune. You saw what animosity Lucullus* directed at L. Quintius* last year. What turmoil is just now stirred up against me! All this was, of course, done to no purpose, if they were trying to end their tyranny before you ended your slavery. Especially since the struggle on both sides during this civil discord, despite other things
12 being said, was about who would be your masters. And so there were other temporary flare-ups caused by privilege, hatred, greed: but only one thing has remained as the object of both sides,* and it has been stolen from you for the future: the tribunician power, a weapon
13 created by your ancestors to protect your freedom. I warn you of this and I beg you not to change the name of things to suit your cowardice, not to call slavery "tranquillity"—a thing for which, if disgrace overcomes the true and noble, there are now no terms of enjoyment. There could have been, if you had acquiesced. But now they are wary and, if you are not victorious, they will bind you more tightly. The more severe the injustice, the safer it is.
14   ' "What, then, do you advise?" some one of you might interrupt. First of all, cease what has become your habit: having a restless tongue, a listless heart, thinking of freedom only when there is an assembly.
15 Next, I do not encourage you to those manly acts* by which your ancestors created the tribunes of the plebs at one point, a patrician magistracy,* elections free of patrician sanction. But since all power is in your hands, citizens, and since the orders that you now endure for others you surely could carry out or not carry out for yourselves, are you waiting for the advice of Jupiter or some other god?
16 The great military commands of the consuls and the decrees of the Senate: you ratify them by following them, citizens, and of your own accord you hurry to increase and aid their unrestrained licence against
17 your interests. But I don't urge you to avenge the wrongs you have

suffered; rather, you should desire a reprieve. Not wanting civil
discord, as they charge, but an end to civil discord, I am seeking
restitution according to the law of nations.* And if they hold back
tenaciously, I do not advise rebellion or secession, but only that you
stop offering your blood. Let them hold and manage in their own way 18
their military commands; let them seek triumphs, and pursue Mithridates, and Sertorius and the rest of the exiles with the help of their
ancestral portraits.* You get no part of the profit, so abandon the
danger and the work. Unless, of course, you think that your services 19
have been paid for by that sudden grain law,* the one in which they
estimated your freedom at five pecks of corn each; I think that's just
about what you get to eat in prison. The reason they do this is that,
just as that meagre supply in prison keeps off death, while strength
deteriorates, so their meagre contribution does not ease any family
worries, while it frustrates the lazy with the tiniest of hopes. But no 20
matter how generous their contribution, it is the price of slavery, and
what sort of idiocy is deceived by it and is willing to be grateful for
getting one's own property when it was stolen? You had better beware 21
of their treachery. They cannot prevail against all of you in any other
way, and they won't try. For this reason they are offering palliatives
and putting you off until Pompey arrives, the very man whom they
carried on their necks* when they were afraid of him;* but now, when
they don't fear him, they tear to pieces. They are pretending to be 22
the avengers of freedom, but they are still not ashamed that, many
as they are, they neither dare to right a wrong nor have the ability to
defend the law without the help of this one man. I think I have seen 23
quite enough of Pompey, a young man of great accomplishments, to
know that he prefers to be a leader with your willing support than
to be their ally in tyranny, and that he will move to restore tribunician power.* But, Romans, previously it was the case that individual 24
citizens found protection in the community, not the whole in a single
person. And no single mortal was able to grant or to take away such
protection.

'And so, enough of words. Ignorance doesn't hamper things, 25
rather some sort of torpor has possessed you, and so you are moved 26
neither by glorious action nor by shameful action; you have traded
everything for this present stupor. You think it the bounty of liberty,
because, of course, they do not lash your backs* and you may go here
and there; the generous gifts of your wealthy masters. And yet the 27

country people don't have the same liberties, but they are slaughtered in the political rivalries of the powerful, and they are sent as a gift to
28 the magistrates in the provinces. And so all the fighting and all the victories are for a few men. The plebs, whatever happens, are treated like conquered people and this will get worse, as long as the few are more eager to hold on to their tyranny than you are to regain your freedom.'

BOOK IV

[The events of 72–68.]

[Sallust's narrative begins with the urban affairs of 72 and the defeat of Spartacus (71). It then includes the urban affairs of 71 and 70, the year of Pompey's and Crassus' consulship, Lucullus' command against Mithridates, and the urban affairs of 69 and 68. There were three Mithridatic wars. In the first, 88–84, Sulla defeated Mithridates' general Archelaus and negotiated the peace of Dardanus (85). He drove Mithridates out of Greece, but returned to Italy to deal with Marius and Cinna before a lasting peace could be enforced. In the second, 83–81, Mithridates reorganized his troops and opposed the Roman annexation of Bithynia. The war began when Murena entered Cappadocia in 83/2 and ended with the siege of Sinope. Murena was recalled to Rome and Aulus Gabinius restored the terms of the peace of Dardanus. The Third Mithridatic War (75–65) began when Mithridates attempted to take advantage of the war against Sertorius. Lucullus was sent to Pontus and was successful in several small engagements. He finally defeated Mithridates at the battle of Cabera (72). He then attacked Mithridates' ally, Tigranes II, and defeated him on 6 October 69 at Tigranocerta. But heavy losses on the Roman side led to several mutinies and Lucullus was not able to follow up his victory. Eventually Pompey was sent (66) to bring the war to an end, which he did.]

69 (67). Letter of Mithridates.

[The letter of Mithridates VI of Pontus (132–63) is dated to the period 69–67. Mithridates is trying to persuade King Arsaces of

Parthia to join his cause after Tigranes II's defeat near Tigranocerta.
Tigranes II has entrusted Mithridates with a new army and they are
trying to create a coalition that will drive the Romans from the east.

King Mithridates sends greetings to King Arsaces.* All who are 1
asked at a time of prosperity to form a war-alliance ought to consider
whether it is possible at that time to maintain peace, and, second,
whether what is being asked is consistent with duty,* possible without danger, glorious, or dishonourable. I would not dare to seek such 2
an alliance from you, and I would not hope to add my misfortunes to
your good fortune, if it was possible for you to enjoy a lasting peace, if
the enemy were not vulnerable and utterly immoral, if your defeat of
the Romans would not bring extraordinary fame. There are apparent 3
reasons to hesitate: your anger at Tigranes in the recent war* and my
less than successful position.* But if you are willing to come to a true
understanding of them, they offer special encouragement. Tigranes 4
is under obligation to accept whatever kind of alliance you want.
As for me, Fortune may have diminished my resources but she has
given me the experience to offer good advice and something else that
successful men should desire: my reduced power provides an example for how to organize your affairs more faultlessly.

The Romans have had a single enduring reason for making war 5
with all other nations, peoples, kings: a profound craving for power
and wealth.* Because of this they first undertook a war with the king
of Macedonia, Philip,* though they had pretended to be allies as long
as they were under pressure from Carthage.* When Antiochus* came 6
to his help, they cleverly diverted him by conceding Asia; and soon,
when Philip's power was broken,* Antiochus was stripped* of all the
land this side of the Taurus along with ten thousand talents. Then, 7
after many battles with varying outcomes, Philip's son, Perseus,*
was brought under Roman protection in front of the gods of Samothrace. But because they had agreed by treaty not to kill him, those
clever men, inventors of new forms of treachery, caused his death
from lack of sleep.* Eumenes,* whose friendship they so ostenta- 8
tiously display, they first betrayed him to Antiochus* in exchange
for peace; afterwards, having made him the custodian of captured
fields, with expenses and insults they turned him from king into the
most wretched of slaves, and using a fake and impious will* they led
his son, Aristonicus,* in triumph like an enemy because he had tried

to regain his father's kingdom. These very men laid siege to Asia.

9 Finally, when Nicomedes* died, they ripped Bithynia to bits, despite the fact that he clearly had a son by Nysa, a woman he had called queen.

10 So, why should I mention myself? I was separated on all sides from their empire by kingdoms and tetrarchies, but it was said that I was wealthy, would not be a slave. For that reason they used Nicomedes* to provoke me to war. I was not ignorant of their criminal actions and had already warned the Cretans about what would happen. They were the only free people at that time. I also told King Ptolemy.*

11 But I avenged the wrongs and drove Nicomedes from Bithynia.* I recovered Asia, the spoils of war taken from King Antiochus, and

12 I freed Greece from a harsh slavery.* The lowest of slaves, Archelaus,* impeded my progress and betrayed my army. And those who did not take up arms out of cowardice or from some twisted scheme to be saved by my efforts now pay the most bitter penalties: Ptolemy* postpones war by making daily payments; the Cretans have already been attacked once and will only find an end of war when they are

13 destroyed.* As for me, I understood that battle was postponed because of their internal problems,* that peace was not offered, and I began to fight again.* This despite the fact that Tigranes refused to help (too late, he now agrees with what I said), you were far away, and everyone else was under Roman power. On land, I routed Marcus Cotta, the Roman leader, at Calchedo; on the sea I stripped

14 him of a lovely fleet.* At Cyzicus* with a great army I ran out of grain while mired in a siege. None of the neighbours brought help; and winter prevented me from taking to the sea. And so I tried to return to my father's kingdom, under no compulsion* from the enemy, but at Parium and Heraclea* lost the best of my soldiers and my fleets in

15 shipwrecks. Then, when I restored my army at Cabera* and fought Lucullus with varying success,* we both were attacked again by a lack of resources. He was supported by the kingdom of Ariobarzanes,* a place untouched by the war, but I was surrounded by devastated territories and withdrew to Armenia. The Romans pursued, not me, but their habit of destroying every kingdom. Because the narrow places prevented Tigranes' massive forces* from fighting, the Romans parade his imprudence as their victory.

16 Now, I ask you, consider this: do you think that our defeat will make your resistance stronger or that there will be an end of war?

I know that you have great resources in men, weapons, and gold. This is the reason that I pursue you as allies, and they pursue you as booty. But my advice is this. Fight this war far from home, with little effort, using the bodies of our men. Tigranes' kingdom is intact and my soldiers are experienced in war. The fact is we cannot conquer or be conquered without danger to you. Or don't you know that the 17 Romans have turned their armies here only after the Ocean brought an end to their expansion to the west? That since their beginning they have possessed nothing except what they stole: their homes, their wives, their fields, their empire? Once they were immigrants without a country or parents; they have been established as a plague upon the whole world; nothing human or divine prevents them from robbing and exterminating allies and friends, people far away and nearby, the impoverished and the powerful. All that is not their slave they consider their enemy, especially monarchies.

Few men want liberty; a great part want a fair master. They are 18 suspicious of us: we could be rivals and in time avengers. But you, 19 who have Seleucea,* the greatest of cities, and the kingdom of Perses, known for its wealth, what do you expect from them except treachery now and war later? The Romans turn their weapons against everyone, 20 most fiercely against those whose defeat means the greatest spoils. They have become great by daring and deception, and by sowing war upon war. Following this custom they will destroy everything or they will die. And this is not difficult. So far their army is safe because of 21 their good fortune or our mistakes, but they have no grain and no reinforcements. You can cut off their army from Mesopotamia and we from Armenia. It will be to your glory that you came forward to 22 help great kings and crushed the plunderers of the world. I warn you 23 and urge you to do this. Do not choose to let our destruction postpone your own; choose rather to be our ally and be victorious.

EXPLANATORY NOTES

References are to the chapter and section numbers of the text. Recurring technical terms may be found in the Glossary. A basic identification of names can be found at the first occurrence in the text.

CATILINE'S CONSPIRACY

1.4 *All human beings . . . brilliant and eternal*: in the opening paragraph Sallust uses well-known Greek philosophical ideas to address both moral questions (What should we as men do?) and political questions (How do we win glory?). However, the exposition is not entirely clear: do we use every available resource or mainly our mind? Inner resources or physical strength? And the final sentence is ambiguous: 'virtue is held . . . eternal' can mean 'virtue is thought to be eternal' or 'virtue is held as an eternal possession'. Some critics believe that a straightforward and familiar argument is obscured by Sallust's presentation. Others believe that there is a more fundamental difficulty, namely: history (fame, glory) does not reward nor is it a record of virtue (what one should do). Those who take the second position can point to the history of Catiline himself as an example of the failure of the preface's relatively straightforward argument about action, virtue, and glory.

2.2 *Cyrus*: known as Cyrus the Great, king of Persia 559–530 BC and founder of the Persian empire. It is noteworthy that the early kings, who are not named and so do not have historical 'glory', lived in a kind of 'golden age'; but, when we come to famous kings and cities, that is kings and cities with names, we also find 'desire for domination' supplanting contentment. The story of Cyrus is, in part, the subject of the history of Herodotus. History and fame arrive at the same time as 'desire for domination'.

Lacedaemonians and Athenians: Lacedaemonia is the ancient kingdom of Sparta in southern Greece. In the fifth century, Sparta and Athens became involved in the Peloponnesian Wars, which were written about by the historian, Thucydides. By referring here to Thucydides and above to Herodotus, Sallust brings the writing of history into the course of history: historians, after all, give glory for great deeds. Sallust addresses the inequity of history (not everyone or every state gets a Thucydides to record their deeds!) in ch 8; Caesar uses the Lacedaemonians as a bad example in his speech, *C* 51.

2.8 *virtue*: the Latin word *virtus*, which becomes our word 'virtue', is difficult to translate consistently: it refers to the manly virtues (like courage, skill, agility) as well as intellectual and ethical virtues. It may be qualified, as in 'mental excellence' or, as here, it can be posited as an absolute category. The problem that the word presents is not one of finding the best English word to translate it in all contexts. The fact is that it entails a view of the world which is not the modern Anglo-American view, one in which ability, performance, and merit; vigour, morality, and manliness; skill and virtue, are imagined under a single rubric, *virtus*. Other words in Latin can and do separate out this complex, but *virtus* names it. Sallust uses the term seventy-seven times in *Catiline's Conspiracy*, *The Jugurthine War*, and the surviving fragments of the *Histories*.

2.8 *soul*: Sallust switches from *animus*, meaning 'mind', 'soul', to *anima*, usually meaning 'soul', 'life spirit'. Some try to make *animus* a human capacity and *anima* the life force we share with animals (hence, anima-l). The problem, of course, is that here, if *anima* is the 'animal life force', it is hard to understand how the unvirtuous find nothing but a burden in their 'animal life force'; it would seem that by using their bodies for pleasure they are enjoying nothing more than what animals enjoy. See next note.

2.9 *breath of life*: again, Sallust uses *anima*, but here it can easily mean 'life principle'. For men, the true enjoyment of the life principle is found in the exercise of virtue (the mind controls, the body obeys). However, by using *anima* above for 'soul', it is now possible for this sentence in Latin to mean that an active moral life is the true life and the true enjoyment of both the life principle and the soul's function as governor of life.

3.1 *to speak well*: the Latin phrase is sometimes taken to mean 'to praise', as in 'to speak well of someone'. Praise is important in oratory as in a republic, but so is blame, and so is clarity and persuasive power. All of these things are part of what it means for 'to speak well'. In the conservative Roman tradition, an orator (which is to say, a lawyer and politician) was defined as 'a good man speaking well'. See Quintilian, *Inst. passim*, esp. 2.17.

3.2 *deeds must find an equivalence in words*: the Latin could be literally translated as 'deeds must be equated with words' or 'deeds must be equated to words': the first is a problem of rhetoric (how do you find the most expressive or accurate words?), the second is the problem of representation (how can words ever be equal to deeds?).

4.1 *a multitude of miseries and dangers*: see Introduction on the life of Sallust, his expulsion from the Senate and his career with Julius Caesar.

4.2 *slavish occupations*: Sallust is criticizing the choices of others, not claiming that Romans thought that agriculture was a 'servile occupation'. In fact, Cato the Elder wrote a book on agriculture, Virgil composed a poem on farming, and many aristocrats retired to their country villas.

5.1 *L. Catiline was born in an aristocratic family*: Catiline's full name was Lucius Sergius Catilina. Virgil traces Catiline's family back to Sergestus, who came with Aeneas to Italy from Troy. The last Sergius to be consul was Sergius Fidenus Coxo in 380 BC. Catiline served in the military during the Social Wars and was a supporter of Sulla in the civil war of 84–82. In 73 he was tried for adultery with one of the Vestal Virgins, but was acquitted. He was praetor in 68 and the propraetorian governor for Africa during 67 and 66. In 65 he was tried and acquitted of extortion charges. He then stood for the consulship in 64 and 63.

The patricians and plebs formed two 'classes' in Rome but their history and composition is not entirely clear. The 'patricians' were those 'fathers' who composed the Senate and controlled access to political office; the plebs consisted of the mass of citizens who had their own political institutions, some for protection from the power of the patricians. By the late Republic, plebeians were allowed to stand for the consulship; in fact, at least one consul each year had to be a plebeian. The class distinction that used to mean power and wealth no longer did so, and by the time of Catiline many old patrician families were poor (as his was) and many plebeians were among the wealthiest Romans. The aristocracy prided itself on military successes, oratorical ability, and religious knowledge. The *nobilitas*, translated as 'the aristocracy' or 'the nobility', may refer either to families of patrician ancestry or it may refer to the ruling elite within the aristocracy. This inner elite, which by the late Republic included plebeian and patrician families, believed itself entitled to political power and magistracies, especially the consulship. Catiline's family, the *gens Sergia* or 'family of the Sergii', was an ancient patrician family, but Catiline himself was not a member of the aristocratic elite, although he believed that he should be.

5.6   *Domination of Sulla*: L. Cornelius Sulla, 138–78; as quaestor to Marius, he was responsible for the capture of Jugurtha. His brilliance as a general during the Social Wars led to his election to the consulship for 88. His command against Mithridates was taken from him through the collusion of Marius and the tribune Sulpicius. This led to his first march on Rome. He consolidated his position and proceeded with his plans to fight Mithridates. During his absence, Marius and Cinna regained control of Rome. Sulla returned to Italy and marched on Rome again. After his second victory, in 82, he was appointed 'dictator' and held power until he voluntarily gave it up in 79. This period, called the 'Domination of Sulla', was a time of great political violence and governmental reorganization.

5.7   *a 'realm'*: *regnum*, like the English word 'realm', implies not just a coercive sphere of imperial influence, but a king. There are three things to keep in mind: (1) Sulla's cruel and deadly tyranny in which thousands of Romans died was called the *Sullanum Regnum* ('Sulla's rule'); (2) for Romans of the Republic, political kingship was anathema, the antithesis of the freedom that they prized and a form of government that they had not known for almost 500 years; (3) the Roman empire could be thought of as the 'sovereign realm of the Roman people', exercising its rights of absolute authority over its subjects. Catiline's desires are for the best and the worst of what Rome has accomplished.

6.1   *as I understand it*: the phrase suggests some disagreement in the sources and in fact there were two mutually exclusive foundation myths: Rome was founded by the Trojans whom Aeneas led from Troy; Rome was founded by Romulus. Cato the Elder attempted to reconcile the stories: Aeneas founded Lavinium and some 400 years later Rome was founded by Romulus, a descendant of Aeneas and his son Ascanius. This later version is followed by Virgil and Livy; Sallust does not follow the conflated version.

     Aborigines: as their name implies ('from the beginning'), these are native peoples. In the elder Cato's version of the foundation of Rome, Aborigines inhabited Italy before the Trojans arrived, but joined with the Trojans.

6.3   *a state*: the Latin *civitas* designates a grouping of 'citizens' entailing legal responsibilities and rights. The sentence is not found in most manuscripts, but it is Sallustian in content and manner, and the relationship between 'harmony' and 'polity' is thematic in all of Sallust's work; note the prominence later of the Temple of Harmony (*Concordia*).

6.4   *neighbouring kings and peoples*: for example, the Sabines, the Albans, the Latins, the Aequi, and the Volscii. The details, which are recounted by Livy, are not important to Sallust's story of Roman political virtue.

6.6   *'Fathers'*: these 'fathers' or *patres* originally constituted the 'patricians'. The advisory body is the Senate, whose name is derived from *senex*, 'old man'. The senators were addressed as 'conscript fathers'; see 51.1.

6.7   *arrogance*: *superbia*. The last king of Rome was Tarquinius Superbus, or 'Tarquin the Arrogant'.

     domination: *dominatio*, the same word that is used for the 'Domination of Sulla'. Here and above, Sallust's language of abstract political forces recalls and refers to actual people and events in the course of Roman history.

     annual offices: according to Cicero, military and civilian powers were distributed to *praetores* (praetors) and *iudices* (judges) respectively.

     two executive officers: the consuls, according to tradition first elected in 509 BC, were the highest civil and military magistrates; they were expected to restrain each other's power and in this way to avoid or limit abuses of power.

8.3   *writers of great talent flourished there*: one thinks especially of Herodotus, 'the father of history', Thucydides, and Xenophon.

9.4   *disciplinary action*: T. Manlius Torquatus ordered his own son to be killed because he attacked the Gauls without orders; the story is referred to by the younger Cato, see 52.30. In 324 BC A. Postumius Tubertus is said to have executed his son for successfully attacking the Volscians without orders.

10.1   *Carthage*: founded according to legend by Dido, it was the centre of Punic culture and the chief military and economic rival of Rome during the second century BC. It was finally destroyed by Rome in 146 after the Third Punic War. Sallust thought that 'fear of an external enemy' kept Roman culture focused and controlled. He returns to this theme at *J* 41 and *H*. 1.12.

11.4 *L. Sulla took control of the Republic*: i.e. after Sulla's second march on Rome following the defeat of Mithridates in 86.

11.5 *luxury and excessive licence*: Sallust connects the decline of the Republic with moral failures, the luxury that became possible at Rome with the fall of Carthage in 146 and the luxury and licence that damaged discipline in the army and brought luxury and avarice back from Asia to Rome. Between the defeat of Mithridates and Sulla's return to Rome in 83, it is said that Sulla allowed his soldiers a dangerous and destructive degree of freedom and luxury. There is, however, evidence in other historians that the Roman army had enjoyed such luxuries and such lax discipline at other times.

12.2 *innocence was taken for malevolence*: this condensed phrase presumably means that the refusal to join others in vicious action (innocence) was thought to be a sign of some malevolent and ulterior motive. Thus, when self-interest is the only paradigm, deviation is construed as another, even more twisted, form of self-interest. An alternative explanation is that abstinence (innocence) was taken as a (malevolent) accusation against the avarice of others.

13.2 *mountains dug up by private men, seas paved over*: there are two issues here: one involves the distribution of wealth, an increasing gap between the rich and the poor, the ostentation of the wealthy, and the connection of wealth and power; the other involves the desire for luxury regardless of economic status. Catiline appealed mainly to the young whose taste for luxury far outran their resources. In the background is the story of Xerxes, the Persian king defeated by the Greeks, who was taken as an allegory of hubris and Asian excess. His defeat, at Salamis (480 BC) and Plataea (479), was seen as retribution for digging a channel through the peninsula at Mount Athos and building bridges across the Hellespont. In Rome, Lucullus (consul in 74) called Pompey the Great 'Xerxes in a toga'; both men channelled sea water into their fishponds. Statius (*Silv.* 2.2) has a description of a friend's seaside villa: colonnade upon the cliffs like a city, countless rooftops, a different view of the sea from every window.

14.7 *other reasons*: Sallust is not forthcoming about what the other reasons were, although it is not hard to imagine, given what he has said above.

15.1 *a virgin from a good family*: identity unknown; this charge is made by others but may derive more from the norms of political invective than from truth.

Vestal priestess: Cicero (*Cat.* 3.9) also notes an affair with a Vestal Virgin in 73 BC; she was Fabia, the half-sister of Cicero's wife, Terentia. The accusation against Fabia was brought by Clodius; she was defended by Cicero, the younger Cato, and Catulus (35.1). The Vestal Virgins were priestesses of the Roman goddess of the hearth, Vesta. They were committed to service before puberty and sworn to celibacy for thirty years. It would follow, of course, that stories of unchaste Vestal virgins were common. In fact, Romulus and Remus were born to Rhea Silvia while she was a Vestal Virgin; she said that the god Mars was their father.

15.2 *Aurelia Orestilla*: the daughter of Cn. Aufidius Orestis (consul in 71), she is mentioned here and in Appian, *B. Civ.* 2. The only other information we have is that the younger Cornificius was engaged to her daughter.

15.3 *criminal nuptials*: Cicero speaks of a former wife at *Cat.* 1.14; Val. Max. 9.1.9 says that the son was poisoned.

16.3 *the innocent as well as the guilty*: an odd expression in the Latin as well. If, as seems likely, Sallust means that Catiline had men killed for no justification, then 'innocent' must mean 'innocent in Catiline's eyes' (i.e. men who were no obstruction to his plans) and 'guilty' must mean 'guilty of opposing Catiline's objectives'. Focalizations like this blur moral categories, but they also reveal the fact that moral categories are often, if not always, positioned: that is, guilt is usually positioned with respect to someone else's interests.

16.5 *Cn. Pompey*: Cn. Pompeius Magnus, 106–48, was a distinguished general and important political figure in the late Republic. In 83 he sided with Sulla, who gave him the cognomen Magnus . He was consul with Crassus in 70, was a member of the first triumvirate with Caesar and Crassus in 59, but eventually came into conflict with Caesar and was Caesar's adversary in the civil war of 49–48 . At this time he was in Pontus and Armenia where he was bringing the third war against King Mithridates to an end.

seeking the consulship: the year is 64; Cicero and Antonius, the winners, were the other two candidates for the consulship this year. Modern historians find it hard to believe that Catiline would simultaneously plot to overthrow the government and run for the consulship at the same time. However, if Sallust were to date the origins of the conspiracy to Catiline's failure to be elected in 63, he could not argue as effectively that Catiline was created by and exemplary of the general moral decline of Rome. Furthermore, the 'unprecedented nature of the crime and the danger' (4.4) represented by Catiline may refer to his efforts to treat the consulship, not as the reward for civic and military service, but solely as a means to political and military power.

17.1 *1 June*: 64 BC. This meeting takes place, according to Sallust, before the elections for 63; in other sources it takes place in 63 before the elections for 62; see Cicero, *Mur.* 50.

L. Caesar and C. Figulus were consuls: L. Julius Caesar was a distant relative of C. Julius Caesar and uncle of Mark Antony; his sister was at this time married to P. Lentulus Sura, one of the conspirators; see below. C. Marcius Figulus was called Minucius Thermus before being adopted by the Marcii. Another C. Marcius Figulus was consul in 162 and 156.

17.3 *senators*: the presence of senators in Catiline's conspiracy suggests that Catiline's appeal was surprisingly broad. Cicero (*Cat.* 1 *passim*) also alludes to this problem in the *First Catilinarian*, when justifying his own hesitation in acting immediately in October 63.

P. Lentulus Sura: perhaps the most important conspirator; he was a member of the *gens Cornelia* (as was Sulla); praetor 74, consul in 71, praetor for the second time in 63, he had been expelled from the Senate by censors in 70. He will be the leader of the conspirators in Rome after Catiline leaves. He was executed for his part in the conspiracy.

P. Autronius: P. Autronnius Paetus was a friend of Cicero and his colleague in the quaestorship for 75. He was elected consul in 66 but convicted of electoral bribery. He was convicted of violence and banished.

L. Cassius Longinus: a member of a noble plebeian family; he was praetor with Cicero in 66, and a candidate for the consulship, again with Cicero, in 64 but lost the election. According to Cicero, he joined Catiline's conspiracy and persuaded the Allobroges to join it. He was not captured on 3 December.

C. Cethegus: a patrician from the *gens Cornelia* and a relatively young man. In the arson and slaughter Catiline planned for December, he was to attack and kill Cicero. He was executed.

P. and Ser. Sulla, sons of Servius: the father, Servius, may have been the brother of Sulla, the dictator. Both sons were tried and banished in 62. This P. Sulla is not the consul-designate of 66 whom Cicero defended.

L. Vargunteius: he may have been involved in the so-called 'first conspiracy' of 66 and in 63 he volunteered to help murder Cicero. He was charged with electoral corruption in 66 and convicted. He was tried for violence in 62 and banished.

Q. Annius: Cicero says that a Q. Annius Chilo was instrumental in soliciting the Allobroges. If 'Q. Annius' is the same man, he was not arrested in December, but was condemned to death *in absentia* by the Senate on 5 December.

M. Porcius Laeca: a member of Cato's family, the *gens Porcia*, and is chiefly known for the fact that the crucial meeting of the conspirators just before Cicero's *First Catilinarian Speech,* when they planned to murder Cicero, took place at his house on the scythe-makers' street. He was condemned for violence and banished.

L. Bestia: L. Calpurnius Bestia, as tribune of the plebs in 62, would have taken office on 10 December 63. He was supposed to give the signal for arson and slaughter in Rome by giving a speech attacking Cicero (43.1).

He may have been one of the tribunes who harassed Cicero in the final days of his consulship for killing Roman citizens.

17.4   *Q. Curius*: Cicero's chief informant (see ch. 23); he was a member of the *gens Curia*, whose most famous ancestor was Manius Curius Dentatus, consul in 290. He had lost his seat in the Senate in 70 (see 23.1).

   from the equestrian order: M. Fulvius Nobilior is not identified with any other known person of this name. The *gens Fulvia* was a noble plebeian family, but they had not produced a consul since 125 BC. L. Statilius was one of the five conspirators executed while Cicero was consul. He was in charge of arson at Rome (see 43.2). P. Gabinius Capito is named by Cicero as 'the most wicked deviser of all sorts of crimes'; he is involved with the Allobroges at 40.6 and is mentioned as one of those executed at 55.5. C. Cornelius was another member of the *gens Cornelia* but from the plebeian branch of the family. He and Vargunteius volunteered to murder Cicero (28.1). He was convicted of violence.

17.5   *aristocrats at home*: local aristocrats would have influence in Rome by virtue of personal ties with Roman aristocrats.

17.7   *M. Licinius Crassus*: thought to be the richest man in Rome; he plays a shadowy role throughout Sallust. He was consul with Pompey in 70 and, together with Caesar and Pompey, would form the first triumvirate in 59 BC; he was consul again in 55 and died in 54 fighting the Parthians. Both he and Pompey had served with Sulla. When Crassus defeated Spartacus, Pompey claimed credit. Relations between the two men were always uneasy.

   a great army: in 66 Pompey had been given an extraordinary command over Asia, Cilicia, and Bithynia in order to prosecute the Third Mithridatic War.

18.1   *a few men likewise conspired*: most modern scholars do not accept this story of a first conspiracy: 'a tissue of improbabilities' (Syme). It appears that something happened in 66: it involved Autronius and Sulla (elected to the consulship of 65 but then convicted of bribery); it may also have involved the tribune C. Manilius, whose trial for extortion was broken up by mob violence on 29 December 66. This violence may also explain the fact that the Senate voted a bodyguard for the consuls of 65. Catiline may have been involved in the violence, but it is unlikely that there was a conspiracy or, if there was, that Catiline had been involved. Nevertheless, the story fits Sallust's narrative and ancient psychological assumptions: Catiline had been a revolutionary at heart since Sulla's domination; therefore, he was always planning to take over the government.

18.2   *as accurately as I can*: Sallust's introductory language suggests that even for him the evidence was not complete or detailed.

   L. Tullus: L. Volcacius Tullus, consul in 66, was the magistrate who refused to allow Catiline to stand for the consulship in 66 on the grounds that he was accused of abusing his power while governor in Africa.

M'. Lepidus: M'. Aemilius Lepidus, a patrician of little importance. During Caesar's civil war, he refused to leave Italy with Pompey and retired to his villa to await the outcome.

P. Sulla: not the same Sulla as that mentioned above at 17.3. This P. Sulla was indicted in 62 for taking part in the Catilinarian conspiracy and defended by Cicero. He married Pompey's sister and fought with Caesar during the civil war. He died in 46.

18.3 *arraigned under bribery laws and fined*: the penalties for a conviction under the bribery laws included forfeiture of the consulship and loss of one's seat in the Senate.

18.4 *the legal deadline*: Catiline had been propraetor in Africa and was tried for extortion, that is, for illegally taking money from the subjects and allies of Rome. It is most likely that he was barred from the supplementary election of 66, the election that was necessary after Autronius and Sulla had been convicted. It is unclear whether Catiline actually stood trial in 66 or in 65. It seems that at the time he was barred from candidacy he was only under threat of prosecution. If so, the consul may have disqualified Catiline without any clear legal precedent. The legal deadline, however, may refer to the original election, one that Catiline may have missed because he did not return from Africa in time. If so, the consul used a technicality to prevent Catiline's name from appearing.

Cn. Piso: Cn. Calpurnius Piso, quaestor in 65, enemy of Pompey; he was sent as *quaestor pro praetore* to govern Nearer Spain.

18.5 *around 5 December*: the dates are suspect and recorded differently in other authors; Sallust does not usually pay close attention to precise chronology.

kill the consuls: one wonders why Catiline would kill the consuls elect. His complaint was against Volcacius Tullus, who had disqualified his candidacy. Furthermore, at his trial in 65 he was supported by a number of consulars, including the consul L. Torquatus, whom (according to Sallust) he had planned to kill. Even Cicero thought of defending Catiline. These details make the conspiracy, as related, quite unlikely.

on 1 January: Cicero (*Cat.* 1.15) says that Catiline appeared armed in the Forum on 29 December 66. There were riots, but they seem to have been connected with Manilius' bill to give Pompey extraordinary powers. The new consuls entered office on 1 January.

18.6 *the two Spanish provinces*: these provinces, Nearer Spain and Further Spain, were created in 197 BC.

18.7 *5 February*: no other source speaks of a continuation of the original plot.

18.8 *the signal too soon*: in other versions of a single plot, the coup fails because Crassus failed to appear and Caesar did not give the signal.

19.2 *quaestor with praetorian powers*: at this time a province was normally administered by an ex-consul or an ex-praetor; he would be aided by a quaestor. If the governor died or left before his term was over, his quaestor took over as a propraetor. Piso would have been sent to Spain as 'acting governor' because the province was without a governor.

19.2 *a bitter enemy of Pompey*: again, Crassus appears in conflict with Pompey. In the period 66–62 the absence of Pompey, his extraordinary commands, and his inevitable homecoming with a victorious army was on everyone's mind; there were references to the similar homecoming of Sulla. Crassus might easily have supported Piso without supporting the so-called conspiracy.

19.5 *old . . . clients of Pompey*: these would be supporters who had become loyal to Pompey during his command in their province against Sertorius, 76–72.

never before perpetrated any such crime: in fact, L. Piso Frugi had been killed as propraetor in Spain in 112 BC.

20.1 *just mentioned*: Sallust returns to the narrative that he left after ch. 17. The time according to Sallust's narrative is early in June 64 , just before the consular elections for 63.

20.9 *How much longer are we still going to put up with this*: some hear in this phrase an echo of the opening to Cicero's *First Catilinarian Speech* ('How much longer still, Catiline, will you abuse our patience?') and find a tendentious imitation of Cicero in Catiline's words. It has been argued, however, that this kind of impatient redundancy ('how much longer still') was characteristic of Catiline. In this case, Sallust would imitate Catiline for verisimilitude, not Cicero to mock him.

20.11 *levelling the mountains*: Sallust has Catiline repeat some of his own criticisms of contemporary Rome; see above, ch. 13, and note. While this does not justify Catiline's conspiracy, it does complicate our understanding of the context.

21.2 *clean slates*: the tablets on which debts were recorded would be wiped clean. Catiline is the first to propose cancellation of debts by armed revolt rather than by legislation. It is not, however, easy to separate his legislative programme as consul from his military programme, since the consulship entailed both civil and military authority.

proscription of the wealthy: Sulla's proscriptions were notorious and inform both Catiline's programme and fears of it. Sulla eliminated his enemies by offering a bounty for their murder: their names were published on lists put in public places, a reward was offered for information leading to their death, and the murderer was allowed to keep part of the property. New names would be added as suggested by Sulla's followers.

21.3 *Piso*: see above, ch. 19. We do not know when Piso was killed, but we do know that he was dead by the time of Catiline's speech.

P. Sittius Nucerinus: a banker who had lent a large sum of money to the king of Mauretania and so may have been visiting Mauretania. He did not have an army until several years later, after he had gone into exile in Africa to avoid prosecution. It was a private mercenary army, which supported Caesar in the civil war.

C. Antonius: C. Antonius Hybrida, praetor with Cicero in 66, became Cicero's co-consul in 63. He had attempted to form a coalition with Catiline against Cicero, and Cicero purchased his support by exchanging proconsular provinces (26.4). He led the Roman army against Catiline although he did not himself participate in the final battle (see 59.4). In 59 he was prosecuted for oppression in Macedonia, convicted, and exiled. In 42 he became censor.

22.3 *the hatred that later rose up against him*: it was illegal for a Roman magistrate to enforce a capital penalty on a Roman citizen without allowing an appeal to the people. In 58 Cicero went into exile when Clodius (tribune of the plebs that year) passed a law threatening exile for anyone who executed a Roman citizen without a trial. At the centre of this legal and constitutional issue is the Senate's 'final decree': did it merely advise the consul to take all steps necessary to protect the Republic, or did it give him constitutional authority to inflict capital punishment?

23.1 *censors had removed from the Senate*: in 70 BC the censors, probably Cn. Lentulus and L. Gellius, purged the Senate, removing, among others, Cicero's colleague in 63, C. Antonius, P. Cornelius Lentulus, and Q. Curius.

23.3 *Fulvia*: otherwise unknown.

23.5 *entrust the consulship to Cicero*: this is unlikely as the sole reason for Cicero's success: he led the poll with the support of all citizen voting blocks. His opponents were: two members of old aristocratic families (Catiline and P. Sulpicius Galba), two plebeian nobles (C. Antonius and L. Cassius Longinus), and two other candidates from senatorial families (Q. Cornificius and C. Licinius Sacerdos). It is more likely that his success depended upon his skill as an advocate, his connections with leading members of the towns and Senate, and his contacts among the mercantile class.

23.6 *'new man'*: in the previous 150 years only ten consuls had been elected from non-senatorial families, and Cicero was the first since C. Coelius Caldus (consul in 94).

24.1 *M. Tullius*: M. Tullius Cicero, known to English-speakers as Cicero. A Roman was typically known by his praenomen and his nomen; the two together were used in the formal address of the Senate to a senator or magistrate.

24.2 *more agitated daily*: Sallust leaves out of his account the fact that after the elections of 64 Catiline was indicted for his part in the Sullan proscriptions. He was tried before Caesar, supported by many ex-consuls, and acquitted. It would seem that his revolutionary plans were not well known at that time.

Manlius: C. Manlius, a veteran from Sulla's army. He had profited from Sulla's proscriptions but had lost his wealth. He was the leader of other

Sullan colonists from Arretium and Faesulae. He took up arms on 27 October 63, before the Catilinarian conspirators meet at Laeca's house on 6 November to receive their orders (see 30.1). This suggests that he was acting independently of Catiline, although from many of the same motives.

24.4 *the urban slaves*: compare Catiline's response to Lentulus' suggestion that he enlist slaves (44), and his refusal to allow slaves to join his army (56.5). The memory of Spartacus' revolt was still fresh and terrifying.

25.1 *Sempronia*: from the family of the Sempronii, a family that included among their ancestors the Gracchi. Her husband was D. Junius Brutus, consul in 77 (see below, 40.5), and one of her sons was the Decimus Brutus who assassinated Caesar.

26.1 *the following year*: Catiline stood in 63 for the consulship of 62. Sallust leaves out the events following the election of 64.

Antonius: Cicero's co-consul; on his character, see 21.3.

26.4 *an agreement about provinces*: the consular provinces for the year were Gaul and Macedonia. Cicero agreed to take the inferior province, Gaul, although Macedonia had fallen to him by lot. We do not know when he reached this agreement with Antonius or when Antonius ceased to be an ally of Catiline. Cicero tells us that Catiline claimed the support of Antonius while canvassing for the consulship in 64 (tog. cand.) and Cassius Dio says that Antonius met with the conspirators as late as November 63 (37.30.3). Cicero, on the other hand, did not seem eager to take a province as early as January 63 (*Leg. Agr.* 1.26).

26.5 *election day came*: normally the elections would be held in July. Cicero had the elections postponed, either because Catiline had uttered threats against the state or, more likely, against Cicero himself. We do not know how long the delay was. On the election day Cicero appeared in the Campus Martius wearing armour to dramatize the danger that Catiline presented to the state and to himself, the consul. Later he claimed that Catiline was defeated as a response to this putative threat. D. Junius Silanus (see 50.4) and L. Licinius Murena were elected consuls for 63.

27.1 *to Faesulae*: at 24.2 Manlius is already at Faesulae and appears to be acting independently. Sallust seems uncertain about when Manlius became Catiline's subordinate.

Septimius of Camerinum: nothing further is known about Septimius; Camerinum is a town of Umbria near Picenum.

C. Julius: otherwise unknown.

27.3 *M. Porcius Laeca*: introduced in 17.3. Sallust puts this meeting before the Senate passes its 'final decree'. The narrative is different in Cicero. On 21 October he warned of danger to the state and predicted Manlius' uprising on 27 October; the Senate then gave him the authority of their 'final decree'. The conspirators met at Laeca's house on the night of 5/6 November; two men tried to murder Cicero on the morning of

7 November and that day or the next Cicero convened the Senate at the Temple of Jupiter and delivered the *First Catilinarian*.

27.4 *in the dead of night*: we know from Cicero's speech for P. Sulla that the night was that of 6/7 November.

28.1 *L. Vargunteius*: Cicero in the *First Catilinarian* speaks of two *equites* (1.9). He names Cornelius as one (*Sull.* 18.9). No other source mentions the senator Vargunteius, although Cicero does connect him with Catiline (*Sull.* 6.67). Plutarch says that the second assassin was named Marcius (*Cic.* 16.2); Appian says it was a Lentulus (*B. Civ.* 2.3)

ceremonial visit: early in the morning clients and others would visit important men to greet them and accompany them to the Forum.

28.4 *they had lost all their fields and property*: land was taken from peasants in Etruria and Campania to settle Sulla's veterans upon his return from the east.

Meanwhile in Etruria . . . appetite and extravagance: this brief paragraph can be seen as summarizing the economic and political difficulties that played into Catiline's hands. Sulla had punished Etruria for its allegiance to Marius by land confiscations for more than 100,000 veterans. At his death, Lepidus led an uprising of the disaffected, who themselves represented a problem going back to the land redistribution programmes of the Gracchi. In the years between Sulla and Catiline many of Sulla's veterans lost or wasted their resources and so added to the problem of the urban poor and the disaffected. Attempts to address problems like this through reforms failed, from the Gracchi down to the land laws of Augustus.

29.2 *before the Senate*: we know from the *First Catilinarian* that Cicero reported to the Senate on 21 October.

29.3 *Let the consuls prevent any damage to the Republic*: this decree, often cited as 'the final decree of the Senate', was used at various times in the late Republic to ward off what the Senate considered deadly threats to the state. It appears that this is the exact wording of the decree.

Otherwise . . . no right to any of these actions: it is generally thought that the Senate's decree was only advisory. One should note, however, that Caesar, in his speech at ch. 51, does not object that capital punishment for the conspirators is illegal, only that it sets a bad precedent. Nevertheless, actions taken under this decree's authority still required a legal defence. Since Roman law did not allow a magistrate to kill or exile a Roman citizen without a trial, Cicero argued that when the law was impotent, extra-legal action was necessary, that the debate about the conspirators in the Senate constituted a trial, and that his action was taken at the behest of the Senate; he also argued that by taking action against the state the conspirators became enemies of the state (*hostes*) and relinquished their rights as citizens.

30.1 *L. Saenius*: otherwise unknown.

30.3   *Capua and Apulia*: we hear at 46.3 that Lentulus had been sent to Apulia
to stir up the slaves. Slave revolts and rumours of slave revolts were a
frequent cause of alarm in the late Republic.

Q. Marcius Rex: consul in 68, proconsul in Cilicia in 67. In 63 he was still
waiting for a triumph he had earned in 67. He died before celebrating a
triumph.

Q. Metellus Creticus: consul in 69, proconsul in Crete and Achaea 68–65.
The family of the Metelli were very important in the late Republic: they
held six consulships in fifteen years at the end of the second century and
five consulships in the 60s and 50s. As proconsul (68), Q. Metellus brought
Crete under Roman control; hence, the cognomen Creticus. He waited
four years for his triumph, which he finally celebrated in 62.

30.5   *The praetors . . . Celer*: Q. Pompeius Rufus was praetor in 63, pro-
consul in Africa in 61; Cicero praises his moderation and integrity.
Q. Metellus Celer was Praetor in 63. He had been legate under Pompey.
In Picenum he raised an army and blocked Catiline's way north with three
legions. He became the proconsular governor of Cisalpine Gaul when
Cicero relinquished the province in 62. He became consul in 60.

30.7   *sestertia*: a *sestertius*, or sesterce, was a small silver coin; 1,000 sesterces
made up one *sestertia*, *HS*. The Senate here offers 100,000 sesterces =
100 *sestertia*. It is difficult to compare the value of coins across different
cultures divided by centuries; however, some figures may be useful: the
poor paid 2 *sestertia* a year in rent in the city of Rome; Caesar gave his
soldiers a military bonus of 24 *sestertia*; 400 *sestertia* was the minimum
requirement for membership in the equestrian order. By any standard,
the Senate's reward was substantial.

gladiatorial troops: gladiators were maintained in 'schools', where they
were trained and supervised. Each trainer had a 'troop' (or 'family'). An
individual might use them for purposes of protection or to threaten violence. It is odd to send gladiators to Capua at a time of unrest.

minor magistrates: aediles, tribunes, quaestors, and all others below the
higher magistrates, the consuls, censors, and praetors.

31.4   *He was arraigned by L. Paulus under the lex Plautia*: L. Aemilius Paulus,
consul in 50, was the brother of Lepidus the triumvir; later he was proscribed by the triumvirs and allowed to go into exile. For the Plautian
law, the *lex Plautia de vi*, see Glossary. This is its first mention in the
ancient sources. The date of this arraignment is not known. Catiline
offered to hand himself over to the custody first of Lepidus, then
Cicero and Metellus Celer; all turned him down. Finally he turned himself over to a certain M. Metellus. One may surmise that the evidence
against him was not strong; he had not, after all, done anything yet.

31.7   *published*: Sallust refers to the *First Catilinarian*, one of four speeches
Cicero delivered during this crisis. It was delivered before the Senate in
the Temple of Jupiter on either 7 or 8 November, just after the attempt
on his life. It is often said that Sallust denigrates Cicero's importance

during these events. If that were so, it would be a great insult to the man who largely defined his practical political contributions to Rome in terms of his success in putting down this conspiracy. It is hard to decide whether Sallust's recognition of Cicero's brilliance and importance here is sufficient to countervail the fact that he does ignore Cicero's contributions elsewhere.

a rental resident citizen of the city of Rome: an insulting reference to the fact that Cicero was the first in his family to attain the consulship. Such an achievement was relatively rare, and men who succeeded were called 'new men'. By referring to Cicero as a 'tenant' or 'rental resident' Catiline implies that he has no deep roots in or commitment to Rome.

31.9 *I'll extinguish my inferno with a general demolition*: the language is metaphoric and ominous. Literally, he refers to the practice of containing a fire (the inferno) by destroying the buildings around it (the general demolition). However, the term for fire (*incendium*) may be used metaphorically for bankruptcy and financial ruin ('he got burned'), while the term for the destruction of buildings (*ruina*) may refer to the destruction of the entire city. According to Cicero, this remark was made in July of 63 to the younger Cato when Catiline was threatened with prosecution.

33.1 *according to ancestral custom*: a law of 326 BC stated that a Roman citizen could not be imprisoned for debt; presumably Catiline's reference to 'personal freedom' refers to violations of this law. At this time interest rates were also regulated and limited to 12 per cent, although there are references in Cicero's letters to a loan at 48 per cent and in Horace's *Satires* to those who charge five times the legal rate.

33.2 *the urban praetor*: Q. Caecilius Metellus Celer (see first note on 30.5) may have been the urban praetor in 63. His edict at the beginning of the year would have determined the regulations governing jurisprudence in his courts. Cicero refers to the problems caused by the urban praetor in 63: men were threatening his tribunal (*Cat.* 1.32) and Cicero even goes so far as to mock those who will fall not only if he shows them the Roman army's battle line but even if he shows them the praetor's edict (*Cat.* 2.5). Some modified form of imprisonment for debt seems to have remained a legal option to insure payment according to Cicero and the *lex Rubria*; see A. H. J. Greenidge, *Legal Procedure of Cicero's Time* (Oxford, 1901), 279.

ancestors pitied . . . the resourceless: a law in 367 allowed interest paid to be deducted from the principal; in 342 interest was temporarily prohibited; and in 217 the value of the *denarius* was inflated to make it easier to pay off loans.

within our own lifetime: the *lex Valeria* of 86 allowed loans to be paid off for one-quarter of the principal; since a silver *sestertius* was worth four bronze *asses*, it amounted to allowing debtors to pay off silver with bronze.

33.4 *seceded from the senatorial fathers*: the language opposes the plebeians to the patricians. There were three secessions that we know about: in 494 BC the plebs seceded to the Mons Sacer because of the severity of creditors; in the second in 449 they seceded to the Aventine Hill in response to abuses of power by Appius Claudius; and the last in 287 to the Janiculum was to protest debt. The last resulted in the *lex Hortensia*, which gave the plebs the right to pass laws (plebiscites) in the plebeian assembly.

34.1   *no one had ever sought their help in vain*: a rhetorical claim that is patently untrue; see the opening chapters of *The Jugurthine War* for the Senate's failure to help Adherbal.

34.2   *Marseilles*: Massilia, a colony that was at this time technically a sovereign state; as a result, it could become the refuge for men exiled from Rome, for instance, Milo in 52 when he was convicted for the murder of Clodius, and Verres in 70 when convicted by Cicero for extortion.

34.3   *Q. Catulus*: Q. Lutatius Catulus, consul in 78, a conservative leader of the opposition to Pompey during the years of his extraordinary commands. Earlier in 63 Caesar had defeated him for the office of *pontifex maximus*; this may explain his efforts to implicate Caesar in Catiline's conspiracy (see 49.1–2).

35.1   *experience*: perhaps an allusion to Catulus' support when the Vestal Virgin Fabia was accused of adultery with Catiline. See note on 15.1.

35.2   *new course of action*: in the Latin, Catiline refers to a *novum consilium*, 'a new plan', which could refer to his apparent change of plans and decision to go into exile or to his revolutionary plans (in Latin, novum, 'new', often refers to revolutionary change).

35.3   *the dignified status I deserve*: literally, 'the status that accords with my dignity'. 'Dignity' (*dignitas*) was an important concept in the Republic: it referred to the worth and prestige that attached to a man either because of his own deeds or because of his family's importance; it was, in this sense, like 'nobility', an inheritance and an achievement. Catiline's ancestors, the Sergii, were an old aristocratic family and, as such, would confer 'dignity' upon their members; Catiline, however, had failed to live up to that family 'dignity', though it was on his mind, even as he died; see 60.7. Another important instance of 'dignity' in the late Republic is Caesar's claim that he started the civil war to defend his 'dignity'— a reference both to what he had achieved as a general and what he was owed in return.

I have publicly taken up the cause of the poor: after his failure to win the consulship in 64 he promoted a political programme that would relieve debt; at a public gathering in 63 he declared himself 'the leader and standard bearer of the impoverished' (Cicero, *Mur.* 50).

men of no worth: that is, men without (inherited) dignity, men, like Cicero, who did not come from the nobility.

36.1   *C. Flaminius*: not otherwise known.

Arretium: a town in northern Etruria through which Catiline would pass on his way to Faesulae.

36.2 *signs of military authority*: twelve lictors with fasces, a curule chair, the military cloak and a sword. Catiline was therefore looking and acting like a magistrate sent out with an army by the Senate.

enemies of the state: such a declaration was implicit in the Senate's emergency decree, but it becomes explicit and precise by this decree. The decree meant that a state of war existed between the state and its enemies. There were legal implications: if the conspirators were 'enemies of the state', arguably they could not be 'citizens'.

36.5 *two decrees that were passed by the Senate*: at 30.6, Sallust records that the Senate offered a reward for information about the conspiracy; and, just above, at 36.2, the Senate offers a pardon to any who lay down their arms.

37.4 *the urban plebs*: the plebs were separated into the 'urban plebs' and the 'county or agrarian plebs'; each group had different needs and suffered from different circumstances.

37.6 *common soldiers had become senators*: we know of only one, a centurion named L. Fufidius. Sulla replenished the Senate, which he had helped to deplete, and increased its membership from 300 to 600, but he probably appointed new senators from the equestrian class.

37.9 *their freedom diminished*: one of Sulla's laws prohibited the sons of the proscribed from holding public office. The law was finally abrogated by Caesar in 49.

37.11 *This . . . evil*: the preference of public turmoil to senatorial ascendancy (or the diminished power of those who opposed the Senate) hinges upon the power of the tribunes: they acted as a check on the abuses (and uses) of senatorial power.

38.1 *tribunician power . . . during the consulship of Pompey and Crassus*: Sulla had diminished tribunicial power by his reforms in the late 80s: he limited the tribunes' right of veto, prevented their initiating legislation, and barred them from holding further offices. By 75, the bar on holding other offices was lifted. Pompey and Crassus, consuls in 70, restored their unrestrained right of veto and their ability to initiate legislation.

39.1 *Mithridates*: this was the Third Mithridatic War; see 16.5 and note. Pompey was away from Rome from 67 to 62. During this period the Senate attempted to secure its position partly out of fear of Pompey's return.

39.5 *someone more powerful*: some believe that Sallust has in mind the danger presented by Pompey, Crassus, and Caesar. Sallust, however, is speaking more generally: he says 'those who attained the victory', and it is not clear that he thinks that a first victory by Catiline would have led to a final victory. He imagines a hypothetical future of two events: first, brutal war that would have been the outcome of Catiline's initial success, caused in part by others who would have joined the conspiracy; second, a brutal exchange of power regardless of who won that first war.

39.5 *Fulvius*: neither the son nor the father is otherwise attested.

40.1 *P. Umbrenus*: Cicero (*Cat.* 3.14) tells us he was a freedman and that
he introduced the Allobrogian ambassadors to Gabinius. He is not
mentioned among the conspirators at ch. 17, at least in part because he
was not a senator or an *eques*.

Allobrogian ambassadors: the Allobroges were a Celtic tribe that lived
in Transalpine Gaul in the foothills of the Alps. They were conquered
in 121 BC by Q. Fabius Maximus. In 64 L. Murena (consul in 62) was
governor and apparently made their financial situation worse by helping
Roman creditors collect debts. The ambassadors were in Rome to seek
relief.

40.5 *D. Brutus*: D. Junius Brutus (consul in 77), husband of Sempronia (see
25.1) and father of the D. Brutus who helped assassinate Julius Caesar.

40.6 *Gabinius*: see 17.4 and note. As a freedman, Umbrenus would not have
much influence; Gabinius was an *eques* and so would lend more weight to
the plan.

they promised to help: Cicero tells us that they were asked to start a revolt
and to provide Catiline with horses.

41.2 *certain rewards*: the Senate voted the ambassadors special rewards on
4 December; see 50.1.

41.4 *Q. Fabius Sanga*: his name suggests that he is a descendant of Q. Fabius
Maximus Allobrogicus, the man who conquered the Allobroges. It would
be typical for the Fabii to become patrons and representatives of the
tribes their ancestor had conquered.

42.3 *C. Murena*: brother of L. Licinius Murena, who had left Transalpine
Gaul to stand for the consulship in 63. Sallust is in error when he says
that C. Murena was in Cisalpine Gaul.

43.1 *Aefula*: the manuscripts, which read *Faesulanum*, are corrupt or Sallust
is in error. In 36.2 Catiline goes to Manlius' camp in Faesulae; his plan
was to march to Rome from Faesulae, 32.2. The emendation attempts to
designate an area near to Rome, which seems required by the sense.

their individual tasks: Cicero says that the massacre and arson were planned
for the Saturnalia, 17 December, when everyone would be relaxed and no
one vigilant. However, since it was illegal to conduct public business on
the day of a public festival, Bestia's speech would have been planned for
16 December, a day on which we know it was legal to address the people.

44.3 *T. Volturcius*: all that we know about this man comes from Sallust, here
and at 45.4.

44.4 *a copy of which*: Cicero also quotes this letter (*Cat.* 3.12). The content is
the same; the wording slightly different.

45.1 *the praetors . . . C. Pomptinus*: L. Valerius Flaccus was son of the *consul suffectus* in 86 who replaced Marius when he died in office and the
author of law referred to at 33.2 which allowed debts to be paid off with

one-quarter of the principal. The son was the urban praetor, later governor of Asia, defended by Cicero against charges of extortion. C. Pomptinus replaced C. Murena in Transalpine Gaul in 62 and repressed a rebellion by the Allobroges in 61. We know of a Pomptinus who served as legate with Crassus in the war against Spartacus; this may be the same man.

Mulvian Bridge: about 3 miles north of the Forum, where the *Via Flaminia* crosses the Tiber.

46.1 *When it was over*: according to Cicero's report in the *Third Catilinarian*, this would have been about three or four in the morning of 3 December.

46.3 *stiffened his resolve*: Sallust does not tell us that he consulted with his brother and with P. Nigidius Figulus (Plutarch, *Cic.* 20.2).

Caeparius of Terracina: Cicero confirms his role in the conspiracy. He and P. Gabinius recruited T. Volturcius (47.1). He was arrested on the Mulvian Bridge and put to death on 5 December.

46.6 *Temple of Harmony*: the familiar name, the Temple of Concord, seems to me to obscure the irony and the thematic importance of this reference. At the foot of the Capitoline Hill, the temple overlooked the Forum. It was built in 367 to celebrate the reconciliation after the first secession of the plebs; it was rebuilt in 121 by L. Opimius (consul in 121) after the murder of C. Gracchus. The reader may recall that according to Sallust it was harmony (6.2, 9.1) that initially created a great state from a diverse population.

summoned the Senate: Cicero appointed four senators to keep a written record of the proceedings at this meeting and also at the meeting on 4 and 5 December. This did not become regular practice until 59 BC. On this occasion, Cicero had the record published throughout Italy.

47.2 *Sibylline books*: a collection of oracles kept in the Temple of Jupiter Capitolinus. They appear to have prescribed the proper response to crises and were consulted only in times of emergency. In 83 BC they were destroyed in a fire in the temple. The Senate commissioned a new collection based on sources in Asia and Italy. There were many forgeries current and Lentulus presumably had found this prophecy in one of them.

three Cornelii: the first was L. Cornelius Cinna, who opposed Sulla and held the consulship from 78 to 84; the second was L. Cornelius Sulla, the dictator (see ch. 5.6). P. Cornelius Lentulus Sura hoped to be the third member of the Cornelii to rule in Rome.

burning of the Capitol: on 6 July 83, as Sulla invaded Italy, the Temple of Jupiter on the Capitoline was burned; Sulla began the rebuilding which was completed after his death by Q. Lutatius Catulus (consul in 78) in 69 BC.

47.4 *'free custody'*: a literal translation of the Latin, referring to the tradition of placing prominent citizens who were awaiting trial in the custody of another prominent citizen in order to guarantee their appearance in court.

47.4 *Q. Cornificius*: one of the six men who ran for the consulship in 64, which means that he would have been praetor in 66 or before.

C. Caesar: i.e. C. Julius Caesar. He may have supported Catiline for the consulship in 64. As praetor designate, he will give the first of the two speeches that Sallust reports in the Senate on 5 December to decide the fate of the conspirators.

Cn. Terentius: otherwise unknown.

48.3 *L. Tarquinius*: otherwise unknown.

48.7 *such an important matter*: in this extraordinary passage, Sallust refuses to arrive at a precise judgement about Crassus. Instead, he gives us the reasons why we will never know if Crassus was involved. The investigation itself examines the cause of something that may not have happened.

49.1 *C. Piso*: C. Calpurnius Piso (consul in 67) opposed Pompey's extraordinary powers and laws to check bribery. As candidate for the consulship he avoided a prosecution with a huge bribe. After his consulship, he was governor of Cisalpine Gaul.

49.2 *a certain Transpadane*: a person from beyond the river Po. Most inhabitants of Cisalpine Gaul had received citizenship in 89, which protected them from summary execution. The Transpadanes had only a limited form of citizenship. Caesar and Crassus supported efforts to make them full citizens. When Piso returned from his governorship in Cisalpine Gaul, he was prosecuted for extortion and murder by Caesar and defended by Cicero. Caesar's position in this trial would have gained support for him in northern Italy.

49.3 *just a young man*: Caesar was 37 or 39 at the time, relatively young to be *pontifex maximus*; Catulus was about 57 (he died in 61). See 34.3.

50.3 *convened the Senate*: Sallust is not specific about the date or place. The meeting took place in the Temple of Harmony on the Capitoline Hill on 5 December. This was the occasion of Cicero's *Fourth Catilinarian*.

50.4 *D. Junius Silanus*: he was married to the half-sister of Cato, Servilia, the mother of M. Brutus, the assassin of Caesar.

first asked his opinion: it was the custom at this time to ask the consuls designate to open discussion of an issue before the Senate, no doubt because the immediate consequences of any decision would fall upon them. Next, the discussion would fall to ex-consuls, praetors elect, ex-praetors, and so on. The presiding consul, however, could determine the order of debate. At this time, after Silanus and Murena, the consuls designate, spoke, fourteen ex-consuls agreed with Silanus' motion. Cassius Dio reports that all who spoke between Caesar and Cato supported Caesar, although Cicero recalls that the motion in favour of punishment had been unanimously supported by all except Caesar.

P. Furius: not previously mentioned. Cicero identifies him as a Sullan colonist from Faesulae who was involved in the Allobrogian affair.

they must pay the penalty: the penalty is 'capital punishment', but that could mean either banishment or death. The expression is itself tendentious: the discussion is about exactly what 'the penalty' is or should be.

Ti. Nero: he served on Pompey's staff in 67 and had served as praetor before 63 (hence, he spoke after Caesar). We do not know how much later than Caesar Nero spoke. Appian (*B. Civ.* 2.5) has Nero speaking before Caesar (probably a misunderstanding of this very passage). In Appian, Nero proposes that the Senate wait until Catiline is defeated and an investigation can uncover more facts. This is interesting because Plutarch (*Cic.* 21) also reports that Caesar made the same proposal. It is unclear whether Caesar suggested life imprisonment (Cicero's 'eternal chains') or whether Sallust misunderstood Cicero's (exaggerated?) report.

51.1 *All human beings who debate . . .*: in form, the opening words of Caesar's speech recall Sallust's preface; the content (recommending dispassionate reason over a hasty emotional reaction) recalls the speech by Cato's great-grandfather, Cato the Censor, on how to respond to the Rhodians who had supported King Perses in his war against Rome.

conscript fathers: the term of formal address to the Senate. The epithet 'conscript' is not fully understood. Livy refers it to the fact that some senators were enrolled from among the plebeians after the expulsion of the kings: the name would be a conflation of *patres et conscripti*, 'fathers and the enrolled'. Others refer the name to a change in admission to the Senate from being automatic for any head of a patrician family to depending upon other criteria, such as electoral office.

51.5 *the Macedonian War*: the Third Macedonian War against Perses of Macedonia was brought to an end at the battle of Pydna by L. Aemilius Paulus (168 BC). The Rhodians had asked to mediate the conflict, but the war was concluded before they could reach Rome. The Senate interpreted this as a hostile act and debated declaring war on Rhodes. The elder Cato successfully opposed this proposal, arguing that the Romans should not react under the influence of emotions that made them arrogant and fierce; they should be patient, deliberate calmly, understand the Rhodian position, etc. That Caesar uses this example to argue a similar position against Cato the Younger, who modelled his own conservative severity upon his great-grandfather's reputation, is rich and can be unpacked as ironic on the part of Sallust, as rhetorical on the part of Caesar (either because he knew Cato would speak with his usual severity or because Sallust presents him in this context as pre-empting Cato), and as a reflection on how traditional Roman virtues (of severity and compassion) have become segregated and are at war with each other.

unpunished: not quite true; Rhodes was stripped of many of her holdings and a rival mercantile centre was created at Delos.

51.6 *more for money than from injury*: Caesar similarly says that he does not want to seem 'more restrained in matters of life and death than in matters of money' (*B. Civ.* 1.23).

51.6 *Punic Wars*: Rome fought Carthage three times: 264–241, 218–201, and 149–146. These wars ended in the destruction of Carthage and Roman ascendancy throughout the Mediterranean.

many horrible crimes: there is not much evidence of this, although it is common in the rhetoric of war and self-justification.

never reciprocated: again, not quite true. Especially during the Third Punic War, the Romans got their way (which meant the destruction of Carthage) by guile and treachery, even forcing the Carthaginians into an impossible situation from which the war began. One might think that, just as the case of the Rhodians works against Cato's position, the case of Carthage might actually support Catonian severity: Cato the Elder was said to have ended every speech at this time with the phrase, 'Carthage must be destroyed!'

51.8 *unprecedented course*: in a conservative society, the unprecedented (the 'new') was potentially revolutionary, destabilizing, undesirable. There may be a veiled allusion here to repercussions.

exceeds our ingenuity: in a sense, the moral fabric of Sallust's view of *civitas* (a community of citizens) is at stake in this assertion. Sallust, in the preface, asserted that men should use their intellectual ability (*ingenium*); it is exactly this 'intellectual ability' (*ingenia*) that is translated here as 'ingenuity'.

established by law: the 'final decree' advised that the consuls take extra-legal action. Caesar is asking that they refrain from such an extreme and, abiding by the *lex Porcia* and *lex Sempronia* laws (which allowed an appeal to the people and alternatives to extreme punishment), apply the legal penalties for treason and violence (normally interdiction from water and fire, i.e. exile). Caesar's objection, therefore, is not to the provisions of or the interpretation of the 'final decree' of the Senate, but to the potential abuses of the power conferred by that decree.

51.20 *death is not a torture but a release from misery*: Caesar introduces here an Epicurean argument that many have found unconvincing. It is, however, logical: if punishment is not merely a personal and passionate act of vengeance, then it should serve some purpose; if death is an end of suffering in this vale of tears, then death serves no larger punitive purpose. It may get rid of the malefactors, but does not punish them. If this is unconvincing, it is because we are still caught up in the emotions of fear and anger. It is because either intelligence does not find the right solution to the problem or we really do want to satisfy our emotions (vengeance), not our mind. Cato will respond by recalling the mythical punishments of the afterlife. The alignment of conservative politics, religious tradition, and capital punishment is one with a long history in the West.

51.22 *lex Porcia*: between 198 and 195 BC, three laws, *leges Porciae*, were introduced (see Glossary). We do not have precise information about them nor do we know which one Caesar has in mind. The name of these laws indicates that they were passed by a member of the *gens Porcia*, Cato's family.

other laws: probably a reference to the *lex Sempronia* that forbade a capital verdict without the people's judgement.

51.29 *after they conquered the Athenians*: when Sparta defeated Athens in the Peloponnesian War (404 BC), they imposed an oligarchy of thirty known as the Thirty Tyrants to govern the city.

51.32 *Damasippus*: L. Junius Brutus Damasippus, praetor in 82, executed supporters of Sulla under orders from Marius (consul in 82), son of the older Marius (consul in 107, 104–100, and 87). In November 82 he was captured by Sulla and executed.

51.38 *the Samnites*: a Sabine tribe from whom the Romans adopted their javelin.

symbols of civil authority from the Etruscans: including lictors, fasces, the curule chair, and the purple-bordered toga.

51.39 *the Greek custom*: there is no reason to assume that the Romans adopted flogging and capital punishment from the Greeks.

51.42 *virtue and wisdom*: these are the same as the virtues that Sallust praises and recommends in his preface: virtue and wisdom act together giving virtue a prudent and intellectual dimension and lending to wisdom an ethical orientation and practical efficacy. See also 53.19.

51.43 *there should be no consultation . . . the people*: this implies life imprisonment, which was not a Roman penalty. Prisons were used to hold the accused before trial. Cicero refers to Caesar's proposal as 'eternal chains', which may be an exaggeration.

52.1 *the other senators*: at this point, Cicero as presiding magistrate would have given his speech, which we have today as the *Fourth Catilinarian*.

M. Porcius Cato: the younger Cato, the great-grandson of Cato the Censor (consul in 195, censor in 184). He was 32 at the time of the Catilinarian conspiracy and had yet to hold any curule magistracy. He spoke as tribune elect for 62, and so spoke late in the debate. Although a junior senator, his speech rallied the Senate by criticizing Silanus, praising Cicero, and attacking Caesar (who, he insinuated, had a personal interest in clemency for the conspirators). He became Caesar's intractable enemy and committed suicide at Utica in Africa in 46 BC rather than accept life under Caesar.

52.4 *nothing left for the defeated*: Sallust uses the same phrase at 11.7 to describe the action of Sulla's army when he took Rome.

52.7 *often spoken*: as mentioned above, Cato was a junior member of the Senate and had probably not participated much in senatorial debates. Either he exaggerates, or Sallust put in his mouth an anachronistic version of his role in the Senate.

extravagance and greed: Cato's great-grandfather similarly complained about 'extravagance and greed' while opposing the repeal of a sumptuary law in 195 BC.

52.11 *true names for things*: Sallust takes up a topos familiar from Thucydides 3.82. There, Thucydides recounts that civil discord at Corcyra resulted in abuses of language. The topos is illustrated at 12.1 and 38.3 above.

52.22 *other things . . . by guilt nor craving*: Cato's list of the causes of Roman success should be compared with Caesar's ('virtue and wisdom' at 51.42).

52.24 *the Gauls, Rome's most bitter enemy*: the Senones, a Gallic tribe, sacked Rome in 390 BC. Here, however, Cato refers to the Allobroges.

52.30 *A. Manlius Torquatus*: other sources give the name as Titus and record that the incident happened in the Latin War (340), not the Gallic War (361). The story is that as consul Manlius Torquatus wanted to restore traditional discipline in the army and ordered the death penalty for any man who left his post without permission. Manlius' son, seeing the enemy in a vulnerable position, forgot the regulation and engaged the enemy, won a victory, and brought the spoils to his father. Manlius summoned the legion, criticized his son for leaving his post, and handed him over for execution. The story is significant for Cato's position: not only does it demonstrate values that are the opposite of 'compassion and mercy' but it shows that ultimately Cato's position depends upon an objectification of the other in terms of the past ('what did they do?' 'who are they?') and the future ('what will they do?'), not upon the internal morality of the subject ('what should we do?' 'who are we?' 'what precedent do we set?').

52.36 *those caught red-handed*: a technical legal distinction. The right of appeal to the Roman people was not available to those who were caught 'in the act'; they could be summarily executed.

53.1 *with his recommendation*: Sallust's narrative speeds to the conclusion. He does not tell us that another motion was made calling for the confiscation of the conspirators' property. Cicero tells us that he put Cato's motion to a vote because it was the best statement of the position (Cicero, *Att.* 12.21). This would be the reason Sallust does not record Cicero's speech: Cato's motion was both the clearest and the one voted on.

54.3 *not bribing*: Suetonius (*Iul.* 19) tells us that Cato approved of bribery to support the election of Bibulus, Caesar's enemy and co-consul in 59.

55.1 *three men*: the *tresviri* were magistrates elected to help the aediles by maintaining the prison and carrying out executions.

55.3 *Tullianum*: the prison was between the Temple of Concord and the Senate house at the foot of the Capitoline. It had two chambers: the lower one, the Tullianum, was subterranean, although not originally (middle of the third century) built underground; the ground level had risen over the years. This was the death chamber. A second chamber was built at the end of the second century to serve as a detention room for those waiting for their sentences.

56.1 *two legions*: a consul commanded two legions, each one of which comprised 4,200–6,000 men. Catiline seems to be maintaining the appearance of a legitimate Roman consul.

56.4 *Antonius began to approach*: Antonius would be coming from the south. Catiline moved around the area near Faesulae where Manlius' camp was. A senatorial army under Marcius Rex (see 30.3) was also in the area of Faesulae.

57.1 *difficult mountains*: it is likely that Antonius kept him from moving more easily across the plains.

 Transalpine Gaul: presumably he was heading towards the Allobroges, who had yet to receive satisfaction from Rome with regard to their complaints.

57.2 *in the Picene field*: Metellus' headquarters were probably at Ariminum, north of Picenum; he could have moved north along the *Via Aemilia* in anticipation of Catiline's movements.

58.4 *Lentulus'*: this portrayal of Lentulus agrees with Cicero (*Cat.* 3.16), who refers to him as 'the sleep of Lentulus'.

59.3 *man from Faesulae*: unknown.

 colonists: if the manuscript reading is accurate, these may be Sullan colonists; an emendation of *calonibus* for *colonis* also seems reasonable and would mean 'attendants'.

 C. Marius: Marius introduced a silver eagle as the standard for the Roman legion. In 102 BC the Cimbri and the Teutones invaded the Roman provinces. Marius defeated the Teutones in Gaul; Catulus defeated the Cimbri. We do not know why Catiline would have this eagle, but it is mentioned by Cicero as well and was apparently for him both a cherished souvenir and a sign of legitimacy.

59.4 *M. Petreius*: Petreius is praised by Cicero for his role in the fight; Antonius' seems to be treated with some mockery by Sallust. Afterwards, Petreius became Pompey's legate and fought against Caesar at Thapsus in 46. After defeat in that battle, he and King Juba arranged to have a duel, so that both would appear to have died a valiant death. Juba killed Petreius, and asked his slave to kill him.

59.5 *insurgency*: in Latin, *tumultus*, that is, a war in Italy or in Gaul which required a troop levy.

60.2 *with hostile standards*: the military standard was the sign of the Roman army in the field. Hostile standards, then, are an emblem of civil war. The sign of the Roman legion appears on both sides in this battle.

60.5 *praetorian cohort*: a special guard unit whose primary purpose was to guard the general's tent (*praetorium*).

THE JUGURTHINE WAR

1.2 *merit*: see note on *virtue*, C 2.7.

3.2 *subjects*: the Latin *parentes* could mean 'parents' or 'subjects'. 'Parents' would, of course, be absurd: how could one either correct abuses or be slaughtered by using force to rule one's parents? Nevertheless, *parentes* has within it an echo of the other meaning, 'parents'; and here the suggestion of using force against one's parent may be felt to add to the 'literal meaning' (it is dangerous to force subjects) another dimension: it is immoral and unnatural.

3.4 *powerful interests of the few*: elsewhere, especially in *Catiline's Conspiracy*, the *paucorum potentia* ('the power of the few') refers to the power and abuses of the ruling oligarchy. Here, it is not clear whether Sallust has in mind these abuses, which mainly postdate *The Jugurthine War* but which may be presaged in the work by references to *pauci potentes* ('the powerful few'), or the history of post-Sullan factionalism. If the latter, it is important to note that at the time Sallust was writing the *J*, the traditional oligarchy was being superseded. For this reason some feel that he must be referring to the second triumvirate and those who merely did their bidding. Given the general nature of Sallust's discussion, it is probably best not to connect this reference to any particular manifestation of 'the powerful interests of the few'.

4.3 *idleness*: the Latin term for 'business' is *negotium*, as in the English word 'negotiate' (to work things out). The opposite of *negotium* is *otium*, a word that can mean 'peace' or 'leisure' or 'freedom from business'. In its pejorative usages it refers to a moral flaw, laziness, indifference to the business of life or state.

4.4 *to court and greet the people and . . . dinner parties*: a general reference to social activities that are part of a political campaign.

4.5 *Q. Maximus*: Q. Fabius Maximus Cunctator. Consul five times (233, 228, 215, 214, and 209), dictator twice (221, 217), and censor (230), he gained his epithet *Cunctator* ('The Delayer') because of his successful strategy in Italy against Hannibal in the Second Punic War. He became legendary for being tough, courageous, and stubborn.

P. Scipio: P. Cornelius Scipio. This could be either of two famous Scipios: (1) Africanus Maior (236–183), who received his cognomen *Africanus* because his strategy forced Hannibal's return to Africa, which resulted in Hannibal's defeat at Zama (202); or (2) P. Scipio Aemilianus (185–129), adopted by Africanus' oldest son, was consul in 146 and commanded the army that finally defeated and destroyed Carthage.

4.6 *images of their ancestors*: the Romans kept wax masks of their ancestors in the atrium of their houses. At funerals these masks were worn by actors who impersonated the ancestors.

5.4 *the Second Punic War*: see note on *C* 51.6 above. The Second Punic War was the great conflict with Hannibal, 218–201, during which Hannibal crossed the Alps with his elephants then spent several years plundering the Italian peninsula until eventually thwarted by Q. Fabius Maximus. The war was brought to an end at Zama.

Syphax: A Numidian chief who sided with the Carthaginians against the Romans. He was defeated in 203, pursued by Masinissa and handed over to Scipio at Cirta. Masinissa was rewarded with Syphax' kingdom.

5.6 *Micipsa*: Masinissa had three sons who shared in ruling Numidia for a short time after his death (in 148). Micipsa was the oldest and was placed in charge of Cirta and the royal treasury. Gulassa was next in age and was put in charge of 'war and peace'; Mastanabal, who was interested in Greek culture and kept alive his father's contacts in the Greek world, was put in charge of justice. After the defeat of Carthage (146), the Numidian kings were rewarded for their help by Scipio: they received lands within the Roman province of Africa and what remained of the library of Carthage.

Mastanabal and Gulussa: they died shortly after their father between 146 and 139.

7.2 *Numantia*: a town in northern Spain on the river Douro. The Numantine War (154–133) ended when this town was taken by P. Cornelius Scipio Aemilianus, after a long and brutal siege, in 133 BC. The Roman victory put most of the Iberian peninsula under Roman control. The events Sallust refers to took place in 134.

9.3 *immediately adopted him*: if Micipsa 'immediately adopted' Jugurtha upon his return from Numantia, that would have taken place in 132. At 11.6, however, Hiempsal, shortly after Micipsa's death in 118, says that Jugurtha had come to power by adoption in the past three years. There is a discrepancy here of about eleven years. The chronological problem has not been solved.

9.4 *after a few years*: in fact, approximately fourteen years passed between Jugurtha's return in 132 and Micipsa's death in 118.

10.2 *has new life*: in 141 three hundred Numidian cavalry helped Fabius Servilianus; he was ambushed and forced into a treaty that Livy considered a stain on his record. It is not clear why Micipsa says that his family's name has been restored. His concern with family glory recalls Roman aristocratic concerns.

12.1 *to divide . . . among themselves individually*: Micipsa's plan was that they rule together (see the contrast between concord and discord in 10.6), not that they divide the kingdom. Partition of the country was difficult because of the uneven distribution of resources and population. Compare Masinissa's arrangements for Micipsa and his brothers in the note to 5.6.

12.3 *Thirmida*: no such town is attested in other ancient sources.

lictor: in Roman practice, the consul was attended by lictors, an official retinue that preceded him. They carried the fasces and stood beside him when he addressed the people; they cleared his path and had the power to arrest and punish. The 'closest lictor', the man who immediately preceded the consul, was a position of prestige.

13.4 *the province*: the Roman province of Africa, a territory created from Carthaginian territory in 146 BC.

13.7 *former hosts*: since Jugurtha had not been to Rome before, these must have been men who knew him at Numantia or who had met him in Numidia.

13.7 *power in the Senate at that time*: the censorship of the following year, 116, suggests that there were some strong political disagreements at work in Roman politics at the time.

14.5 *friendship*: in international politics 'friendship' meant the reciprocal understanding that the two parties would maintain peaceful commerce and diplomatic relationships.

14.6 *Masinissa*: Masinissa established Numidia's connection with Rome during the Second Punic War. He was, however, Jugurtha's grandfather as well, and Jugurtha had himself served Rome at Numantia.

15.4 *Aemilius Scaurus*: M. Aemilius Scaurus, consul in 115; censor in 109. A patrician, whose family had not held office in three generations, he was born in 162 to a father who dealt in charcoal. He studied oratory and succeeded politically and financially. He appears to have supported L. Opimius (see note on 16.2) and to have been friends with the Metelli, which would have aligned him with the Senate and patrician interests.

15.5 *polluted licence*: that is, the pollution of their otherwise legal licence to act by bribery. Scaurus prevents the pollution of his aristocratic licence by refusing bribes.

typical self-indulgence: avarice.

16.2 *ten legates*: these would be relatively young men, indicating that the Senate did not consider the task a matter of great seriousness; compare the later embassy at 25.4 where Sallust specifies that the embassy was composed of 'older aristocrats'.

L. Opimius: as consul in 121, Opimius had been responsible for acting on the Senate's 'final decree', the first instance of this being passed (see Glossary). He had C. Gracchus, Fulvius Flaccus, and about 3,000 of their followers killed. He was tried the following year for these pre-emptive actions and acquitted. The commission referred to here took place in 116. It was suspected at the time that Opimius had been bribed by Jugurtha and in 110 or 109, when the *lex Mamilia* called for an investigation of those who had abetted Jugurtha, he was forced into exile.

C. Gracchus: he was tribune of the plebs in 123. His reforms, which included grain at low prices, new colonies in Italy and abroad, and changes in tax collection, were opposed by the aristocracy. He and about 3,000 of his followers were killed in 121 when Opimius acted under the Senate's 'final decree'.

M. Fulvius Flaccus: consul in 125 and supporter of C. Gracchus in 123–121. He had tried to solve the problem of the Italian allies who were demanding citizenship. He was killed along with C. Gracchus in 121.

16.5 *given to Jugurtha*: Sallust seems to believe that the settlement was in Jugurtha's favour; this is not the opinion of contemporary scholars. The western part of the province was not, at this time, richer in agricultural resources. It was populated by nomads, who may have been more useful in guerrilla war tactics, but the more important ports (Hippo Regius,

Rusicade, Chullu, Tucca) were in the eastern territory. This does not mean that Sallust is wrong to believe that Jugurtha benefited from the aid of supporters he had bribed. Having acted both illegally and with violence, he was fortunate to avoid reprisals and to receive any portion of the empire.

17.3 *most people*: Strabo (17.3) accepts three continents; Varro (*LL* 5.31) two. Herodotus (2.16) criticizes the threefold division.

17.4 *our sea and the Ocean*: the strait is the Straits of Gibraltar, 'our sea' is the Mediterranean, and the 'Ocean' is the Atlantic.

17.5 *Catabathmos*: the name, meaning 'the descent', refers to an inclined plateau which stretches from the border of Libya into Egypt. It often refers to the boundary between Cyrenaica and Egypt or between Africa and Asia.

17.7 *Hiempsal*: not the brother of Adherbal who was murdered by Jugurtha, but Hiempsal II, the grandson of Masinissa and son of Gulussa who succeeded Jugurtha.

18.1 *Gaetuli*: the Gaetuli were unknown to Herodotus, but lived south of Numidia and Mauretania (Strabo 17.3) just north of the Sahara. The name refers loosely to indigenous inhabitants of the area who were not under the control of Numidian or Mauretanian kings.

Libyans: the term applies either to Africans in general or the inhabitants of the north coast of Africa.

18.8 *Nomads*: the etymology is fanciful. The Persians would not use a Greek name to 'call themselves' by, but a Persian name. The logic of the derivation comes from the apparent echo of *nomadas*, the Greek term that does mean 'nomads', in the name *Numidas*, which does not mean 'nomads'. According to Festus (179L) 'nomads' received their name from the Greek term for 'pasture' (*nomadas*) either because they pastured animals or because they ate fodder like their animals.

18.10 *Mauri*: a fanciful derivation.

18.11 *the Persian state*: that is, the Persians who intermarried with the Gaetuli.

18.12 *both populations*: the Persian Numidians near the Mediterranean and their colonists, the Numidians, near Carthage.

19.1 *Hippo*: either Hippo Regius or Hippo Diarrhytus near Utica.

Hadrumetum: on the east coast of modern Tunisia, south of Carthage.

Leptis: Leptis Minor, between Syrtis minor (the Lesser Syrtis) and Carthage.

19.3 *as you follow the sea-coast*: the current along the coast flows west to east. Sallust, however, is moving from east to west. The confused geography can be unconfused by reference to a minority view that the current along the coast flowed out to the Ocean. In that case, 'along the coast' could mean 'from east to west'.

19.3 *Cyrene*: Thera (modern Santorini) founded the city of Cyrene around 650.

two Syrtes . . . Leptis . . . Altars of the Philaeni: from east to west: the Greater Syrtis (modern Gulf of Sidra), Altars of the Philaeni, Leptis Magna (Lebda), the Lesser Syrtis (Gulf of Gabes, Tunisia). The geography is confused. The Altars of the Philaeni are the first important place after the Greater Syrtis.

19.5 *the Spains*: there were two Spanish provinces.

19.7 *territory that the Carthaginians had recently possessed*: that is, land controlled by the Carthaginians between the Second and the Third Punic wars.

river Muluccha: the boundary between Algeria and Morocco.

20.3 *he invaded*: the invasion took place in 113 BC, three years after the division of the kingdom.

20.6 *already tried*: see 13.3–4.

21.2 *Cirta*: modern Constantine; it was important for the grain trade.

crowd of togas: these would be Italian and Roman businessmen (see ch. 26). The toga was the national dress of Romans and Latins and in the provinces distinguished Roman citizens and Italians from provincials.

21.3 *to pre-empt the legates*: variously taken to mean that Jugurtha wanted to take the town before the legates got to Rome or before they returned with the reply of the Senate.

21.4 *three young men*: three is a common number for an embassy. They would normally be senators, and the reference to their age suggests both that they are early in their political career and still prone to the faults of youth.

23.1 *Cirta's position*: Constantine is surrounded by deep ravines.

25.2 *the same men*: see 13.8, 15.2, 16.1, 27.1.

25.4 *older aristocrats*: compare the embassy of three junior senators, 16.2.

above: see 15.4.

25.5 *leader of the Senate*: Livy tells us that the 'leader of the Senate' was the man whose name was entered first in the censor's books. Originally this honour was reserved for the oldest living censor; later (after 544) it was only a mark of honour (Livy, 27.13). The honour was usually retained for life, and the term, *princeps Senatus*, was adopted by the Roman emperors. See also Livy, 34.44; 39.52.

Utica: the capital of the Roman province of Africa.

27.2 *C. Memmius*: tribune of the plebs in 111. In addition to his opposition to the aristocrats who were aligned with Jugurtha, he ran for the consulship in 100. He was killed in a riot designed to support the re-election of the tribune, Saturninus.

tribune elect: at this time tribunician elections seem to have been held during the summer.

27.3 *lex Sempronia*: passed in 123 by C. Gracchus, the law required that two consular provinces be selected before the consular elections. After the election, the provinces would be assigned to the individual consuls by lot or agreement. In this way the consuls could not select their own provinces to serve their self-interest.

27.4 *P. Scipio Nasica . . . elected*: consular elections were held in October or November. Scipio Nasica was the son of the senator who was responsible for the death of C. Gracchus; he died in office. L. Bestia Calpurnius was tribune in 121; he sided with the Senate against C. Gracchus. He was later accused and condemned for receiving bribes from Jugurtha (see Cicero, *Brut.* 34).

27.5 *An army was then enlisted*: Sallust fails to tell us when war was formally declared.

28.1 *a son*: Jugurtha had more than one son. At least two appeared in Marius' triumph.

after killing Hiempsal: see 13.6.

28.4 *his staff*: these would be the commander's legates, his military staff.

28.5 *I mentioned above*: see 15.4. Legates were typically of lower rank than their commander and so the appointment of Scaurus, an ex-consul, was unusual.

28.6 *personal assaults*: another reading, *insidias*, would mean 'in face of . . . treachery'.

The legions: for 'legions', see Glossary. Typically a consular army was composed of two legions. We do not know how many legions were enrolled for the Jugurthine War.

28.7 *men*: Sallust writes *mortalis*, the Latin word for humans when distinguished by their mortality, a mortal (as opposed to a god). The term is also used in a reduced sense for 'human being' without particular emphasis on mortality; thus, Cicero says of his prosecution of Verres: 'I am defending many men, many states, the entire province of Sicily' (*Div. in Caec.* 5). In instances like this, 'mortals' for the Latin *mortales* is as much of an over-translation as 'men' is an under-translation. I have not found a satisfactory solution.

29.4 *Sextius*: uncertain; perhaps P. Sextius, convicted of bribery as praetor designate, *c.*90.

Vaga: a town that had in earlier days been part of the Carthaginian territory; it was an important market town and will appear again in Sallust's narrative at 47 and 66 ff.

29.5 *Council*: an army commander had a war council, composed of legates, the quaestor, the tribunes, the prefects, and the chief centurions; they would advise the commander, not on terms of surrender, but on whether to accept surrender (which would normally be unconditional).

omnibus bill: that is, the Council was not asked to vote on individual items but only on the entire deal.

29.7 *a small amount of silver*: surrender to the Romans was not normally a conditional affair. Livy gives the formula: 'Do you surrender yourself and the people of your town, the city, its fields and water, its boundaries, temples, and utensils, all things human and divine into my power and the power of the Roman people?' (Livy 1.38).

the elections: probably sometime in October; the elections were held close to or in November.

Peace: not a formal peace, which would have to be ratified by the Senate, but a cessation of hostilities.

30.3 *we mentioned above*: see 27.2.

31.1 *If my concern . . . addressing you*: the speech begins in imitation of Cato the Elder speaking against S. Sulpicius Galba on the occasion of another surrender: 'Many things discourage me from coming forth here . . .' Sallust's language and moral posture seems to imitate Cato elsewhere, which would indicate, among other things, that this is not a literal transcript of the speech given by Memmius.

31.2 *these past fifteen years*: Memmius is speaking in 111. Fifteen years would take us back to 126 or 125, which would be about the time that C. Gracchus began advocating for the Latin allies. Important as this action was, it could not be fairly considered the beginning of a period of aristocratic abuse of the plebs. The events that most affected the plebs were the death of Ti. Gracchus in 133 (twenty-two years earlier) and the death of C. Gracchus in 122 (eleven years earlier). Sallust may have made a mistake, the time may have been rhetorically exaggerated (if Memmius means the murder of C. Gracchus) or have become proverbial (if Sallust refers to the murder of Ti. Gracchus), or there may be an error in the manuscripts: XV written for XX.

31.6 *your ancestors often did*: see note on the secession of the plebs at *C.* 33.3.

31.7 *prosecuted the Roman plebs*: Ti. Gracchus was killed in 133; a tribunal was formed to prosecute his supporters. The tribunal was conducted by the consuls of 132, P. Popillius Laenas and P. Rupilius.

M. Fulvius: M. Fulvius Flaccus; see note on 16.2.

31.11 *empire . . . servitude*: the contrast of *imperium* and *servitium*, empire and slavery, control and servitude, is a prominent feature of Sallust's preface to *C* and of Catiline's speeches. In fact, Memmius' speech should be compared with Catiline's speech at *C* 20.

31.15 *friendship*: see note on *J* 14.5.

31.16 *favours*: it is part of the rhetoric of electoral politics at Rome to call the election to political office a 'favour' granted by the people.

31.17 *the Aventine*: of three secessions of the plebs (see note to *C* 32.3) only one was to the Aventine.

31.21 *in your own destruction*: compare Cato in *C* 52.11–12, 52.27.

32.1 *L. Cassius*: L. Cassius Longinus, Marius' colleague in the consulship, in 107. He had a reputation for severity and, according to Cicero, was 'the most accurate and wisest of judges' (*Rosc. Am.* 30).

33.2 *C. Baebius*: tribune in 111, otherwise unknown; the name is a common one.

33.3 *in the ancestral manner*: a euphemism for capital punishment, usually preceded by scourging.

35.1 *Massiva*: Jugurtha's cousin.

35.2 *Sp. Albinus*: consul in 110.

Q. Minucius Rufus: Sallust has the name wrong. Quintus was the brother of the consul with Sp. Albinus in 110; the consul's first name was Marcus, who may have been the tribune of 121. Both brothers were associated with settling border disputes in Italy in 117 and Quintus was his brother's legate in Macedonia and Thrace.

35.4 *Bomilcar*: Jugurtha's lieutenant. He fights Rutilius at 49.1 ff. (esp. 52.5–53.3), but is not very effective; his loyalty to Jugurtha is compromised by Metellus, 61.4.

35.9 *as sureties*: perhaps a reference to Bomilcar's first appearance in court at 35.7. Typically a 'surety' guaranteed someone's appearance in court by pledging a sum of money to be forfeited if the defendant did not appear. The number 'fifty' is very high.

35.10 *a city for sale and soon to fall, if it could only find a buyer*: in some manuscripts, and in Livy and others, this famous quote is recorded as an exclamation: 'Oh, city for sale and soon to die, if only she can find a buyer!'

36.4 *Aulus*: the career of Aulus Albinus is not certain. He may have already been praetor; the disgrace in Numidia may have ended his career; he may have been consul in 99.

set out for Rome: October or November 110.

37.1 *P. Lucullus and L. Annius*: both otherwise unknown.

37.3 *January*: this is January 109, the month in which new consuls would take office. In ch. 43, however, Metellus and Silanus are still 'consuls designate'. If Sallust's chronology (the only precise date in the entire work) is correct, we must assume that the failure of elections referred to just above meant that the consuls were not elected until 109 and therefore did not take office until later in the year.

winter camps: the Roman army did not normally campaign in the winter, but Africa seems to be a different case. Metellus leaves his winter camp (68.2) and Marius goes on an expedition during the winter of 106–5 (103.1). Other winter campaigns in Africa are known from Caesar and Tacitus.

37.3 *severe winter weather*: in northern Africa the severe weather would be caused by rain during October and November and during April and May. Presumably Aulus was misled by a dry spell.

37.4 *Suthul*: a fortified town on the river Ubus, between Cirta and Hippo and nearly 40 miles south of Hippo Regius.

where the king's treasury was kept: another ancient source, Orosius, says (5.15.6) that the treasury was at Calama, which was also the site of conflict. Neither place can be identified with certainty.

38.1 *the legat's*: here referring to Aulus, a junior officer serving a consul in the province.

legates: here, the members of Jugurtha's embassy.

38.2 *[Thus . . . more hidden.]*: this is thought to be a scribe's comment, not part of Sallust's text.

38.6 *those whom we said above*: see 38.3.

Ligurians: at least four cohorts served under Metellus, and Ligurian forces had served in both the Carthaginian and Roman armies. According to Virgil they were hardy people, accustomed to hardship (*Georg.* 2.168).

Thracian cavalry: at this time the Romans were at war with several Thracian tribes.

centurion of the first rank: the commander of the first century of the first file of a legion. See Glossary.

38.10 *in exchange for their fear of death*: the expression is trenchant and harsh.

39.2 *the Latins*: the ratio of allies to Romans has been variously calculated, but all agree that the brunt of the war was borne by the Italian allies and the Latins, from just south of Rome, who enjoyed a limited kind of citizenship.

40.1 *C. Mamilius Limetanus*: tribune in 109, author of a law regulating boundaries (hence, his cognomen, which means 'the boundary man').

those who had advised Jugurtha: this would include all those mentioned since 13.8, new men and old aristocracy, who had encouraged Jugurtha. Cicero (*Brut.* 128) records the names of the condemned: C. Galba, L. Bestia, C. Cato, Sp. Albinus, and L. Opimius. The condemnation of Opimius was the first conviction of a legate while part of an embassy. This appears to have established the precedent for holding ambassadors responsible for their conduct in the same way that governors and magistrates were responsible.

those who had returned his elephants and deserters: presumably relatively obscure men.

40.2 *those who had reached agreements . . . or war*: Bestia and A. Albinus.

friends: here in the political sense, political allies and clients.

the Latins: literally, 'men of Latin name'. The form of Sallust's expression 'men of Latin name and the Italian allies' is unparalleled although the expression has several other variants. The phrase 'men of Latin name' means 'men of whatever is considered Latin'; cf. 'hateful to the Roman name', which means 'hateful to whatever is Roman'. The aristocracy would exert its influence through 'clients' (see 8.1: 'powerful among the allies'), but it is not clear how the Italians and Latins would benefit from opposing the *lex Mamilia*. Most would not receive the right to vote for another twenty years and so, whatever they were urged to do, it was probably illegal and violent.

40.4 *who we said above*: see 15.4.

40.5 *one of the three commissioners*: this is so surprising that scholars have suggested that Sallust mistook M. Scaurus for M. Aurelius Scaurus, suffect consul in 108. The 'commissioner' (quaestor) oversaw the tribunal; the jury was composed of 'equites' (the mercantile class), whose interests in Africa were harmed by senatorial misconduct of the war. While there seems to have been no active hostility between the Senate and the 'equites' between 121 and 109, that is, before Marius' campaign for the consulship, this tribunal appears to have played a role in worsening relationships.

41.1 *a few years earlier*: as becomes clear, Sallust ascribes the beginning of Roman decline to the destruction of Carthage in 146. It was a commonplace in ancient thought to value 'the fear of an enemy' (*metus hostilis*) as a restraint on moral degeneration. In fact, the preservation of Carthage as a salutary source of danger to Rome was advocated as early as 201. Sallust's relatively idealistic picture of the period before the fall of Carthage is, of course, belied by the abundant evidence of strife and conflict between 202 and 146. Nevertheless, after 133 major changes were introduced by the Gracchi and by the opposition to them, and their political programme cannot be divorced from the defeat of Rome's most significant external enemy.

41.5 *'dignity' ... 'liberty'*: these are political catchwords, the slogans of partisan conflict. 'Dignity' refers to the prestige, rank, privilege, and reputation of the nobility; 'liberty', of course, is the term used to resist any restraints that come from another party or interest. Reference to them here is also a reference to the debasement of political vocabulary, a common theme in Sallust (see *C* 38.3 and 52.12).

41.6 *had more power*: the ruling oligarchy was generally willing to close ranks to protect its privileges.

41.7 *among the multitude*: one should add that many of the plebs were clients of the aristocracy; this too would dissipate any opposition to oligarchic power.

A few men ... triumphs: compare Catiline, *C* 20.7.

41.8 *poverty*: Sallust's interpretation is supported by historical evidence for resistance to military service and a growing gap between the rich and the poor.

41.10 *men were found*: the reference is to men like the Gracchi and M. Fulvius Flaccus.

42.1 *Ti. and C. Gracchus*: see Introduction. pp. viii–x.

42.1 *ancestors*: these ancestors would include the consuls of 238, 215, 213, 177, and 163, and Scipio Africanus, who defeated Hannibal at Zama in 202 and was their maternal grandfather.

coalition: the Senate and the *equites* opposed Ti. Gracchus in 133–132. C. Gracchus proposed legislation regarding the provinces and public farmlands that gained equestrian support, but Opimius could still count on the equestrians in his prosecution of C. Gracchus in 121. What was the 'coalition'? Perhaps it was senatorial support for equestrian juries or the promise to include some equestrians in the Senate.

42.3 *but it is better . . . in a vicious manner*: the Latin has a typical Sallustian obscurity and subject to many interpretations.

42.5 *I am returning to my initial topic*: this ends the first phase of the war and the first major division of Sallust's monograph. Phase II may be divided as follows: 43–5, Metellus and the army; 46–62, the first campaign; 63–5, Marius and Metellus; 66–82, the second (and third) campaign.

43.1 *egregious flight*: the Latin for 'treaty' is the noun *foedus*; the Latin for 'foul, shameful' is the adjective *foedus*. Sallust puns by referring to *Auli foedus* ('Aulus' treaty') and the *foedam fugam* ('foul flight') of the army.

Metellus and Silanus: Q. Caecilius Metellus, consul in 109, was later named Numidicus for his successes in Numidia against Jugurtha. He will be the general whose presence organizes chs. 43–83. The Metelli were dominant in Roman politics of the time, holding six consulships in the period 123–109. M. Junius Silanus was consul in 109, and was the first member of his family to reach the consulship; he was defeated in the battle against the Cimbri in 109 or 108. The Cimbri defeated the Romans at Arausio in 105, a disaster which resulted in Marius' election to his second consulship (104). These events will mark the ending of Sallust's monograph.

the consuls designate: if the January date above (37.3) is correct, then 'consuls designate' is difficult to understand.

43.2 *entered his term of office*: normally, the consul would enter office on 1 January.

43.3 *a common interest in everything else*: meaning that he believed he had no special responsibility for anything but the war; he thought his colleagues could take care of all other matters in accordance with their common interests.

44.2 *delay in the elections*: elections typically took place in October or November; in 110 they may have taken place between 10 December and 1 January (see 37.2–3). Further delays would have been caused by the preparations and Mamilius' tribunal. Metellus left Rome in April and took over command in early June.

45.2 *transverse marches*: the Latin is as obscure as the English. Presumably, Metellus is getting his army in shape by marching back and forth across the direct path to his destination, a task whose purpose would be to enforce physical exercise and discipline.

46.2 *asking only for the life of Jugurtha*: a precondition for surrender was the surrender of the enemy leader, typically without terms. One might have some moral expectation of leniency and the Roman commander might promise leniency, but complete and unconditional surrender was the only legal condition of those offering surrender. See above, 29.5.

46.3 *through prior experiences*: either Metellus had served in Numidia before or Sallust is referring to the experiences of others, for instance, Bestia's unfortunate dealings with Jugurtha (see ch. 29).

46.5 *mapalia*: see 18.8: nomad huts that look like boat hulls.

46.7 *C. Marius*: this is the first mention of Marius, the general who will play a central role in both the Jugurthine War and Roman domestic politics. See further, Introduction, pp. xi–xiii.

auxiliary cavalry: cavalry raised from the provinces and from among foreigners. The regular cavalry came from the Italian allies and from citizens.

47.1 *Vaga*: it was at Vaga that the Bestia accepted Jugurtha's sham surrender (29.4).

48.1 *with his own methods*: both the adoption of enemy methods (Roman battle formation was adopted from the Greeks, the Roman navy was modelled after the Carthaginian navy) and the use of treachery (e.g. Tullus Hostilius' war against Alba or Scipio at Zama) were traditional features of how the Romans understood their military success. Here, it is an effect of this war that in defeating Jugurtha, the Romans became (and perhaps needed to become) like him.

48.3 *Muthul*: usually identified with the Oued Mellègue, although not without problems. Sallust does not tell us what Metellus' strategic aims were or what direction he was travelling in, or give us enough information to discover the precise site of the battle. His topography is often cited as a weakness of his 'military history' and, judged by modern desires for 'the objective facts', this is true. It is also a clear indication that Sallust is not really interested in topographical accuracy in the same way a modern historian is. In fact, one might suppose that our two-dimensional, linear cartographic notions of territorial space would be foreign to a culture that thought of the world (*orbis terrarum* = 'the circle of lands') in terms of a Roman centre surrounded by lands that were either domesticated (Romanized, civilized) or hostile (barbarian).

†*twenty*†: the distance seems much too great and editors suspect an error in the manuscripts.

in the middle: it is not clear whether Sallust means in the middle of the mountain range or in the middle of the plain.

49.1 *which we described as extended on a transverse course*: see the description in 48.3: the hill extended from the middle of the mountain range, which was parallel to the river. The Latin is not clear and is taken to mean either that the hill lay between Metellus and the river Muthul at right angles to Metellus' route, or that the hill lay at right angles to the river and flanked Metellus' route.

49.6 *in its new formation*: the marching formation appears to have been a triple column of *hastati* (spearmen), *principes* (experienced fighters), and *triarii* (the best veterans), grouped as companies (maniples) each with its own baggage in front. They marched behind their baggage with the *hastati* on the side from which they expected danger. Metellus appears to have expected Jugurtha to attack from the river side in an effort to cut him off from the river. If attacked, each maniple (of *hastati*, *principes*, and *triarii*) moved to the right or left of its baggage (the side from which danger arose) to form a fighting line of *hastati* (H), backed by *principes* (P), with *triarii* (T) in the rear. In this instance, when Metellus turned left to descend the mountain toward the river, Jugurtha was now in the hills on his right. Metellus then changed order of his marching line from H, P, T to T, P, H or P, T, H, placing the *hastati* in position to be the front line against Jugurtha. They, then, moved to protect their baggage with slingers and archers between each maniple. Metellus then moved the cavalry to the wings. Now, with Metellus marching toward the river with Jugurtha in the right, the scene was as follows (where * indicates baggage, 'sl' = slingers; 'ar' = archers):

```
M
O
U   H                                                   H   R
N   O   T*sl*T*sl*T*sl*T*sl*T*sl*T*sl*T*sl*T            O   I
T   R   P   P   P   P   P   P   P   P                   R   V
A   S                                                   S   E
I   E   H ar H ar H ar H ar H ar H ar H ar H            E   R
N
S       ∧∧∧∧∧∧∧∧∧∧∧∧∧∧∧∧∧∧∧∧∧∧∧∧∧∧∧∧∧∧∧

        HILL WITH JUGURTHA HIDDEN
```

Each maniple, consisting of two centuries, was generally formed in a quincunx, so that each line protected the spaces between the centuries of the prior line:

T T

P

H H

Reconstruction of troop movements like this is always open to reinterpretation. Sallust's Latin is not always precise or clear about military movements.

50.1 *Rutilius*: praetor in 118, consul in 105; an enemy of Marius. Historians speculate that Sallust may have relied upon his biography as a source for this battle, since Marius is present but plays a very small part in Sallust's narrative.

50.2 *behind the front line*: the 'front line' refers to the fighting order, not the marching order. Marius would have been in the centre of the marching line, just behind the 'front lines' if they had to turn and face an enemy on the right.

52.5 *we noted above*: see 49.1. It is not clear what Bomilcar's strategy was in allowing Rutilius to pass his position. On the one hand, he did not trust his troops, as Sallust will say shortly; on the other, once Rutilius has passed Bomilcar and pitched camp, Bomilcar can keep him from bringing aid to Metellus.

52.6 *battle growing louder*: if the battle takes place close to the mountains, and the mountains are 20 miles away from the river, it would be impossible for Rutilius, who is now at the river, to hear the battle, as Bomilcar fears. For this reason, some suggest that the correct reading should be 'II' not 'XX' miles.

54.3 *an army larger in numbers*: one of Jugurtha's signal advantages was the ability to raise troops.

55.1 *Metellus' accomplishments*: it had been a difficult year for Rome. In 109 the Cimbri had defeated two Roman armies and there had been losses in Macedonia. Given the management of the war against Jugurtha before Metellus' arrival, relief is understandable; joy is perhaps an over-reaction.

55.2 *a thanksgiving to the immortal gods*: a 'thanksgiving' consisted of three to five days of public prayers decreed by the Senate and proclaimed by a magistrate. All the temples in the city were opened; wine and incense might be provided at public expense.

55.4 *out of formation*: both a strategically smart move and an indication that the number of his troops was dangerously low.

55.5 *Marius led the rest*: Rutilius had seniority, since he had held the praetorship before Marius, but he is not mentioned again, except at 86.5. There, when Metellus hands over his army to Marius, who succeeds him as commander, Rutilius is described as 'second in command'. The prominence of Marius here is particularly striking, especially when one considers that many scholars believe that Sallust's source is Rutilius' account of the war. Sallust has a thematic interest in opposing Metellus and Marius.

56.1 *Zama*: this is probably Zama Regia, the capital of Juba's kingdom. The site is disputed. Of the most commonly suggested possibilities, two do not fit Sallust's description (and yet Sallust must have known the place, if it was the capital of the province) and the third does not have any late-Roman remains at the modern site (although Zama was an important city in imperial times and a colony under Hadrian).

56.3 *Sicca*: see Map 3. A town between fertile plains and on the road from Carthage to Cirta, it had economic and strategic importance. It was the market for cereals grown in the area.

57.6 *by machine*: sophisticated war machinery, like catapults, may have been adopted from the Carthaginians.

58.1 *with a great force*: Metellus' strategy in attacking Zama had been to provoke Jugurtha into a battle (see 56.1). It is surprising, then, that Jugurtha's arrival is unexpected, especially after Jugurtha had attacked Marius at Sicca (56.4). Perhaps Sallust is more interested in drama than in details; perhaps there was some negligence.

58.5 *begged Marius in the name of their friendship and the Republic*: Marius, who will be the central figure in the third phase of the war, when military power is transferred from the patrician general, Metellus, to the 'new man', appears unemphatically throughout the second phase. The relationship between Metellus and Marius is difficult to gauge, either in fact or in Sallust's narrative. Metellus was contemptuous and haughty (64.1); Marius was a 'new man'. In 119 Marius as tribune passed a law to limit the influence of money in elections; this was opposed by Metellus. Then, in 116 Marius was prosecuted for electoral corruption by a member of the Metellus family. He was, however, chosen as Metellus' legate in 109. There must have been some reconciliation and they both had reasons to work together under the present circumstances. Still, it is our knowledge of what will come that adds depth to these scenes. For instance, one may wonder if Sallust is here suggesting that Metellus (the fierce but wise aristocrat) and Marius (the talented *popularis*) should and could have been able to work together at other times 'in the name of friendship and the Republic'.

59.3 *In this way . . . .*: the interpretation of the text is open to much discussion. The most important matter concerns the determination of who is winning and to what degree. Either the Numidians resist and nearly win—but then it is unclear how they were finally beaten off—or the Romans resist 'the Numidian' (that is, Jugurtha) and the Roman infantry and cavalry join forces; either the Roman light-armed infantry conquer a nearly defeated foe or they nearly conquer them. I have adopted an interpretation that makes the most sense to me; there are other ways to read the Latin.

60.3 *You would have seen them*: Sallust's description here is written in imitation of Thucydides' description of the siege of Syracuse, 7.71.1–4.

61.2 *in winter quarters*: this is the winter camp after Metellus' first year of campaign, 109/8. His winter quarters for the second year, 108/7, are not mentioned.

61.4 *to avoid trial for the murder of Massiva*: see 35.5–9.

61.5 *opportunity for duplicity*: the scene recapitulates Metellus' first efforts to turn Jugurtha's legates against him; see 46.3 and 47.3. For Bomilcar's friendship with Jugurtha, see 35.4.

62.1 *bemoaning his fate*: Metellus had ravaged the countryside, but Jugurtha had held Zama. Metellus' victory at the Muthul was costly and he had not secured any territory in Numidia. Jugurtha's anxiety must reflect either real economic losses, loss of prestige, and foreboding about the future or Sallust's sense of drama and foreshadowing.

in every battle: an exaggeration; Jugurtha had just held on to Zama.

62.5 *in the manner of our ancestors*: compare Jugurtha's surrender to Bestia, especially 29.5.

62.7 *King Bocchus*: except for the mention of Bocchus at the end of the African ethnographic digression (ch. 19), this is the first mention of a man who will play an important role in the final phase of the Jugurthine War.

Mauretania: see above, 19.7. Bocchus was ruler of the Moors who, according to Sallust, knew nothing of the Romans before the Jugurthine War.

62.8 *Tisidium*: not otherwise known.

62.10 *assigned Numidia to Metellus*: a general's command would typically last until he was replaced. Since the Senate assigned provinces before the elections, according to a *lex Sempronia*, in this case, all the Senate needed to do was to leave Numidia out of the consular provinces for 108 and Metellus would keep his command. By assigning Numidia to Metellus, they indicated their confidence in him. This was the first time during the Jugurthine War that the general in command was prorogued. In Sallust's narrative, it is a particularly important moment: it follows a failure to capture Jugurtha by treachery and precedes Marius' aspirations. Marius will eventually replace Metellus and his legate, Sulla, will capture Jugurtha by treachery.

63.1 *During this period*: Sallust's expression, even in the Latin, is vague; this allows him to connect Metellus' success with Marius' growing ambition. Plutarch (*Mar.* 45) dates the oracle to the evening of Marius' departure for Rome to stand for the consular elections in 108. It is unclear why Marius is in Utica or how he got there.

Utica: see Map 3. Utica was a port with large numbers of Roman citizens; it is generally regarded as the capital of the province of Africa.

63.2 *test his fortune*: the role of fortune is important and thematic in Sallust's preface. It is striking that Marius' career from this point on is frequently marked by references to some form of good fortune (65.5; 85.48; 90.1; 92.2, 6; 93.1; 94.7). It is also noteworthy that Plutarch (*Mar.* 45) recounts that Marius said that wise men do not trust in luck.

for the consulship: having been elected tribune in 115, he would have been eligible to stand for the consulship in 112.

his lineage: Marius was a 'new man', meaning that no member of his family had ever been elected to the consulship or the Senate.

not a victim of lust or wealth: Marius' virtues should be compared with Jugurtha's virtues; see 6.1.

63.3 *Arpinum*: A small town about 60 miles south-east of Rome, the birthplace of the famous orator Cicero. See Map 2.

Greek eloquence or urban polish: such claims are common for a 'new man' who wishes to succeed in a system that privileged the conservative aristocracy; the elder Cato made them, though he studied Greek rhetoric and had his sons taught Greek. Marius, too, shows evidence of sophistication: his speech at ch. 85 is modelled on the elder Cato and, despite his claim to know no Greek, it contains reminiscences of Greek authors: Demosthenes at 85.12, Plato at 85.21 and 49, and perhaps Lysias at 85.4.

63.4 *military tribune*: we do not know the date when Marius first held this office. Scholars offer dates from 134 to 119.

63.6 *worthy of a higher office than the one he held*: the evidence does not confirm this: he was tribune in 119, failed to be elected to either the curule or the plebeian aedileship, was barely elected praetor in 115, and was tried for electoral corruption in 112.

destroyed by ambition: compare Sallust's view of ambition in *C* 10.5 and 11.1–2.

the aristocracy . . . among themselves: Sallust was himself of a non-consular family, and, perhaps more important, of a non-senatorial family. He exaggerates, however, the difficulties of a 'new man'. In the second century a 'new man' reached the consulship every three or four years (see E. Badian, *Gnomon*, 36 (1964), 384). A non-senatorial 'new man', however, found the odds much more difficult: it had been twenty years since Rupilius was elected consul in 132, the last consul from a non-senatorial family.

63.7 *unclean*: compare Catiline's attitude toward Cicero, *C* 31.7.

64.1 *he asked Metellus for a furlough*: Cicero (*Off.* 3.79) says that Metellus sent Marius to Rome.

64.4 *Metellus' son*: Metellus Pius: praetor in 89 or 88. He could have expected to reach the consulship in 86, when Marius would have been 80. In fact, Metellus did not become consul until 80.

regiment: the Latin *contubernium* refers to a body of soldiers who occupied the same tent.

64.5 *looser discipline than before*: Marius' reaction to Metellus' arrogance is to undo the military discipline that had been the hallmark of Metellus' generalship. Other traditions portray Marius as a general who was willing to share his soldiers' burdens, and was affable and generous. Compare Metellus (45.1) and Sulla (96.3).

Traders: the Latin term would cover traders, merchants, bankers, and moneylenders.

dragged on the war: the war, begun in 112, had been in progress for three years.

65.1 *Gauda*: Jugurtha's half-brother. He was left in charge of Jugurtha's kingdom after the war.

65.5 *lex Mamilia*: see note on 40.2.

66.1 *Meanwhile*: Jugurtha's intrigues and the rising at Vaga take place during winter, 109/8.

66.2 *the leaders of the state conspired together*: these may be magistrates or members of the town council. Since we do not know anything about the administration of the town, it is hard to say.

a festival day: we do not know what festival this was. Scholarly opinion suggests a festival for Ceres, the goddess of grain, or for Tinnit, an African fertility deity. The reference to licentiousness may support the latter.

66.3 *T. Turpilius Silanus*: otherwise unknown. At 69.4, Sallust says he was a Latin, but it is unlikely that a Latin would be prefect of the city or commander of Roman troops (67.3). Plutarch and Appian say he was a Roman.

67.3 *a life of turpitude*: Sallust uses the word *turpis*, meaning 'ugly, repulsive, dishonourable', to pun on the name *Turpilius*.

wretched and despicable: the Latin terms *improbus intestabalisque*, are legal terms taken from the Twelve Tables; they designate a person of such disgraceful character that he was not allowed to give evidence in court.

68.2 *Numidian cavalry*: the Numidian cavalry could have been comprised of deserters or enlisted from communities not under Jugurtha's control.

69.3 *a citizen from Latium*: the Latin presents a problem. See 67.3 on Turpilius' status as prefect and commander. If Turpilius was a Roman citizen, he should not have suffered capital punishment; if he was not a Roman citizen, he should not have been prefect.

70.2 *Nabdalsa*: we know nothing of this man except what Sallust tells us here.

73.2 *dismissed to go home*: Sallust leaves the impression that Marius was sent to Rome while Metellus was in winter quarters; Plutarch (*Mar.* 8) reports that it was just twelve days before the elections in October or November.

73.4 *added to his appeal*: Marius was married to Julia, the aunt of C. Julius Caesar; this gave him patrician credentials which are ignored in the narrative, and were perhaps overlooked in the campaigning as well.

73.5 *seditious magistrates*: presumably tribunes of the plebs.

73.6 *the plebs*: the plebs could be and should be here taken to include the *equites*, Rome's wealthy mercantile class.

73.7 *T. Manlius Mancinus*: tribune of the plebs in 107. He may be the same man as C. Manlius; see 86.1.

they voted: the tribune would have taken office on 10 December 108. Sallust's narrative has skipped a year: he has moved from the events at Vaga (winter, 109/8) to the following winter, without mention of Metellus' campaigns of 108–107 or his winter quarters in 108/7. As 107 ends, Metellus returns to Rome.

Numidia to Metellus: this would be the second prorogation of Metellus' command, but the formal prorogation does not appear in Sallust's text.

74.2 *Metellus appeared*: apparently Metellus did not know that his command had been taken away. Alternatively, this action took place in 108 before Manlius transferred the command to Marius. Presumably Metellus heard of his lost command in January 107; Marius probably arrived in Africa late in 107.

75.1 *Thala*: we do not know where ancient Thala was; modern Thala does not conform to Sallust's description. The word *thala* is Berber for 'spring' and so may have been a common name in antiquity. This Thala was apparently in the south, since Jugurtha flees south to the Gaetuli after escaping.

77.1 *Hamilcar*: otherwise unknown; his description indicates that he was probably a member of the town senate or town council. Political events in Numidia frequently parallel political problems in Rome.

77.2 *the beginning of the war with Jugurtha*: this would be in 111, when Bocchus too asked for a treaty with Rome, but was refused. See below, 80.4–5.

77.4 *C. Annius*: the name is common; see the unrelated tribune of the plebs, L. Annius, tribune of the plebs in 110, 37.2. Further identification is speculative.

78.1 *Sidonians*: the Sidonians are also known as the Tyrians; the names are used interchangeably for Phoenicians.

78.4 *'dragging'*: the etymology is Greek: *syrein* means 'to drag'.

79.1 *the extraordinary and marvellous deed*: excursuses or digressions like this are felt to have structural significance in ancient history and often to elucidate the narrative in thematic terms. This excursus acts structurally to set off Metellus' final military accomplishment with a tale that may be felt to create a thematic contrast between the self-sacrificing patriotism of the Carthaginians and the self-serving motives of the current war. For the places named here, see the geographical excursus at chs. 17–19.

80.3 *to persuade the close friends of King Bocchus*: Jugurtha and Bocchus did not make a formal alliance until after Marius took command. This may reflect earlier connections and aid.

81.1 *Perseus*: king of Macedonia, 179–168, with whom the Romans fought the Third Macedonian War.

81.2 *Cirta*: Cirta was brutally captured by Jugurtha at the beginning of the war; see chs. 21–6. Sallust does not tell us when it was retaken by the Romans.

86.2 *to set sail*: it is a sign of Marius' sense of urgency that he sends his legate ahead before the infantry levy was completed. A. Manlius is otherwise unknown; he was perhaps related to T. Manlius Mancinus, tribune of the plebs in 107; see 73.7. He probably left Rome sometime in February or March 107.

from the headcount: Roman society was divided into five classes based on property qualifications and a sixth, unpropertied class. The landowners were called *assidui*, 'settlers'; those without property were called *proletarii*, 'breeders', and were *capite censi*, 'counted by head'. It was the custom, but not a legal requirement, to enrol an army from the *assidui*. The 'headcount class' was exempt from military service, except in an emergency. The requirement for the lowest class of *assidui* was property in the amount of 1,500 *asses*, an amount so small that it did not meaningfully distinguish the 'settlers' from the 'headcount'. The military and political effects of Marius' enrolment of the 'headcount' became increasingly evident later: it allowed for uniform armament, increasing professionalism, client armies, and the development of cohorts. At the time, the Senate did not oppose Marius and even seems to have accepted the new method of enrolment (see Plutarch, *Mar.* 9).

86.4 *larger than decreed by the Senate*: the total enrolled, about 5,000, was not large in comparison with the numbers already under arms.

87.1 *his legions*: there is no evidence that Marius had more than the typical consular army of two legions.

full strength: see Glossary under 'legion'. It seems likely both that Marius needed to make up for losses suffered and that the legions originally sent were understaffed.

87.2 *They saw . . . and all else*: an odd instance of military rhetoric, like that of Catiline at *C* 58, appearing in a narrative.

88.1 *greatest rejoicing*: Metellus was awarded a triumph in 106 and received the honorific cognomen *Numidicus*. This triumph was opposed, probably by the tribune T. Manlius.

89.4 *Capsa*: modern Gafsa, the main town of the region and the only town of any importance. It was at the meeting point of several roads.

90.2 *Lares*: identified with modern Henchir Lorbeus, about 11 miles south-east of Sicca.

90.3 *Tanais*: this river cannot be identified because Sallust does not provide us with enough information about Marius' movements.

91.7 *contrary to the laws of war*: an exaggeration. The treatment of those who surrendered was always subject to the needs of public policy. Still, there appears to have been an increasing opposition to unjustified harshness on the part of individual generals during the last century of the Republic.

92.4 *after capturing many places*: the campaign took the remainder of 107 and part of 106.

92.5 *Not far from the river Muluccha*: from Capsa to the Muluccha is 750 miles. It would have taken nearly six months to travel back and forth from Capsa, and, if one allows for skirmishes in hostile country, ignorance of the terrain, and the need for rest and foraging, the whole expedition seems to have occupied the normal campaigning season of 106. This means that the fall of Capsa must have taken place during the winter of 107/6. It is possible that Sallust has confused the Muluccha with some other river.

93.2 *furthest from the fighting*: the capture of a well-guarded fortress by attacking from a steep and poorly guarded side of the fortress is a common topos in ancient history; G. M. Paul (*A Historical Commentary on Sallust's* Bellum Jugurthinum (Liverpool, 1984), 231) cites Herodotus 1.84, Polybius 7.15, and Livy 5.47.2.

95.1 *L. Sulla*: L. Cornelius Sulla Felix ('The Lucky'): born 138, quaestor at 30. Later he was the first general to march on Rome with an army and impose his reforms with violent proscriptions. He was responsible for a reign of terror known as the 'domination of Sulla', a period of civil war that haunted the Romans throughout the rest of the last century of the Republic.

95.2 *L. Sisenna*: L. Cornelius Sisenna, praetor in 78, wrote an account of the Social Wars and Sulla's civil war.

95.3 *concerning his wife*: it is not clear what Sallust refers to; Sulla was married five times and was a notorious womanizer.

95.4 *most fortunate*: a reference to Sulla's cognomen Felix. Once again Sallust's thematic interest in fortune and luck appears.

97.3 *as he was heading for his winter camps*: September–October 106 BC.

100.1 *because of their provisions*: Sallust says at 102.1 that Marius was headed for Cirta; it may be that he was to winter there with part of the army, the rest in the coastal towns, but the coast is 53 miles away by road. See Map 3.

a squared line: the phrase does not appear in Caesar, seems to be misunderstood by Livy, and is used metaphorically by Cicero. Hence, it is probably not a technical term. It refers to a formation first recorded in relation to Lucullus in Spain in 151: the three columns of infantry formed a long rectangle ('squared') with baggage preceding each maniple and with cavalry and light infantry surrounding as a protective screen. See note at 49.6.

101.6 *wheeled towards the infantry*: there is some debate as to whether this is his own or the Roman infantry, who will hear his words. It seems to me that 'secretly' indicates that he turns to his men so that in that position ('then') he may be overheard by the Romans.

in Numidia: see 7.2 ff. The Numantine campaign had ended in 134, about twenty-seven years earlier.

101.7 *with some vigour a foot soldier of ours*: there seems to be some sarcasm in this description.

the cruel deed: presumably they observed the slaughter of the foot soldier.

101.11 *drenched in blood*: ancient sources report that Jugurtha and Bocchus lost 90,000 men in the second of two battles with Marius (Orosius 5.15.8) and speak of the death of many tens of thousands of Libyans (Diodorus 36.1).

102.2 *matters of interest to himself and the Roman people*: according to Diodorus (fr. 89.5), Bocchus first asked for Jugurtha's kingdom as the price of his cooperation; when Marius refused he tried to come to a more mutual agreement.

102.4 *Sulla's eloquence*: Sallust is the only author to speak of Sulla's eloquence, except perhaps Sulla himself in his *Commentarii*, which Sallust may be using. In Cicero's *Brutus*, a work on Roman oratory, Sulla's name does not appear, nor does he appear in Quintilian, except as a dictator.

102.9 *Fortune*: here, near the end of the work, the man who will be responsible for bringing Jugurtha under Roman control, himself called Sulla Felix, 'Sulla the Lucky', contradicts the moralistic concerns with self-determination and chance that occupied Sallust in the preface to the work.

102.13 *from which he had forcefully expelled Jugurtha*: the text and the meaning are unclear. Some read 'from which [Marius] had driven Jugurtha'. Some think that Bocchus is inventing fictions.

102.14 *an alliance had been rejected*: such a refusal may reflect the Senate's indifference to certain foreign entanglements, especially since Bocchus had not demonstrated his value to Rome. Besides, Jugurtha had already done service to Rome; see ch. 7.

103.1 *winter camps*: the winter of 106/5.

103.3 *if Marius agreed*: as above (102.14), the Senate did not deal directly with belligerents. Negotiations were started with the commander in the field.

103.7 *as signs of goodwill*: and yet at 80.3, 97.2, and 102.15, Jugurtha is said to have bribed the Moors.

104.1 *L. Bellienus*: perhaps the uncle of Catiline who is said (Asc. *Tog. Cand.* 91 C) to have killed Q. Lucretius Ofella on orders from Sulla in 81.

104.3 *Cn. Octavius Ruso*: he entered the quaestorship on 5 December 106; he may also have been the legate of Cn. Pompeius Strabo, praetor between 94 and 91.

  who had brought the soldiers' pay to Africa: Marius, just referred to as 'consul', was at this time proconsul. His command had been prorogued, and, when this happened, additional money for pay and supplies would be brought from Rome by a magistrate or legate.

105.1 *Balearic slingers*: inhabitants of the Balearic Islands, men famous for their ability in using slings.

105.2 *Paelignian cohort*: soldiers from a territory in central Italy.

105.2 *light armour*: this consisted of a shield, 3 feet in diameter, a leather helmet, seven light throwing spears, each about 4 feet long, and a short Spanish sword.

107.5 *to pass openly through Jugurtha's camp*: safe passage through the midst of an enemy camp is commonly associated with supernatural help. The topos goes back to Priam's journey to Achilles' tent in the *Iliad*.

108.1 *Aspar*: this is our only information about this Numidian.

  Dabar: Massugrada may have been a son or grandson of Masinissa. Dabar seems to have been a rival of Jugurtha.

108.2 *he should not fear Jugurtha's legate*: there seems to be some unnecessary confusion in the commentators about this passage. Bocchus, through Dabar, tells Sulla not to be afraid of Jugurtha's legate, Aspar—meaning that his presence and, one assumes, his familiarity with Bocchus' own legate, does not indicate either fidelity to Jugurtha or a means of communication between Bocchus and Jugurtha. The appearance of good relations between Bocchus and Jugurtha is a ruse; otherwise, Bocchus would find himself subject to Jugurtha's treachery, if Jugurtha suspected his allegiance.

114.2 *Q. Caepio and Cn. Manlius*: Q. Servilius Caepio, consul in 106, was from a prominent patrician family, and was the author of a law that changed the composition of juries. Cn. Mallius Maximus, consul in 105, was a 'new man'; we know from epigraphical evidence that the Sallust manuscripts have the incorrect nomen.

  defeated by the Gauls: the defeat at Arausio occurred on 6 October 105.

114.3 *on 1 January*: 104 BC.

HISTORIES

BOOK I

1 *the consular year of M. Lepidus and Q. Catulus*: i.e. 78 BC, the year of Sulla's death. For M. Lepidus and Q. Catulus, see below.

7   *vice of human naure*: commentators discuss Sallust's pessimism in
     the *Histories*: is Sallust sceptical about the nature of man? Or does he
     still hold on to the possibilities of human excellence that inform his
     earlier works? It is generally thought that the *Histories* are darker and
     more pessimistic. However, one should recall that already in *Catiline's
     Conspiracy* he claimed that the question of whether the mind or the body
     was the best means to excellence was solved when history began, and
     it began with men and states (that is, Cyrus in Herodotus and Athens
     and Sparta in Thucydides) who were dissatisfied with what was their
     own and who considered 'the craving for domination' to be a 'reason
     for war'.

     liberty or glory or domination: the sequence, liberty, glory, domination, is
     itself a brief on the causes of civil war.

11   *in the consulship of Servius Sulpicius and Marcus Marcellus*: i.e. 51 BC.
     Sallust goes on to explain why this year marked the height of Roman
     military power. Servius Sulpicius Rufus was one of the leading lawyers
     in Rome. In the civil war, he supported Pompey and was pardoned by
     Caesar. Cicero eulogizes him in the ninth Philippic. Marcus Claudius
     Marcellus was adamantly opposed to Caesar and proposed, unsuccess-
     fully, Caesar's recall. He had declared Caesar's colony at Novum Comum
     illegal and flogged a citizen of Novum Comum to demonstrate his belief
     that he did not consider the man a Roman. He did not participate in the
     civil war.

     all Gaul this side of the Rhine: the year 52 ended with Vercingetorix'
     final surrender at Alesia (see book 7 of Caesar's *The Gallic War*). At this
     point, one could argue that all Gaul was under Roman power. Book 8
     of *The Gallic War*, written by Caesar's general Hirtius, records various
     mopping-up actions necessary in Gaul during 51 BC. The next year, 50,
     would see hostilities between Pompey and the Senate on one side and
     Caesar on the other progress to the impasse that resulted in civil war.
     Caesar crossed the Rubicon on the night of 10/11 January 49. Thus, the
     year Sallust has chosen is intimately connected to Caesar's career both in
     terms of external empire-building and the internal dissension that ended
     in the fall of the Republic.

     between the second and the last Punic war: i.e. between 201 and 150 BC.
     It was a commonplace of Roman history that 'fear of an external enemy'
     was the cause of internal harmony. This was such a prevalent view,
     even at the time, that Scipio Nasica argued that Carthage should not be
     destroyed precisely for this reason.

     the destruction of Carthage: 146 BC. Different historians cited different
     dates as the beginning of the Roman decline: Livy ascribed it to 187 and
     the return of Manlius Vulso's army from Asia; Polybius saw the crisis of
     the late Republic as beginning after 168; Piso set 154 as the beginning
     of degeneration. While Sallust rejects the dominant annalistic tradition,
     later writers follow him in seeing 146 as a pivotal year. See also the note
     on *J* 41.1.

the secessions of the plebs: the plebs seceded from the 'fathers', that is, from participation in the senatorial control of Roman society and from service in the army, as an extreme form of civil disobedience. They did this three times: in 494 (due to rampant debt), in 449 (due to the harsh enforcement of debt laws by Appius Claudius, the consul for 495), and in 287 (due to disputes over public land). The first secession resulted in the establishment of the tribunate, an institution that was protected by 'sacred laws'. It is not certain whether the secession took place to the Mons Sacer or to the Aventine Hill. The second secession was to the Aventine and resulted in the end of the 'Gang of Ten' (decemvirate), a board of ten patricians with consular powers who were originally to codify Roman law but who had become tyrannical. The third secession was to the Janiculum and resulted in plebiscites having the power of law.

the expulsion of the kings: tradition held that there were seven kings of Rome. The last, Tarquinius Superbus, was expelled from Rome in 510/9 by Brutus, who then founded the Republic, led by two executive officers (consuls).

fear of Tarquin: after he had been expelled from Rome, Tarquinius Superbus, backed by the Etruscan Porsenna, attempted but failed to re-establish his position as king. He died in 496. Sallust is supporting his claim that 'fear of an external enemy' is the basis of domestic harmony at Rome.

tribunes of the plebs: the tribunate was not a magistracy, i.e. it could not propose measures to the people for a vote. It was, in effect, a protection for the people, originally consisting of two, four, or five tribunes. By 449 the number had become ten, which it remained for the rest of the Republic.

the Second Punic War: 218–201. During this war Hannibal's presence in Italy and his devastation of the countryside led to a sense of unity and common cause that, according to Sallust, brought a temporary end to the struggle between the different orders in Roman society.

12 *were called*: for Sallust's interest in the corruption of language caused by civil strife, see *C* 38.3 and 52.12. The theme derives from Thucydides 3.82.

13 *exchange value*: see Jugurtha's exclamation that everything at Rome was for sale, *J* 35.10.

47 *with great violence about the prefecture of the city*: the consuls, when they entered office, set the date for the 'Latin Holidays', a festival commemorating the union of Rome and Alba. These celebrations took place on the Alban Hill (13 miles south of Rome) and required that the consuls be absent from the city. This absence entailed the need for a 'prefect of the city', a deputy to act in their absence.

55 *Lepidus*: M. Aemilius Lepidus, consul in 78.

55.3 *descendants of the Bruti*: Brutus was responsible for helping to found the Republic and was one of Rome's first two consuls. Among his descendants was D. Junius Brutus, consul in 77, whose wife is said to have helped Catiline.

Aemilii: one of the most important aristocratic families of Rome, said to have been descended from a son of Numa (Rome's second king). They gave their name to the Via Aemilia, Via Aemilia Scauri, and the Basilica Aemilia in Rome. Mamercus Aemilius Lepidus Livianus, consul in 77, may have captured Norba for Sulla in 82; he was an enemy of Lepidus.

Lutatii: an old Roman family, but not aristocratic. They were plebeians who rose to prominence during the First Punic War. Q. Lutatius Catulus, consul in 78 and colleague of Lepidus, was the fifth member of the family to become consul. He opposed Lepidus and later Caesar.

55.4 *Pyrrhus*: king of Epirus at the beginning of the third century. He aided Tarentum and himself invaded Italy in 280. His victory in Apulia in 279 was so costly that thereafter a crippling victory was called a Pyrrhic victory.

Hannibal: the Carthaginian general who led his army with their elephants over the Alps into Italy during the Second Punic War and spent about fifteen years devastating the Italian countryside.

Philip and Antiochus: in 201 Philip V of Macedonia and Antiochus III of the Seleucid empire signed a treaty of cooperation; this led to the Second Macedonian War which ended at Cynoscephalae when Philip was defeated by Flaminius. Philip was thereafter forbidden to interfere in matters outside his boundaries. Antiochus invaded Greece as part of a general expansion of his empire in 192. He was defeated in 191 and forced to withdraw to Asia. The following year he was defeated by Scipio Asiaticus at Magnesia and forced to abandon all of his territory in what is now central and northern Turkey.

55.5 *Romulus*: founder and first king of Rome (753–715), known for his military prowess. Sulla is called a 'perverted Romulus' because he attempted to present himself and his reorganization of the state as a restoration of Romulian ideology. The Latin here translated as 'perverted' literally means 'left-handed'.

from foreigners: the point is that Sulla treats citizens as if they were foreign enemies, not as political opponents. In other words, when the 'fear of a foreign enemy' disappears, the citizen is treated as a foreigner.

so many armies and consuls: among those who were killed in Sulla's civil wars were four consuls: L. Cornelius Cinna in 89, L. Valerius Flaccus in 86, the younger Marius and Cn. Papirius Carbo in 82.

and other leaders: the list of prominent orators and politicians that can be amassed is substantial; see McGushin's note on this passage (M 1.48.5) and at 1.77.19 (= 1.69.19).

55.6 *before life is certain*: Sulla passed legislation that barred the sons of the proscribed from seeking public office. This law was finally abrogated by Caesar in 49.

55.9 *peace and leisure with freedom*: an echo of a Ciceronian phrase *cum dignitate otium* ('leisure with dignity'), where *otium* refers to political tranquillity and personal leisure and *dignitas* refers to the prestige and influence one has inherited as well as earned. This became a slogan of the aristocrats, useful no doubt because of its flexible ambiguity. Lepidus substitutes 'liberty' for 'dignity' and explicitly adds 'peace'.

55.11 *empire, glory, law*: Sulla's reforms limited the power of all magistrates: the censorship became ineffective; new regulations governed the order of offices, the age of the candidates, and the intervals between offices; the tribunes were denied the right to initiate legislation or to hold any further office.

55.12 *a slave's rations*: Sulla ended the corn dole. The grain law of 73 limited the amount given to the needy to about five bushels per month, an amount that was equivalent to what a master gave a slave to live on, according to Seneca (*Ep.* 80.7, *c.* AD 64).

grant of citizenship: the *lex Iulia* of 90 effectively brought the Social Wars (between Rome and her Latin allies) to an end by granting citizenship to the Latins. Sulla barred from citizenship all those who had opposed him in Etruria, Campania, and Latium. The process of enrolling new citizens was not complete until 70.

a few of his followers: landowners were evicted to provide homes for Sulla's veterans, but even after the veterans were settled land was provided at bargain prices for those who would support Sulla.

55.15 *stained with civil blood*: Sallust reports that Gratidianus, tribune in 87, had his eyes gouged out and his arms and legs broken 'so that he could die limb by limb' (fr. 44 (36)); others tell of bloodshed everywhere, in temples and homes (Plutarch, *Sulla* 31.5, Dio 30–5, fr. 109.8); L. Cornelius Merula is said to have splattered the altars when he opened his veins to commit suicide (Vell. Pat. 2.22).

55.16 *Sulla says*: Lepidus is justifying his opposition to Sulla in light of his own survival and profit from Sullan proscriptions. He grants that he did benefit from the rewards of 'turmoil', but asserts that it was necessary as the only way to survive (they were selling the goods of the proscribed; if you did not buy, you were at risk). In other words, he says that he now opposes the immorality that had become a norm from which it was dangerous to deviate.

55.17 *Vettius Picens*: an equestrian follower of Sulla; he acquired Catulus' villa and later sold it to Cicero.

Cornelius: one of 10,000 slaves freed by Sulla ('Cornelius' is Sulla's family name, and would be the name taken by any of Sulla's slaves). Cicero, lamenting that the rewards of civil war keep the seeds of civil war alive, says that Sulla's secretary was elected quaestor in 44 (*Off.* 2.29).

55.18 *Cimbrian booty*: Rome fought against the Teutones and Cimbri from 113 to 101. The Cimbri were defeated and nearly annihilated by Marius in 101.

55.20 *Fortunate*: Sulla's cognomen was Felix, 'The Lucky'.

55.21 *except the victory*: however much one might deplore Sulla's actions in Rome, he was a gifted general. He was instrumental in the war against the Cimbri and Teutones, responsible for important victories in the Social Wars, and against Mithridates and Archelaus. One might even include his victory over Cinna and Marius in the civil war as something that one would not want changed: it ended the fighting, though it began the proscriptions.

Tarula and Scirtus: nothing else is known of these slaves. The point, however, is that the soldiers who won Sulla's victories would certainly want everything but the victory changed, since they got nothing but death and wounds while Sulla's slaves got wealthy.

Fufidius: he is supposed to be the man who urged Sulla to publish the proscription lists; he was praetor in 81, propraetor in Spain in 80.

a shameless working girl: common political rhetoric. Calling Fufidius a 'working girl' insults both his masculinity and his independence.

55.24 *peace and harmony*: a slogan of aristocratic interests.

77 *Philippus*: L. Marcius Philippus, tribune of the plebs *c.*104, praetor 96, consul in 89, censor in 86, and 'leader of the Senate' at this time. He was a supporter of Sulla and considered the most eloquent speaker of his time. He delivered Sulla's funeral oration.

77.2 *Unless perhaps*: irony and mockery seems to inform Philippus' style.

77.3 *for the destruction of freedom*: Philippus uses the slogan of the *populares* to support the 'freedom' of the *optimates*, that is, their freedom to continue the control of political and economic life.

incantations: this cannot be a reference to the Sibylline books, which were destroyed when the Capitol burned in 83. It is not necessary to have a precise reference for these 'incantations' in order to understand Philippus' general tone of mockery and contempt.

77.4 *from plunder, he got the consulship*: the implication appears to be that Lepidus extorted money from Sicily while governor in 80 and used this money to get the consulship by bribery. There is some evidence that he attained the consulship with the help of Pompey and that he had inherited wealth. The facts do not, however, stand in the way of inflammatory rhetoric.

from rebellion, he got a command with an army: the meaning is not entirely clear, since the Latin translated here as 'command' could also mean 'province'. This could be Lepidus' proconsular province of Gaul, allotted in 78, but according to Sullan law the consular provinces were determined before the consuls were elected. An alternative is that it refers to the revolt of citizens, evicted by Sulla's veterans, in Faesulae. The Senate sent both consuls, Lepidus and Catulus, to restore order. This was unusual, and it is suspected that the Senate was afraid either to send Lepidus alone with an army to Etruria or to leave him alone in Rome without a colleague to restrain him. The revolt was quickly contained. Catulus returned to Rome, but Lepidus stayed in Etruria, where he promised reforms and built support.

77.5 *those who decreed legates*: Philippus is again being sarcastic: Lepidus was not grateful to the senators who tried to negotiate a peace. While he stayed in Etruria, he promised to recall exiles and restore property; he raised an army and offered money to the populace. The Senate ordered him to disband his army and return to Rome. He refused. The Senate then sent an embassy to maintain 'peace and harmony' and to avert civil war. Whatever promises were made by the legates, the Senate did not ratify the terms.

77.6 *proscribed recalled*: an exaggeration; Lepidus only promised to recall the proscribed.

praising . . . the Aemilian family: some aristocrats continued to support a fellow aristocrat until hostilities actually broke out. Lepidus came from a distinguished family: his father had been consul twice, censor, *pontifex maximus*, and leader of the Senate, and his son would become consul in 46.

to destroy liberty: again, Philippus uses the slogan of the other side in support of the powers of the oligarchy.

77.7 *thief*: the Latin *latro*, which means 'thief', 'bandit' in the classical period, originally meant 'a mercenary soldier, one who fights without rules or legitimate cause'. It was a common term of political abuse.

now he is a proconsul: Philippus distinguishes the actions Lepidus took as consul in 78, when the Senate missed its first opportunity to deal with him, from his actions as proconsul in 77. He was proconsul when he refused to return to Rome and, instead, joined the Etruscan rebels and began to build an army with 'private arms'.

most corrupt men of all the orders: not all of Lepidus' followers were corrupt, dispossessed, or classless. M. Junius Brutus (father of the Brutus who killed C. Julius Caesar) was Lepidus' legate; M. Perpenna Veiento, governor of Sicily and member of an important Etruscan family, was also a legate and later joined Sertorius in Spain; L. Cornelius Cinna, brother-in-law of C. Julius Caesar, also joined Lepidus.

Saturninus: L. Appuleius Saturninus, tribune of the plebs in 103 and 100. In 103 he introduced a law granting land to Marius' veterans and a grain law; in 100 Marius again relied upon him to supply land for his veterans. He won the election for 99, but amid electoral violence which resulted in the death of one of the candidates for the consulship, he lost Marius' support and was eventually killed while being held in prison.

Sulpicius: P. Sulpicius Rufus, tribune of the plebs in 89, was responsible for transferring Sulla's Mithridatic command to Marius and so setting in motion the events that led to Sulla's civil war.

Marius: pairing Marius with Damasippus indicates that Sallust has in mind Marius' son, C. Marius Minor. He became a leader of his father's faction upon his father's death in 86. His army was defeated by Sulla and he committed suicide in 82.

Damasippus: L. Junius Brutus Damasippus, praetor in 82, executed several leaders of the Senate under Marius' orders, and was killed at Sulla's command after the battle of the Colline Gate, 82.

77.8 *Spain is stirred to arms*: since 80, Sertorius had been active in Spain.

Mithridates: the First Mithridatic War had been concluded by Sulla in 88; the second, 81, was also concluded by Sulla; the third broke out in 74. Philippus is noting the policy of expansion followed by Mithridates VI after the second war, a policy that would continue to bring him into conflict with Rome.

at the borders: Philippus refers to the peoples first affected by Mithridates' expansionist policies. Cicero notes that the revenues from Asia surpass those of other provinces, that they are what makes war possible and peace honourable (*Leg. Man.* 14).

77.10 *peace and harmony*: the aristocratic slogan again.

77.14 *the property of others*: see Lepidus' speech, 55.17, where he both defends the property he purchased as legally his and promises to return it.

all our civil discord: clearly the oligarchical point of view. Tribunician power was used on both sides to promote factional interests: the Senate wanted to weaken it since it limited their power, the plebs wanted it restored since it gave them some protection against senatorial abuses.

77.15 *a second consulship*: Marius held the consulship continuously from 104 to 100. Sulla regarded this as a serious threat to constitutional process and required a ten-year hiatus between repetitions of the same magistracy.

the first: Lepidus refused to return to Rome to conduct consular elections in 78. Upon the end of his term as consul, he took proconsular command of his army in Etruria and his province of Gaul. In holding on to this proconsular army and not returning to Rome when the Senate required it, he can be said to have not given up his first consulship.

perjury: a standard piece of political abuse; however, in this case, it may refer to Lepidus' decision to ignore the terms of the oath that he and Catulus took upon setting out for Etruria.

77.17 *how long will we delay*: see note to *C* 20.9 on the possible echo of the
opening words of Cicero's *First Catilinarian*. One should not be too hasty
in assuming that Sallust makes Lepidus (or Catiline, for that matter)
echo Cicero. It is equally possible, and perhaps more likely, that Lepidus
echoes Catiline (and that Cicero mocks one of Catiline's mannerisms).
In any event, the ending of the last section is filled with rhetoric that also
recalls Cicero's attack on Catiline.

77.19 *crimes of Cinna*: L. Cornelius Cinna, consul in 87, attempted to enrol
new citizens and to recall Marius. He was expelled from Rome by his
colleague, Cn. Octavius. Supported by the army of Ap. Claudius, he
was joined by Marius, and returned to Rome where, after five days of
looting, rape and murder, he instituted a reign of terror (86–83). During
this period he killed many leading men of Rome, here called 'the glory
of this order'. His control of Rome was brought to an end by Sulla's
return.

77.20 *Cethegus*: P. Cornelius Cethegus, proscribed by Sulla in 88, later became
a follower. After Sulla's death, he was influential in senatorial circles,
though he never held office.

77.22 *Ap. Claudius as interrex*: Ap. Claudius Pulcher was praetor in 89,
consul in 79. As consul, he was a 'Sullan' and after Sulla's death was made
interrex. He died in Macedonia in 76, leading an army against attacks
from the Thracians. Because of civil unrest, the year 77 opened without any elected consuls. An *interrex* was appointed by the Senate as a
provisional office whose responsibilities included consular authority
while elections were held. The appointment was for only five days. This
dates Philippus' speech to the early days of 77.

that the Republic is not damaged in any way: these are the terms of the
Senate's 'final decree'.

88   *As military tribune . . . T. Didius*: Sertorius served under Q. Servilius
Caepio in 105, and under Marius against the Germans from 105 to 101.
We do not know where he served 101–98, but he probably joined
T. Didius in 97. Didius was a successful general and politician. Praetor
in 101, he celebrated a triumph in 100; he was consul in 98, governor of
Spain 97–93, and celebrated another triumph in June 93. He was a legate
in the Social Wars, serving under Sulla in 89. Sertorius probably served
under him from 97 to 93.

Marsic War: that is, the Social Wars, 91–87.

BOOK II

17   *domination*: the Latin *dominatio* refers to the exercise of absolute power
in political and military spheres. The years of Sulla's dictatorship were
known as the 'Domination of Sulla'.

19   *in using a crowbar with the muscular*: I have not been able to improve on
McGushin's translation, so I have simply adopted it.

(19) *he*: this fragment has been variously assigned and there is no certainty about whom Sallust is describing, but a good case can be made that this reflects Pompey's cruel and insulting treatment of men like Carbo. The placement here follows McGushin.

47   *C. Aurelius Cotta*: a member of a distinguished plebeian family, he stood for the tribuneship in 90. We do not know if he won the office that year, but Cicero reports that he was expelled from the tribuneship (some later year?) because of personal animosity. He went into exile when charged with encouraging the allies to revolt, but returned in 82. In 79 he opposed Cicero and supported Sulla in a lawsuit concerning citizenship (*Caecin.* 97); Cicero called him 'the most eloquent man of the state'. He continued to be prominent in politics: he defended Dolabella against charges brought by Caesar (77), was elected to the College of Priests, elected praetor (78) and consul (75). As consul, he alienated the Senate by abrogating Sulla's law disqualifying tribunes from other magistracies. He received Gaul as his province and was awarded a triumph. He died from 'friendly fire' when he was impaled through the back by one of his soldiers.

      mourning: his change of clothes reflected his assumed position as a mourner.

47.2 *old age*: born in 124, Cotta would be 49 at the time. The Romans marked 60 as the beginning of 'old age'; Cotta's exaggeration may be an appeal to pity, as is his use of the word 'miseries'.

47.3 *your parricide*: the Latin term *parricida*, literally 'patricide, killer of one's father', is a highly charged term of political abuse, one that couples fear of the death and destruction that war brings with the impiety of killing not only one's own father, but all who are in the role of father: the 'conscript fathers' or 'fathers of the Senate', the fatherland, as well as close relatives, and so citizens.

      given a second birth: a reference to his return from exile in 82. Both exile and execution were considered 'capital punishment' in Rome, since both ended what was considered one's real life, the life of a citizen.

47.4 *you . . . gave me back again*: not quite true: Cotta returned from exile because of Sulla's victory.

47.6 *Our generals in Spain*: Sertorius was dominant in Spain from 83 to 77, when he was joined by M. Perperna Veiento with some members of the Roman aristocracy and a Roman army. Metellus was sent in 79 to put down his rebellion, and Pompey was sent in 77 to reinforce Metellus. Sertorius continued to elude capture and defeat. In fact, he defeated Pompey at Sucro and he defeated the combined armies of Pompey and Metellus at Saguntum. Gradually his coalition weakened through rivalries and he was assassinated in 72.

      defection of allies: the people of Spain sided with Sertorius, which made it difficult to gather supplies locally.

47.6 *flight . . . through the mountains*: Sertorious was notorious for his guerrilla tactics.

47.7 *Asia and Cilicia*: Asia was a province that included Pergamum, Phrygia, Lydia, and the colonies and islands on the coast of Ionia. Cilicia was between Pamphylia and Syria on the south-east coast of Asia Minor.

Mithridates: at this time Mithridates was negotiating a treaty of cooperation with Sertorius. Of the three Mithridatic wars, this was the third. Lucullus and eventually Pompey were sent to fight the king, who was not defeated until 65, by Pompey.

Macedonia: border wars with the Thracian tribes were being prosecuted by C. Scribonius Curio.

Italy and the provinces: the pirates had their headquarters in southern Asia Minor and troubled commerce from Gibraltar to Syria.

47.11 *dedicating my life to the Republic*: Cotta refers to the act of *devotio*, a ritual dedication of one's life to the gods of the underworld in return for their support in war.

70 *sling*: the meaning of the Latin word *transenna* is disputed. Here, Macrobius seems to mean 'in a sling'; Servius uses the word to mean 'an extended rope'; in Plautus it seems to refer to a net or snare.

embroidered toga: as was worn by generals in triumphs.

98.4 *more enthusiasm than strategy*: since this was the complaint made against Pompey on all sides at the beginning of the civil war with Caesar, it is reasonable to see in his acknowledgement a character trait.

a titular command: Pompey claims that he received the title without an army; he provided an army from his own resources. In fact, he kept the army that he had been given to fight Lepidus, despite orders to disband it, until the Senate gave him a command to reinforce Metellus against Sertorius in Spain.

within forty days: early in his career, Pompey was noted for the speed with which he conducted his campaigns; at the end of his career, he succumbed to the greater speed of Caesar's campaigns.

98.5 *different from Hannibal's path*: the determination of Pompey's route depends on Hannibal's route from Spain to Italy, and we do not know which path Hannibal took.

I recovered Gaul: an exaggeration; there were only local disturbances in Gaul.

Lacetania, the Indigetes: Lacetania was a remote area in the north-east of Spain; the Indigetes ('Natives') were a remote people bordering on Lacetania.

first attack of . . . Sertorius: in the battle of Lauro earlier during the year, Pompey had been outwitted and severely defeated. After the battle his foraging parties were ambushed and a legion sent to rescue them was annihilated.

new: untrue; his army was the one that he had used against Lepidus.

98.6 *popularity*: that is, popularity with his troops, who would prefer to winter in the towns.

Sucro: Pompey, having just won a battle at Valentia, attempted to attack Sertorius at Sucro before Metellus could arrive. Sertorius routed Pompey's troops on the left wing and Pompey himself was wounded and forced to flee without his horse. Afranius on the right wing succeeded in taking Sucro, but could not control his troops, who were attacked by Sertorius on his return. Pompey was forced to abandon Sucro.

Turia: the river runs through the Valencian province and empties into the sea at Valentia. Pompey's list here seems to set forth several military successes, but all are really only the individual elements of the same campaign. The object was to control the east coast of Spain. The fighting took place outside the town of Valentia, between the walls and the river Turia.

C. Herennius: praetor in 80, a supporter of Sertorius. Pompey's victory over Sertorius' generals, Herennius and Perperna, took place at Valentia and caused the death of 10,000 rebels, including Herennius.

98.9 *supplied Metellus' army*: although Pompey seems to assume that political motives are responsible for his lack of supplies, this reference indicates that other contingencies were operating as well.

98.10 *the following year*: i.e. 74, in which L. Licinius Lucullus and M. Aurelius Cotta were the consuls.

The consuls: i.e. the consuls of 75, C. Aurelius Cotta and L. Octavius.

BOOK III

48   *C. Licinius Macer*: author of a history of the struggle between the orders and an orator of some experience, rather than talent (so Cicero, *Brut.* 238).

48.1 *seceded*: for the three secessions of the plebs, see above, fifth note on *H.* 1.11.

48.2 *freedom*: these rights include the right of appeal to the Roman people from any sentence of execution, exile, or flogging and the right of a tribune to prevent a magistrate from coercing a citizen.

48.3 *empty appearance of a magistracy*: Macer means that the tribunate has been so weakened that it is only an empty name. It was not, however, a real magistracy (like the office of aedile, quaestor, praetor, and consul) which entailed statutory power and insignia.

48.4 *alone*: during the years 76–73 we know of only one tribune for each year. It has been suggested that Sicinius in 76, Quinctius in 74, and Macer in

73 agitated for the restoration of tribunician rights on their own, that the other tribunes steered clear of conflict.

48.8 *Cotta*: see his speech, above, 2.47. Cotta represented the most conservative wing of the ruling aristocracy. The fact that he was motivated to make some concessions indicates, according to Macer, that the aristocracy is afraid of the plebs.

L. Sicinius was silenced: L. Licinius (or Cn. Licinius; his name is uncertain) was tribune of the plebs in 76. The Latin says that he was 'circumvented', which could mean that he was killed, cut off, or prosecuted.

48.9 *Catulus*: C. Lutatius Catulus, colleague of Lepidus as consul in 78 and his chief opponent. See 1.55.

48.10 *A revolt intervened*: Lepidus' rebellion prevented any attempt to restore tribunician powers in 77.

Brutus and Mamercus: Decimus Junius Brutus came from a consular family (his father had been consul in 138 BC) and was the father of the Decimus Brutus who assassinated Caesar. Mamercus Aemilius Lepidus Livianus, consul in 77, was the husband of Sulla's daughter.

C. Curio: himself tribune of the plebs in 90, he was Sulla's legate and elected consul in 76. He supported Cicero during the Catilinarian conspiracy and was an opponent of Caesar. He apparently eliminated Sicinius, the 'innocent tribune'.

48.11 *Lucullus*: L. Licinius Lucullus, consul in 74, was the military commander who fought Mithridates until replaced by Pompey in 66. He was a military tribune under Sulla, who dedicated his memoirs to him.

L. Quintius: tribune of the plebs in 74, he attempted to restore the tribunician powers.

48.12 *both sides*: see above, *H* 1.12: 'while the few who had power . . . aspired to domination under the honourable pretexts of "the Senate" or "the people" '.

48.15 *those manly acts*: i.e. acts of armed resistance and secession.

a patrician magistracy: following McGushin, I take this to mean that the ancestors created three rights for the people: the tribunate, the ability to stand for the consulship, which until 367 had been a patrician magistracy, and elections free from senatorial review.

48.17 *I am seeking restitution according to the law of nations*: the appeal is to a supposedly common law of behaviour between nations. Macer uses the formula that was used by the priest in demanding restitution from foreign nations for stolen property or redress of grievances. Though he does not desire or seek civil discord, he does portray the relationship between aristocracy and plebs as one between antagonistic states.

48.18 *ancestral portraits*: see note on *J* 4.5. The aristocracy kept images of their famous ancestors in their houses; these badges of nobility were trotted out for funerals and other official occasions. For Macer to imagine the nobles fighting a war with their ancestral portraits is a contemptuous reference to their pomp.

48.19 *sudden grain law*: the grain law was interpreted as a conciliatory action. It was sponsored by the consuls of 73, M. Terentius Varro Lucullus and C. Cassius Longinus.

48.21 *on their necks*: as if they were the men who carried Pompey around in his litter.

   afraid of him: Pompey was always a source of ambivalence to the nobility. He was used against Lepidus and then extorted the Spanish command by refusing to disband his army. See his letter, above, 2.98.

48.23 *to restore tribunician power*: something he did do, but not until his consulship in 70.

48.26 *not lash your backs*: M. Porcius Cato, praetor in 198, had prohibited the scourging of citizens without appeal to the people.

BOOK IV

69.1 *King Arsaces*: a dynastic name for the Parthian kings, the Arsacids. This king is probably Phraates III, the twelfth Arsacid.

   consistent with duty: the Latin term *pius*, cognate with our word 'pious', refers to the active fulfilment of one's obligations to family, state, and gods; in other words, beyond the meaning 'legitimate' there is an exhortatory sense to the term, 'what one should do'.

69.3 *recent war*: hostilities between Parthia and Armenia went back to 88–87, when Tigranes II, on the death of Mithridates II of Parthia, attacked and occupied Parthian territory.

   my less than successful position: Mithridates refers to his defeat by Lucullus at Cabera (72) and Tigranes' subsequent defeat at Tigranocerta (69).

69.5 *craving for power and wealth*: see *C* 11–13 and *J* 41 for similar comments on Roman degeneration. Note as well, however, that history itself begins for Sallust when 'craving for domination began to be considered a justification for war' (*C* 2.2).

   Philip: Philip V of Macedonia allied himself with Hannibal and expanded his territory and influence in the Aegean and Anatolia. In 201, Rome, at the request of Pergamum and Rhodes, sent an embassy to him with terms for maintaining peace. He ignored diplomatic overtures and Rome declared war in 200. The Romans had defeated Carthage the year before, in 201.

69.6 *Carthage*: the period 205–202 was the final crucial period in the Second Punic War. For this reason, Rome had in 205 offered Philip liberal terms in the peace treaty of Phoenice.

69.6 *Antiochus*: Antiochus III, king of Syria, offered Philip a secret alliance against Egypt in 203/2. It is unlikely that Rome conceded all interests in Asia to Antiochus; more likely, the Romans were occupied with the Second Macedonian War against Philip.

Philip's power was broken: Philip was defeated in 197. From 196 to 192 Rome used diplomacy to avoid armed conflict with Antiochus. War finally broke out in 192.

Antiochus was stripped: Antiochus was defeated at Thermopylae in April 191 and again at Magnesia in December 190. He was forced to withdraw from Asia on the western side of the Taurus mountains.

69.7 *Perseus*: Perseus succeeded his father in 179/8. War with Rome broke out in 171 (the Third Macedonian War); Perseus enjoyed erratic success, but was overwhelmingly defeated at Pydna in 168. He fled to the protection of a temple in Samothrace and was persuaded to give himself up to the good faith of the Romans. He attempted a negotiated surrender but was forced to surrender unconditionally.

69.8 *death from lack of sleep*: other historians report that he committed suicide. Plutarch (*Aem.* 37.2–3) knows both traditions but says that the guards became angry with Perseus and kept him from sleep until he died. There is no evidence that his death was the official policy of Rome.

Eumenes: Eumenes II, son of Attalus I of Pergamum, succeeded in 197. Rome intervened on his behalf with Bithynia and no doubt promised the benefits of Roman friendship when trying to persuade him to ally himself with Rome.

betrayed him to Antiochus: the charge cannot be substantiated. A change in Roman policy came about at the conclusion of the war with Perseus in 167/6. The Romans suspected Eumenes of betraying the cause of Rome; thereafter, he was humiliated and insulted.

a fake and impious will: according to the will of Attalus, the Roman people were the heirs of the kingdom of Pergamum.

Aristonicus: the illegitimate son of Eumenes, he attempted to seize the throne by violence in 133. The consul P. Licinius Crassus was sent with an army in 131, but was defeated and killed. Crassus' successor, M. Perperna, defeated Aristonicus in 130. Manius Aquillius brought the war to an end in 129. According to some, Aristonicus died before victory celebrations were held; according to others he was led in Aquillius' triumph and was strangled at Rome by order of the Senate.

69.9 *Nicomedes*: as one of his last official acts, Nicomedes IV (Philopater) left the entire kingdom of Bithynia to Rome in his will. Mithridates' interest in Bithynia led directly to the Third Mithridatic War.

69.10 *they used Nicomedes*: in 89 the Romans restored Nicomedes IV to the throne of Bithynia and encouraged him to raid the territory of Mithridates. This led to the First Mithridatic War.

Ptolemy: Ptolemy VIII of Egypt rejected a request from Rome to aid in the First Mithridatic War.

69.11 *drove Nicomedes from Bithynia*: in 88 Mithridates' generals, Archelaus and Neoptolemus, defeated Nicomedes and drove him from Bithynia.

69.12 *freed Greece from a harsh slavery*: Mithridates presents his war in Asia as a war of vengeance and his war in Greece as a war of liberation. As one might expect, the sources present different versions of Athenian loyalty or revolt.

Archelaus: one of Mithridates' generals, defeated in Greece in 86. It was several years after the peace of Dardanus (85) that he deserted to Rome. It seems that incompetence, not treachery, was the reason for his defeat.

Ptolemy: Ptolemy XI (Auletes). From 81, when he succeeded to the throne, until 59, when Egypt was granted status as 'friend and ally', there was a long period of uncertainty and insecurity, during which Ptolemy tried to secure his status with bribes.

69.13 *when they are destroyed*: in 69 Metellus was given command against the Cretans. The war dragged on until 67, when Crete appealed to Pompey. Metellus ignored any terms of settlement and insisted on finishing the war before Pompey arrived.

internal problems: i.e. the civil wars of Sulla, Cinna, and Marius.

I began to fight again: Mithridates admits aggression, but blames Roman intentions for it. He seems to view the Third Mithridatic War as a continuation of the first war.

69.14 *On land . . . of a lovely fleet*: Cotta attacked Mithridates before Lucullus' army (including both veteran legions and fresh recruits) arrived. He suffered a total defeat, including the loss of a fleet collected from the allies. Mithridates destroyed 4,000 ships, according to Appian (*Mith.* 71).

Cyzicus: Mithridates allowed Lucullus to take a position that controlled the supply routes. He had been misled by Magius, either a counsellor from Sertorius or a deserter, into believing that he could win a quick and bloodless victory.

under no compulsion: in fact, he attempted a secret escape from Lucullus' siege, was pursued, and lost 6,000 horse and 15,000 men who were captured.

Parium and Heraclea: at Parium, Mithridates lost about 30,000 infantry while crossing the rivers Aesepus and Granicus which were flooding; at Heraclea he survived a powerful storm by abandoning his heavy ship for a light pirate boat which took him to safety.

69.15 *Cabera*: Lucullus pursued Mithridates, who had his main force at Cabera in Pontus. Lucullus was forced by Mithridates' cavalry to travel through the hills, but aided by Greek prisoners he took up a protected position overlooking Cabera. The routes south to Cappadocia were controlled by Mithridates' cavalry.

varying success: not quite true. Mithridates had some initial success with his cavalry, but was soon overwhelmed by Lucullus' superior abilities. He was forced to retreat into Armenia, which was ruled by his son-in-law, Tigranes.

Ariobarzanes: king of Cappadocia, supported by Rome and restored to the throne in 92 by Sulla when he had been expelled by Tigranes. Expelled again by Mithridates, he was restored in 89. The peace of Dardanus (85) placed him again on the throne. His aid to Lucullus was repayment for Roman patronage.

Tigranes' massive forces: Lucullus besieged Tigranocerta with 6,000 men under the assumption that Tigranes, contrary to his own best interests, would come down from the mountains to protect the town. The strategy worked. The Armenian forces included many neighbours, Medes, Arabs, Albani, and Iberians. Plutarch reports that, as Tigranes came down from the mountains, he expected to destroy the Roman army and contemptuously said, 'If they are come as ambassadors, they are too many; if as soldiers, too few' (Plutarch, *Luc.* 27, McGushin's translation *ad* 4.64–6). Lucullus' speed and tactics won a crushing victory. Many areas of Tigranes' kingdom went over to the Romans; Tigranes' subjects sent envoys to Lucullus; various allied rulers sued for terms; and Lucullus opened negotiations with the new king of Parthia.

69.19 *Seleucea*: the customary residence of Parthian kings on the river Tigris; a centre of trade.

GLOSSARY

aedile There were two ranks of aedile, the curule and the plebeian; the designation depended upon how one was elected and conferred prestige, but did not distinguish duties. Both were concerned with the care of the city (streets, sewers, markets, etc.), the care of grain (distribution of the grain supply), and the care of the annual public games. Election to the office was not required by the *cursus honorum*, but it did confer membership in the Senate, and both the supervision of public games and the distribution of grain could be useful to a politically ambitious man. The office was usually held after the quaestorship and before the praetorship.

aristocracy, see *nobiles*

Athens One of the two great Greek city-states of the fifth century. It was exemplary of Greek culture and civilization, for Sallust in part because it produced Thucydides, the Athenian historian whose style Sallust imitated.

Carthage Phoenician colony in northern Africa, which controlled the sea-routes of the Mediterranean until it came in conflict with Rome. The fall of Carthage changed the political and cultural face of Rome and, according to Sallust, was the beginning of Roman decline.

censor Elected magistrate, responsible for keeping the census (a registry of citizens and their property), for supervising public morality, and for the administration of some finances.

centurion Senior commander of a century (80 men in Marius' time). Just as centuries had hierarchical importance, so a centurion's importance depended on the century he commanded. The century of the first file (*primus pilus*) was the most prestigious; in a Roman legion there were only eight men with authority superior to his.

century The smallest unit of a Roman legion. Its size was variable, due to the problems of recruitment, losses from casualties, and historical changes, but despite the name, in the late Republic 60 to 80 men were considered a full century.

cognomen A Roman's third name, indicating his appearance, standing, origin, and so on, additional to the NOMEN and PRAENOMEN.

cohort In the Republic a cohort consisted of three MANIPLES; each maniple was made up of two CENTURIES, each century of 60–100 men. Ten cohorts made up a LEGION. The cohort formed a 'triple line' of *hastati*, *principes*, and *triarii*; these 'lines' were defined by the experience and armour of the men. One result of Marius' reforms was that the legion abandoned its organization by maniple and was reorganized in terms of cohorts. The battle at *J* 49.6 is said to be the last one in which maniples were used as such.

consul The chief civil and military office of the Roman state during the Republic. The consulship was an annual office (limiting the duration of power) and included a colleague (limiting the exercise of power). These principles of annuality and collegiality were the Republic's answer to the unlimited power of a monarchy.

consul suffectus A consul elected to complete the term of a consul who died in office or was removed from office.

decemvirate Any of several magistracies held by ten men. One decided whether a man was slave or free; another kept the Sibylline books; a third governed the state when the constitution was suspended in 451 BC.

decree A senatorial decree, or *consultum*, was technically advice given to a magistrate. It did not have the force of law and did not need to be obeyed, but in practice it was generally obeyed.

eques, equites, **equestrian order** The equestrian order may be thought of as the Roman middle class. Originally it was a military class, comprising the cavalry and those financially capable of providing their own horse. Later, it included all who met a specified property qualification: for instance, during the Empire it took 400,000 sesterces to be an *eques*, while the requirement for a senator was 1 million sesterces. The equestrians (singular, *eques*; plural, *equites*) were influential but not a formal part of the governing class; they included the *publicani*, who farmed taxes in the provinces, and the financiers involved in banking and commerce. Throughout the late Republic control of the courts moved back and forth between the senators and the *equites*, each having their own interests in the administration of the provinces. To distinguish themselves in public, the *equites* wore a gold ring (that of the patrician was of iron) and they had a narrow black band on their tunic.

Etruria The territory occupied by the Etruscans. After a period of expansion from 750 to about 500, they inhabited northern Italy from the river Po to Campania; during the Republic their territory extended north of Latium and Rome to the river Arnus.

Etruscans According to the Roman understanding, the earliest occupants of the site of Rome and early rivals for control of Italy. Their empire (c.500 BC) consisted of a loose federation of states from the river Po to central Campania. They provided Rome with many of its civil and religious institutions.

fasces Originally an Etruscan emblem of the monarchy, they were a bundle of rods tied together with an axe by a red ribbon or thongs; the symbol of the power of government or magistrates to punish and kill.

They were carried by lictors in front of all magistrates with an active command. Early in the Republic the axes were removed within the city walls.

'final decree' of the Senate The *senatus consultum ultimum*, a decree passed by the Senate at times of constitutional crisis and danger to the Republic enjoining the consuls to 'see to it that the Republic be not harmed'. Whether this decree conferred any legal authority or just advised the consul and magistrates on the gravity of the situation was a matter of debate and legal argument. It was first used against C. Gracchus, and thereafter against Saturninus, Lepidus, Catiline, and Caesar.

Gaetuli Nomadic tribes of an area in northern Africa from the southern slopes of Mount Atlas to the northern Sahara.

governor The man elected or appointed to be the chief administrative officer in a Roman province. He was responsible for taxation and fiscal management, for the administration of justice, and for the military. Typically, he was aided by an executive council and a quaestor, who was second in command, and could appoint a prefect to govern a sub-section of his province. A governor was frequently able to amass great wealth from the provincials. As a result, there were courts in Rome to try ex-governors for extortion.

Lacedaemonians Alternative ancient Greek name for the Spartans, the citizens of Sparta in the Peloponnesus of southern Greece. During the Peloponnesian War they fought Athens for hegemony in the Greek world.

legate The term, literally 'one who is selected', refers during the Republic to any of three offices: (1) An envoy or ambassador on official business. (2) A senior military officer, usually two or three in number, proposed by a commander and appointed by the Senate. These military legates would assist the commander in the field, often commanding troops, and they served on the commander's council. (3) Senior members of a provincial governor's staff.

legion The Roman fighting force of approximately 4,000–6,000 men. Its tactical unit was the MANIPLE, which had its own emblem and was composed of two CENTURIES of 60 to 100 men each. The legion was drawn up in three lines, each composed of ten maniples: the *hastati* (spearmen), the *principes* (chief men), and the *triarii* (the third line). The *hastati* were the least experienced; the *triarii* were the veterans. They were deployed in a staggered formation (*quincunx*) such that the gaps in the line of *hastati* were covered by the *principes*, and the gaps in the *principes* were covered by the *triarii*. The legion was typically supported by about 1,200 light-armed troops. Each century was commanded by a centurion, each maniple had one superior and one inferior centurion. Each legion was commanded by six MILITARY TRIBUNES. A CONSUL was normally given command of two Roman legions and a similar number of allied troops. Marius changed the tactical structure of the legion from maniples to cohorts. He also replaced the light armed troops and cavalry with auxiliary troops from foreign people.

lex Mamilia Mamilian law, passed in 110 or early 109, established a court to determine who had helped Jugurtha with resources or counsel. We know of five who were condemned: C. Galba, a priest, and four ex-consuls: L. Bestia, C. Cato, Sp. Albinus, and L. Opimius.

lex Manilia Manilian law, a law of 66 BC which transferred the large army Pompey had enlisted in the war against the pirates to his command in the Third Mithridatic War.

lex Plautia de vi A law dealing with acts of violence, probably passed by a tribune in 70 BC. It covered the unlawful use of a weapon and the use of armed men in public spaces. The Catilinarian conspirators were tried under this law.

lex Porcia Any one of a series of laws that limited the power of Roman magistrates against Roman citizens. In 199 BC a *lex Porcia* extended the right of appeal to the people in capital cases to Roman citizens in Italy and in the provinces. The next year a *lex Porcia* prohibited flogging a Roman without appeal. Another *lex Porcia* in the second half of the second century prohibited military officers from summarily executing citizens in the army.

lex Rubria Passed in 122, this law authorized a colony on the site of Carthage.

lex Valeria A law of 86 BC which permitted debts to be settled for one-quarter of the remaining principal.

magistracy Any elective office invested with rights, duties, and executive power by the mutual agreement of the people and the Senate. A magistrate's executive power was limited by two principles: collegiality, that is, a fellow magistrate who could prevent any abuse of power; and the right of appeal to the people that any Roman citizen had. Technically speaking, the tribuneship was not a magistracy since it did not have either specific duties or executive power.

maniple Literally, a 'band' or 'handful' of men; technically, an infantry unit in the Roman army. It consisted of two CENTURIES. In the middle Republic the maniple was the strategic fighting unit; after Marius' reforms the COHORT became the primary strategic unit.

mantlets Movable sheds; *vinea*, siege shelters. These structures were approximately 8 feet wide, 7 feet high, and 16 feet long. The frame was covered with vines (hence the name) and leather, and had an open back. They were fairly lightweight and soldiers could carry them by hand. During a siege a number of *vinea* would form a protected, roofed passage along which soldiers could move toward the enemy's fortifications.

military tribune The six senior officers in a LEGION, attached to the legion itself, not commanding subdivisions of the legion. They were ranked as magistrates. The tribunes for the four 'urban legions' were elected by the people; other tribunes that would be needed when the number of legions was increased were nominated by the commander.

Mons Sacer The 'Sacred Mountain', a hill near Rome, just beyond the Anio which joins the Tiber north of Rome.

new man A *novus home*, a 'new man', was, strictly speaking, a consul who comes from a non-consular family. The term is also used of the first member of a family to hold an office qualifying him for membership in the Senate. (Cicero was both.) In the late Republic, access to the Senate and to the consulship was restricted mainly to members of the nobility, that is, to senatorial families. Sallust regularly contrasts the 'new man' with the nobility.

nobiles The 'aristocracy'; the term refers, strictly speaking, to the descendants of CONSULS. It seems at times to be used to refer to the descendants of any curule magistracy. It was not, however, a legal concept and, like so much in Roman politics, depended upon recognition and prestige: you were a *nobiles*, if the *nobiles* recognized you as such. Linguistically, the name *nobiles* (English, 'nobles') is the same as 'knowable' in English; it means that you have a name (a nomen); that is how you are 'known'.

nomen A Roman's second name, the name of his clan.

optimates Also known as 'the powerful few' and 'the good men', they comprised a faction in the late Republic whose power base depended upon the traditional prerogatives of the Senate and collusion with powerful and successful members of the 'aristocracy'. See also POPULARES.

parricide Technical term for the killing of a father or any close relative; by extension the killing of anyone who stands in a paternal relationship to the murderer. In political rhetoric, this can include fellow citizens, since the state (the *patria*, or the 'fatherland') is like a father to its citizens.

patricians The name seems to derive from the name for senators, *patres conscripti* or 'conscript fathers', and it is thought that it originally referred to families that had produced senators. These men held magistracies and religious offices in the early Republic and were contrasted with the plebs. They could renounce their status, as the tribune

Clodius did, or be adopted into a plebeian family. Their power diminished as their numbers did, and by the end of the Republic there were only fourteen patrician clans with thirty families. Catiline's clan, the Sergii, was a patrician gens.

plebs The general body of Roman citizens, those who were not the patricians. Originally the plebs were excluded from all magistracies and could not marry patricians. During the period of conflict among the orders, they organized into a separate entity with assemblies and officers. By 287 BC they had attained all their political objectives. Thereafter, the term 'plebeian' began to refer, not to the plebeian class, but to members of the lower classes.

populares The designation by the OPTIMATES of the faction that opposed them, men who, contesting senatorial power, found their own power base in the tribunate and the votes of the people.

praenomen A Roman's first name or personal name.

praetor Originally the name of Rome's chief executive officer. By the fourth century BC, the *praetor urbanus* (or 'urban praetor') had special responsibility for the administration of justice. He could command an army, summon the assembly to vote, and initiate legislation. He had six lictors. In the third century a second praetor was created to deal with lawsuits that involved foreigners. In 227 the number of praetors was increased from two to four, to provide governors for Sicily and Sardinia; in 197 it was increased to six to administer Spain. Sulla increased the number again to eight, but required that they all spend their year in Rome to administer justice; the following year they were sent to the provinces as governors.

prefect A person appointed by one with higher authority to command a military unit. Frequently they were officers of equestrian rank in charge of cavalry units or auxiliary forces.

Prefect of the City A temporary substitute for the consuls when they needed to be absent from Rome. After the institution of praetors, this office was needed only once a year when all magistrates were required to attend the Latin Holidays on the Mons Albanus.

propraetor A magistrate or officer in the provinces with the civil or military authority of a PRAETOR.

proscriptions Originally a notice of sale. During Sulla's dictatorship these published lists were used to declare citizens outlaws, meaning that they could be killed with impunity. The murderer was rewarded and the victim's property was sold at auction. Sulla's proscriptions were designed to give him the money and land he needed for his soldiers and his programmes, and as an act of revenge for the murders committed by Cinna and Marius. The practice was repeated by the second triumvirate.

province In general, the sphere of activity in which a magistrate exercised his authority. The term came to refer primarily to the units of foreign territory by which Rome through her governors exercised control. In the late Republic provinces were generally administered by ex-consuls and ex-praetors.

quaestor An office typically held at the age of 27 which, being the lowest magistracy, earned the holder the right of entry into the Senate. Sulla made the office compulsory in the *cursus honorum*, and set the minimum age at 30. He also fixed their number at twenty. They were primarily financial officers, stationed in various towns and provinces. Magistrates could choose a quaestor for personal reasons. Such a quaestor was expected to serve his commander, even commanding military forces himself, until the commander gave up office. Such a quaestor was expected to remain a client of the commander for the rest of his life.

Romulus The first king and founder of Rome.

secession of the plebs The withdrawal of the Roman plebs from the community, i.e. from political life and military responsibilities, in order to gain political rights and freedom from the pressures of debt. Five secessions are recorded between 494 and 287.

Sempronian laws Any of the laws passed by T. or C. Gracchus including those that enforced a limited use of public land, that assured a reasonable price for wheat, and that excluded senators from some juries and restricted their right to establish special tribunals.

Senate A political institution going back to the monarchy. It was composed of elders (hence the name) and advised the king and elected new kings. During the Republic its primary function was to direct the Roman magistrates especially in military conflicts, to propose legislation, to manage state finances and foreign policy, and to supervise civil government. During an emergency, the Senate could appoint a dictator. It did not, however, pass laws.

senatus consultum ultimum, see FINAL DECREE OF THE SENATE.

Social Wars Wars waged by Rome's Italian allies (91–87) for Roman citizenship. Rome gained the victory primarily by granting citizenship through a series of concessions.

standards (military) Symbols that a Roman army followed, rallied around, and recognized in the chaos of battle; they represented both the army and Rome herself.

tortoise Protective covering formed by the interlocked curved body shields carried by Roman legionaries.

tribune (of the plebs) An officer elected by the plebeian assembly to protect the people from abuses of power by magistrates. Tribunes had the right to veto any action by the Senate or a magistrate and to bring legislation before the people, and they asserted a right to enforce decrees of the people. Each tribune could block the action of another tribune. The powers of this office were first systematically exploited by the Gracchi brothers. See also MILITARY TRIBUNE.

Trojans The enemy of the Achaians (or Greeks) in Homer's *Iliad*. According to legend, the Trojan Aeneas escaped from Troy with his father and his son, wandered the Mediterranean and eventually settled in Latium where his descendants founded Rome.

INDEX

The Oxford World's Classics Website

www.worldsclassics.co.uk

- Browse the full range of Oxford World's Classics online

- Sign up for our monthly c-alert to receive information on new titles

- Read extracts from the Introductions

- Listen to our editors and translators talk about the world's greatest literature with our Oxford World's Classics audio guides

- Join the conversation, follow us on Twitter at OWC_Oxford

- Teachers and lecturers can order inspection copies quickly and simply via our website

www.worldsclassics.co.uk

American Literature

British and Irish Literature

Children's Literature

Classics and Ancient Literature

Colonial Literature

Eastern Literature

European Literature

Gothic Literature

History

Medieval Literature

Oxford English Drama

Poetry

Philosophy

Politics

Religion

The Oxford Shakespeare

A complete list of Oxford World's Classics, including Authors in Context, Oxford English Drama, and the Oxford Shakespeare, is available in the UK from the Marketing Services Department, Oxford University Press, Great Clarendon Street, Oxford OX2 6DP, or visit the website at www.oup.com/uk/worldsclassics.

In the USA, visit www.oup.com/us/owc for a complete title list.

Oxford World's Classics are available from all good bookshops. In case of difficulty, customers in the UK should contact Oxford University Press Bookshop, 116 High Street, Oxford OX1 4BR.

Bhagavad Gita

The Bible Authorized King James Version
  With Apocrypha

Dhammapada

Dharmasūtras

The Koran

The Pañcatantra

The Sauptikaparvan (from the
  Mahabharata)

The Tale of Sinuhe and Other Ancient
  Egyptian Poems

The Qur'an

Upaniṣads

ANSELM OF CANTERBURY   The Major Works

THOMAS AQUINAS   Selected Philosophical Writings

AUGUSTINE   The Confessions
  On Christian Teaching

BEDE   The Ecclesiastical History

HEMACANDRA   The Lives of the Jain Elders

KĀLIDĀSA   The Recognition of Śakuntalā

MANJHAN   Madhumalati

ŚĀNTIDEVA   The Bodhicaryàvatàra

	Travel Writing 1700–1830
	Women's Writing 1778–1838
WILLIAM BECKFORD	Vathek
JAMES BOSWELL	Life of Johnson
FRANCES BURNEY	Camilla
	Cecilia
	Evelina
	The Wanderer
LORD CHESTERFIELD	Lord Chesterfield's Letters
JOHN CLELAND	Memoirs of a Woman of Pleasure
DANIEL DEFOE	A Journal of the Plague Year
	Moll Flanders
	Robinson Crusoe
	Roxana
HENRY FIELDING	Jonathan Wild
	Joseph Andrews and Shamela
	Tom Jones
WILLIAM GODWIN	Caleb Williams
OLIVER GOLDSMITH	The Vicar of Wakefield
MARY HAYS	Memoirs of Emma Courtney
ELIZABETH INCHBALD	A Simple Story
SAMUEL JOHNSON	The History of Rasselas
	The Major Works
CHARLOTTE LENNOX	The Female Quixote
MATTHEW LEWIS	Journal of a West India Proprietor
	The Monk
HENRY MACKENZIE	The Man of Feeling

Late Victorian Gothic Tales

JANE AUSTEN
Emma
Mansfield Park
Persuasion
Pride and Prejudice
Selected Letters
Sense and Sensibility

MRS BEETON
Book of Household Management

MARY ELIZABETH
BRADDON
Lady Audley's Secret

ANNE BRONTË
The Tenant of Wildfell Hall

CHARLOTTE BRONTË
Jane Eyre
Shirley
Villette

EMILY BRONTË
Wuthering Heights

ROBERT BROWNING
The Major Works

JOHN CLARE
The Major Works

SAMUEL TAYLOR
COLERIDGE
The Major Works

WILKIE COLLINS
The Moonstone
No Name
The Woman in White

CHARLES DARWIN
The Origin of Species

THOMAS DE QUINCEY
The Confessions of an English
   Opium-Eater
On Murder

CHARLES DICKENS
The Adventures of Oliver Twist
Barnaby Rudge
Bleak House
David Copperfield
Great Expectations
Nicholas Nickleby
The Old Curiosity Shop
Our Mutual Friend
The Pickwick Papers